Popes and the Papacy:
A History
Part I

Professor Thomas F. X. Noble

THE TEACHING COMPANY ®

PUBLISHED BY:

THE TEACHING COMPANY
4151 Lafayette Center Drive, Suite 100
Chantilly, Virginia 20151-1232
1-800-TEACH-12
Fax—703-378-3819
www.teach12.com

ISBN 1-59803-159-7

Thomas F. X. Noble, Ph.D.

Professor of History, Notre Dame University

Thomas Noble is the Robert M. Conway Director of the Medieval Institute and Professor of History at the University of Notre Dame. He assumed his current position in January of 2001 after teaching for 20 years at the University of Virginia and 4 years at Texas Tech University.

Professor Noble earned his B.A. in history at Ohio University and his M.A. and Ph.D. in medieval history at Michigan State University, where he studied with the distinguished medievalist Richard E. Sullivan. During his years as a graduate student, Professor Noble held a Fulbright-Hays Fellowship, which took him to Belgium for a year and gave him the opportunity to study with François-Louis Ganshof and Léopold Génicot. Subsequently, he has been awarded two fellowships by the National Endowment for the Humanities, two research grants by the American Philosophical Society, and a visiting fellowship in Clare Hall (University of Cambridge).

Professor Noble's research interests are concentrated in the late antique and early medieval periods (A.D. 300–1000). He has worked on religious history, the history of Rome and the papacy, and the age of Charlemagne. His first book, *The Republic of St. Peter* (1984; Italian translation, 1997) explored the origins of papal temporal rule. Dr. Noble has also edited four volumes and has written more than a dozen articles on Roman and papal history as a preparatory to a history of the papacy from its origins to 1046. Shortly, Dr. Noble will complete a long monograph, *Images and the Carolingians*, itself preceded by six articles, which explores controversies over religious art in the 8th and 9th centuries, set against the background of late-antique and Byzantine art discourse. In 2004, Houghton-Mifflin published the fourth edition of his successful coauthored textbook, *Western Civilization: The Continuing Experiment*.

Dr. Noble has been a member of the Institute for Advanced Study (Princeton) and the Netherlands Institute for Advanced Study (Wassenaar). In 2002, he was elected a Fellow of the Societa Internazionale per lo Studio del Medioevo Latino (Florence) and, in 2004, was elected a Fellow of the Medieval Academy of America. Dr. Noble currently serves on the editorial boards of *Speculum* and

Church History and has held offices and/or served on committees in the American Academy of Religion, the American Catholic Historical Association, the American Historical Association, and the Medieval Academy of America.

Professor Noble has taught courses in Western civilization for more than 25 years, along with surveys of medieval Europe and Church history. He has also taught advanced courses in late antiquity and Carolingian history. In 1999, Professor Noble was presented with the Alumni Distinguished Professor Award at the University of Virginia, that institution's highest award for teaching excellence, and a Harrison award for outstanding undergraduate advising. Dr. Noble has supervised 11 dissertations, and his Ph.D. students now teach at colleges and universities across the country.

Table of Contents
Popes and the Papacy: A History
Part I

Popes and the Papacy: A History

Scope:

The papacy is the oldest continuously functioning institution in the world. Indeed, in all the world's history, only a few institutions can trace so long an unbroken history. This fact alone commands attention. And if anyone wonders whether that story still matters, we have only to think about the rapt attention that the world lavished in 2005 on the death of Pope John Paul II and the election of his successor, Benedict XVI. Four million people streamed into Rome, and many people waited up to 30 hours to pay their respects to John Paul. Media outlets all over the globe devoted almost continuous coverage to the solemn events that marked the passing of one pontificate and the inception of another.

What, then, is papal history? At its core, it is four histories. The first is the history of an idea, the idea of the *Petrine Office* and of the *ecclesiology*—that's a theologian's word for the theory of Church government—that flows from that office. Second, it is the history of an institution. The Catholic Church has one pope at a time (albeit sometimes, there have been two or more men claiming to be legitimate pope!), but the papacy is an institution that transcends time. Americans are familiar with separating presidents from the presidency. So, too, we shall learn to distinguish between popes and the papacy. Third, it is the serial biography of 265 men, some holy and some wicked, some efficient and some incompetent, some learned and some simple, some visionary and some blinkered. There were also more than 30 antipopes from 217 to 1447, and we will meet some of them, as well. Fourth, the history of the popes and the papacy is, in some ways, a mirror of the history of Western civilization itself. At every great moment and turning point, the popes were there as participants, promoters, or critics. Viewing Western civilization through a papal lens will open for us unique perspectives on the end of the Roman Empire; the evangelization of Europe; the Crusades; the Renaissance; the Reformation; the Enlightenment; the great movements of modern times, such as industrialization, urbanization, science, and mass politics; and finally, the world wars and the collapse of communism.

Papal history has tended to be written in huge volumes, sometimes many-volume collections, or in highly specialized studies in many languages. As a result, the suggested readings at the end of each lecture in this course often refer to chapters in larger works, as well as to particular studies. Books that themselves contain rich bibliographical information are marked with an asterisk (*) in the bibliography.

Lecture One
What Is Papal History? When Did It Begin?

Scope:

This lecture provides some opening, orienting reflections on two basic issues. First, the lecture establishes the four basic themes that will, in differing measures, inform every lecture in the course. That is, the lecture seeks to define papal history in four ways: as an idea, as an institution, as a series of biographies, and as a vantage point for the whole history of Western civilization. Second, the lecture examines the first evidence we have, and the oldest evidence the Roman Church itself has always adduced, for the beginnings of the story. I refer to Christ's words to Peter in the 16th chapter of Matthew's Gospel: "For you are Peter and upon this rock I will build my church." What might these words have meant when they were spoken? How were those words interpreted down to the middle of the 3rd century? How did a persecuted Church survive at the very heart of the Roman world? What support can archaeology and other historical sources bring to our understanding of the first two centuries of papal history? What is at stake, historically and theologically, in how we answer these questions, for not everyone, let alone all Christians, answers these questions in the same way?

Outline

I. The papacy is the oldest continuously functioning institution in the world.

    A. Consider that when George Washington took office as the first president of the United States, the 250th pope was reigning and that Pope Benedict, elected in 2005, is the 265th pope.

    B. The demise of the papacy has often been predicted and—as we shall see—occasionally seemed imminent.

    C. One interesting subject that we will follow is precisely why the papacy has proved so durable.

II. To study the history of the papacy is actually to follow four histories at once. Perhaps in this complexity lies some of the explanation for the papacy's longevity.

A. First, the history of the papacy is the history of an idea: the *Petrine idea*.

    1. This idea takes its name from Peter, the leader of the apostles and, supposedly, the first pope.

    2. The *Petrine Office*—the office that comes down from Peter—is the term used by specialists in *ecclesiology* (the theory of Church government and organization).

B. Second, the history of the papacy is the history of an institution.

    1. Peter had no staff or departments to help him, but gradually, the papacy became one of the most sophisticated and impressive institutions in the world.

    2. The history of any institution must be both bound to and separated from the people who at any moment make up that institution.

C. Third, the history of the papacy is the serial biography of 265 men from Peter to Benedict XVI.

    1. Of some of these men, particularly in early times, we know very little.

    2. Many popes were remarkable, interesting, impressive, and memorable characters, while others were regrettable or forgettable. We will offer some thoughts on why a particular pope might command our attention, but we cannot talk about more than a few of them in any detail.

    3. Sometimes the institution and the men have collided: Between 217 and 1449, some three dozen *antipopes* have laid claim to the papal office.

D. Fourth, the history of the papacy is almost the history of Western civilization in microcosm.

    1. The popes have patronized architects, artists, and builders.

    2. The popes contributed powerfully to the political and legal culture of Europe.

    3. The popes have put their imprint—now approving, now disapproving—on every significant intellectual movement in the last two millennia.

4. The world is more secular and less Catholic today than formerly, but no figure compares to the pope in prestige and influence.

III. Now, to the beginnings of the history itself: We must start with Peter. Who was he?

A. Only a few details can be pinned down with some certainty.

    1. He was a fisherman named Simon from Bethsaida who moved with his family to Capernaum. He was born circa 4 B.C.

    2. He had a brother, Andrew, and was married. Tradition accords him a daughter, Petronilla, but this is shaky.

    3. He met Jesus in about 28 A.D., and on an early occasion, Jesus asked who people said *he* (Jesus) was. Simon said Jesus was the son of the living God, and Jesus announced that God alone had revealed this to Simon: "You are Simon, the son of John; you will be called Cephas which is rendered Peter" (John 1:42).

    4. The Gospels provide a somewhat obscure account of Peter's dawning awareness of Jesus' identity and significance.

    5. In Matthew's Gospel (16:16–18), Jesus assigned Peter a leader's role, once again for recognizing his identity: "You are Peter and upon this rock I shall build my church and the gates of Hell shall not prevail against it. I will entrust to you the keys of the kingdom of heaven...."

B. Peter did exercise some sort of leadership among Jesus' early followers.

    1. Jesus put direct questions to Peter alone among the apostles.

    2. The accounts of the Resurrection of Jesus feature Peter.

    3. Peter is the first apostle reported to have performed a miracle. He explained the Pentecost event to the crowds, took the lead in electing Matthias to replace Judas Iscariot, and passed judgment on Ananias and Saphira.

    4. Paul (Galatians 2:7–9) recognized Peter as special leader for Jesus' Jewish followers, but in the Acts of the Apostles (15:7), Peter calls himself the leader of Jew and Gentile alike.

IV. We have encountered at the beginning a person and, perhaps, an idea and an institution.

    A. Peter was an unlettered fisherman portrayed as a man of both deep faith and cowardice, a bumbler, but also a man of courage and decency.

    B. But the first faint stirrings of the Petrine idea are present, even if opaque.

V. Popes belong in Rome, we assume. How did Peter get there?

    A. Roman tradition makes Peter the first bishop of the city; hence, the first pope.

    B. His dates are given as 42 to 67, but this is unlikely because Peter was probably in Antioch and Corinth at some point during that time and in Jerusalem in 49.

    C. Peter did not found the Roman community, and there is no good evidence that that community had a bishop—an "overseer"—in the 1st century.

    D. Peter may well have been martyred—traditionally crucified upside down—in the persecutions of Nero between about 64 and 67.

VI. Powerful traditions about Peter grew up in Rome very early, but none of them has any direct basis in New Testament writings.

    A. A stone in the Mamertine prison supposedly has the imprint of his head. The Church of Nereus and Achilleus has the *fasciola* of Peter—his leg wrappings or bandages. There is the "Quo vadis?" church (San Sebastiano) on the Appian Way, where it is said that Jesus appeared as Peter fled persecution in Rome and Jesus asked Peter, "Quo vadis?" ("Where are you going?"). The "Separation Church" near St. Paul's Outside the Walls is where Peter and Paul separated. Peter's chains are said to be in San Pietro in Vincoli, and a stone with imprints of his knees is found at Santa Francesca Romana.

    B. Another tradition says that Peter was crucified in the circus of Nero on the Vatican Hill.

    C. It remains for us to explore how the historical Peter and a batch of traditions that surely have some foundation even if they cannot be proved (or disproved!) turned into "the papacy."

Recommended Reading:

Brown, Donfried, and Reumann, *Peter in the New Testament.*

Shotwell and Loomis, *The See of Peter*, pp. 3–207.

Questions to Consider:

1. What interpretations of Peter's role in the early Church will the New Testament support?

2. What can the *historian* learn from the early legends of Peter?

Lecture One—Transcript
What Is Papal History? When Did It Begin?

Hello, and welcome to this course of 24 lectures on the history of the popes and of the papacy. My name is Thomas Noble. I'm the director of the Medieval Institute at the University of Notre Dame, professor of medieval history there, and for a little over 30 years I have been reading about, and writing about, and teaching about the history of Rome and the popes and the papacy. So it's a great pleasure for me to have an opportunity to share some of my interests, some of my obsessions, some of the things that have engaged my attention over a long period of time.

I think it's fair to say that this is, in a lot of ways, a pretty compelling subject. The papacy is the oldest continuously functioning institution in the world. That's a fairly grand claim. Consider, for instance, that when George Washington was elected president of the United States, the 250th pope, Pius VI, was reigning. The papacy's demise has often been predicted, and as we'll have occasion to see in some future lectures, it was occasionally imminent. But one interesting question, and we'll follow this in some detail, was why has the papacy proved so durable? Think of all of the changes, all of the dramatic changes in the last 2,000 years—in the last generation, let alone the last 2,000 years—and there, in stately splendor, stand the popes.

To study the history of the papacy is actually to follow four histories at once. Perhaps—a little puzzle about this later—some of this complexity is responsible in some ways for the papacy's very longevity. In the first place then, the history of the papacy is the history of an idea, of the "Petrine" idea. This idea takes its name from Peter, the leader of the apostles and supposedly the first pope. It goes without saying, Peter didn't have a museum or a post office or a radio station or a Popemobile, and probably would be very surprised to learn that he was the first pope. But in any case, there he was. The Petrine Office, the office that comes down from Peter, is the term used by specialists in the discipline called ecclesiology. That's a big fancy name for the study of how and why a church is organized as it is. Every church has an ecclesiology, a theory of how it's organized, so in the Roman Catholic Church, the Petrine Office is how we talk about the ecclesiology of the papacy, the theory behind it. And we'll be much occupied with the Petrine Office in later lectures, a little bit in this one, but especially in a number of later lectures.

In the second place, the history of the papacy is the history of an institution. Again, Peter had no staff, he had no departments, but gradually the papacy became one of the most sophisticated and impressive institutions in the world. The history of any institution, of course, must be both bound to, and separated from, the people who make it up in any given moment. As Americans, we're very familiar with this. We draw a distinction between the president and the presidency; we have a notion of individuals as mortal and institutions as immortal. But that, of course, brings us to people. The history of the papacy is the serial biography of 265 men, from Peter to Benedict XVI, elected in April of 2005. Of some of these men, particularly in very early times, we know almost nothing. Many popes were remarkable, interesting, impressive, memorable, and some were regrettable, some forgettable.

We'll offer some thoughts as we go along on why particular popes might attract our attention, why we might devote a little consideration to them. But I think it goes without saying we can't talk about all of them in detail And then there're not only the 265 recognized popes; beginning in the early 3rd century, going down until the year 1449, some three dozen antipopes have laid claim to the papal office. What's an *antipope*? Well, in various political circumstances or ecclesiastical circumstances or military circumstances or diplomatic circumstances, multiple people have laid claim to the papal office. Eventually, the official line of popes was registered at 265, and those who raised but failed in their claims to be popes have been sort of put on one side as antipopes. We will, from time to time, encounter some of these antipopes.

Fourth and finally then, the history of the papacy is almost the history of Western civilization in microcosm. The popes have patronized, for example, architects, artists, builders: Fra Angelico, Bramante, Michelangelo, Raphael, Tiziano, Bernini, Borromini; the list goes on and on and on and on. The popes also have contributed powerfully to the political and the legal culture of Europe. Rome, both in pagan imperial times and in papal Christian times, has been in one sense like a great sponge; it soaked up a great deal from its environment. But in other respects, Rome was like a great pipeline, sending things out, and so, too, the papacy has learned from the world around it and has taught that world much. The popes have put their imprint—now approving, now disapproving—on virtually every significant intellectual movement in the last two millennia. Some would say the popes have sometimes put their nose where it didn't belong. Some would say that the popes have taken the view that it was their duty and responsibility to comment on the great issues of the day.

It goes without saying, I think, that the world today is more secular and less catholic than in former times. But there is still no figure on the world stage who commands the prestige, the interest, or the influence of the pope. One has only to think about those remarkable days in April of 2005, when the world's attention and all the world's media was riveted on Rome, day after day, 24 hours a day, when four million people went to Rome simply because they wanted to be there. They had no formal role to play, oftentimes no place to sleep, very hard to find a place to eat, but still they went. There's just nothing comparable. So in some respects, one part of the burden we carry in this course is to explain not only why that sort of thing was interesting, important, true a long time ago, why it's still true in the early 21st century.

In the very last place, we might say that papal history is a bottomless well of curiosities. How are popes elected? Where do they get their names? Who reigned the longest? Who reigned the shortest? Was there a Pope Joan? Well, we won't miss opportunities as we go along to drop in lots of these fascinating little factoids of papal history. I can almost promise you that I will probably, in the course of these lectures, miss a few of your favorites, but I'll also tell you about a few you don't know. We won't primarily focus on the interesting curiosities because we could fill these 24 lectures just with those. Let's go back to the beginning then, and see if we can start building this nearly 2,000-year-old history.

We must start with Peter. Who was he? There're only a few details that we can pin down with some degree of certainty. He was a fisherman; his name was Simon; he came from Bethsaida; he moved with his family to Capernaum on the Sea of Galilee. He was born in about 4 B.C. He didn't know it was 4 B.C.; that's, of course, our dating system. He's almost exactly contemporary with Jesus; they're born at almost the same time. He had a brother named Andrew, and he was married, apparently. Tradition gives him a daughter named Petronilla. This is a little shaky. We can't say for sure that Peter had a daughter named Petronilla, but tradition indeed believed that he did. He met Jesus in about 28 A.D. On a very early occasion, reported in the Gospels, Jesus asked Peter who the people said he, Jesus, was. Simon said Jesus was the son of the living God. Jesus announced that God alone had revealed this to Simon. He said to him, "You are Simon, the son of John. You will be called Cephas, which is rendered Peter." The Greek word means rock, and *petros* is another word for rock, from the first chapter of John's Gospel.

The Gospels provide a rather obscure account of Peter's dawning awareness of Jesus's identity and significance. But one thing that's quite interesting is that in the three so-called Synoptic Gospels— Matthew, Mark and Luke—synoptic, can be seen with one eye—the three narrative gospels, the three gospels that basically tell the story in more or less chronological order of Jesus's life—and then John's Gospel—the fourth gospel, the more theological gospel, the more theoretical gospel, which leaves a great many biographical details on one side—we know that we can lay these documents out parallel and they don't all tell all the same stories. One theme that runs through all four of them is Jesus's awareness of Peter's dawning awareness of Jesus's identity. This, it would appear, means something.

In Matthew's Gospel, the 16th chapter, Jesus assigned Peter a leader's role. We are here at the very faint beginnings of our Petrine Office. Once again, Peter had acknowledged who Jesus was, and Jesus said to him, "You are Peter, and upon this rock I shall build my church, and the gates of Hell shall not prevail against it, and I shall entrust to you the keys of the kingdom of Heaven." How exactly to understand those lines has been one of the central cruxes in Christian history for now some 20 centuries, and we'll have lots more reflections on what those words might mean, what they meant at different times and places as we go along, but here they are at bottom the origins of the Petrine Office.

It seems pretty clear that Peter exercised some sort of a leadership role among Jesus's early followers. For instance, Jesus put direct questions to Peter alone among his disciples. The accounts of the resurrection all feature Peter: the first Easter morning, Jesus rising from the dead. There are other people there: the women at the tomb, the apostles on the road to Emmaus. Other people figure in those stories; Peter is the only one who figures in all four of them. Peter is the first apostle reported to have performed a miracle. It was Peter who explained to the gathered crowds the Pentecost experience, that is to say, the descent of the Holy Spirit on the disciples after Jesus's ascension into heaven.

It was Peter who took the lead in electing Matthias to replace Judas Iscariot, the apostle who had betrayed Christ. It was Peter who, for instance, and I'm just choosing really a few examples at random, passed sentence on Ananias and Saphira. This is from the "Acts of the Apostles." The early Christian community had decided that all would hold everything in common, so everyone was to sell all of their property, sort of pool the resources, and then the community would live off this pool of resources. Ananias and Saphira sold their property, to be sure, but they tucked away a little for themselves. This was revealed to Peter, he accused them each in turn of having done this, and they dropped dead at his feet.

Paul—Saint Paul—in the Epistle to the Galatians, the second chapter, recognized Peter as a special leader for Jesus's Jewish followers. This is rather interesting in a number of respects. There clearly was some kind of rivalry, some kind of tension, some kind of awkwardness between Peter and Paul. Paul we know as the great missionary to the Mediterranean world, the apostle to the Gentiles, those persons not Jewish, par excellence, so Paul appears to have tried to paint Peter into a corner and make him the apostle to the Jews. But Peter insisted that he was leader of Jew and Gentile alike, and it's interesting, for instance, that he presided at the baptism of Cornelius, a Gentile and a man who was permitted to become a Christian without being circumcised. In other words, he didn't have to pass through Judaism on his way to Christianity, but was accepted as a Christian from the very beginning.

So Peter had some kind of a prominent position, some kind of a leadership position. That helps us, I suppose, with the Petrine part. Can we extrapolate from that to an office? Can we get from there to a papacy? That's something that we'll be pursuing a little bit in this lecture, quite a bit in the next lecture, and in quite a few of the lectures ahead of us. But one of the things that I want you to be able to see is that we're going to be sort of building a story here. It won't come to us fully developed at any one moment.

We've encountered a person, certainly an idea, and maybe the first faint hint of an institution. Back to Peter for a second; he's a quite remarkable character in a lot of ways. As I said, we don't really know all that much about him, but the way he is portrayed is interesting. He's an unlettered fisherman. He is portrayed as a man of deep faith, but also a coward. Peter denied Christ repeatedly. He was a bumbler, but also a man of courage and of decency. One has to wonder if, on that day when, in the presence of the other apostles, Jesus said, "You are Peter, and upon this rock I will build my church," the other apostles didn't have a good laugh.

If the first faint stirrings of the Petrine idea are present, even if opaque, let's shift the prism, refract the light a little differently, and ask another question. Surely, we think, popes belong in Rome. Rome is an important part of the story. How did Peter get there? By boat I suppose, but actually the question is really, what was Peter doing in Rome? How did he come to be in Rome? Why didn't he go someplace else? The fact is, of course, for a period of years he did go other places. Roman tradition makes Peter the first bishop of the city. We will, in due season, talk much more about bishops and what bishops are. For the moment we'll just say Roman tradition makes Peter the first bishop of the city of Rome, hence the first Pope. His dates are given in tradition—the traditions descend from the 3rd century—his dates are given in tradition as 42–67.

This almost certainly cannot be. Peter was in Jerusalem in 49. There's a great council, sort of the early apostles in the generation immediately after Jesus's death and resurrection and ascension. Peter was there. This took place in Jerusalem in 49. Peter certainly spent some years in Antioch. Peter apparently was also, for a while, in Corinth, so he couldn't have been in Rome for the whole of this period, no matter what else. Though the very fact that tradition accorded him 25 years, 42–67, is interesting because beginning in the Middle Ages, it became traditional that when a man was elected pope, one of those in attendance said to him "You will not see Peter's years." The idea was to keep him humble; you weren't going to be around very long. Interestingly enough, it was not until the end of the 18th century, Pius VI, that we had a pope who reigned longer than Peter did in tradition.

What other things can we say about this rather murky Roman community? Well, Peter didn't found it; almost certainly, Peter didn't found it. He went there to join a community that was already in existence. You'll recall perhaps that Paul wrote a letter to the Romans. Paul himself, of course, also visited Rome. There's no evidence that when Peter went to Rome, however, there was already a bishop there. The word "bishop" in Greek means overseer. Again, we'll have lots more to say about bishops in due course, but there's no evidence that when Peter got there, there was a bishop. Was he recognized as a particularly important, significant person—was he accorded some kind of precedence, was he treated with great honor and respect—possibly, but there's just no evidence.

Peter may very well have been martyred. Tradition says that he was crucified upside down, that he refused to be crucified erect because he wouldn't imitate the death of his lord. Now, probably we can say that if Peter was martyred, and if he was then in Rome, then the only thing that fits is the Neronian persecution, the persecution under the emperor Nero. That persecution really cranked up in the year 64; by 67, it had pretty well run its course. So if one were to try to make an estimate of when Peter died on the basis of sort of ambient historical circumstances, you'd be better off betting on 64 than the traditional date of 67. But one cannot demonstrate either of those dates to be strictly true.

Powerful traditions about Peter grew up in Rome very early. This we know and this can be very, very important and revealing. Every people, every institution, every club, every group has its story or its stories, has its traditions, has the ways it reflects on its own past. If we take something, let's say, out of American history as simple as George Washington and the cherry tree, I think most people would agree, we don't actually know if that story is true or not. In a certain sense, it doesn't matter if it's true or not because the story is meant to tell us something about George Washington and about us. So when we notice—and we'll notice in just a second—these traditions about Peter that began to emerge clearly in the 2nd century and then just come on apace from then until now, when we notice these stories, we notice the way the Roman community wanted to think about itself, the way they thought about their past, the way they thought about their history. It doesn't mean that none of this is true, but it doesn't mean either that we can prove any of it.

What are some of these traditions, then? What do I have in mind here? What am I referring to? Well, there's a stone in the Mamertine Prison in Rome. The Mamertine Prison was a prison in Rome where who we might call state prisoners were held. There's a stone in the Mamertine Prison that supposedly had an imprint of Peter's head; he had used it as a pillow stone. The Church of Nereus and Achilleus in

Rome had his fasciola, his leg wrappings. Peter had been bound with chains, and his legs had been rather badly torn up by these chains, so they had been wrapped in bandages, and the Church of Nereus and Achilleus has always claimed they have those bandages. There's the "Quo vadis" church, which is actually the Church of San Sebastiano on the Appian Way, "Quo vadis?" "Whither goest thou?" This is the story of Peter, of course, fearing the persecution in Rome and fleeing from the city, going out through the Appian Way, the great road that goes south from Rome. Peter was on his way out from Rome when Jesus appeared to him and said "Quo vadis?" Very interesting; in this telling of the story, of course, Jesus is speaking Latin. But anyway, he says to him, "Quo vadis?" "Where are you going?" So Peter turns around, goes back to the city and faces his execution.

There is the "Separation Church" just near the Great Basilica of Saint Paul, San Paolo fuori le Mura, "Saint Paul Outside-the-Walls," the church where Peter and Paul separated and went their separate way. Peter's chains are alleged to be in the Church of San Pietro in Vincoli, "Saint Peter in Chains" in Rome. They're still there; you can go and see them. Are they Peter's chains? Well, maybe; they have been shown in that place for a very long time. Just outside the Church of Santa Francesca Romana, which in the Middle Ages was the Church of Santa Maria Nova, "New Saint Mary's"—as opposed to Santa Maria Antiqua, which was about 100 yards away, but was destroyed in 846 by an earthquake—just outside Santa Francesca Nova is a stone with two imprints, supposedly from Peter's knees because he knelt there to pray. You can still see that stone to this day.

There were a lot of stories about Peter, a lot of physical reminiscences of Peter, a lot of attempts to connect him to specific places, to connect specific objects with him, with his life, with his activities. These things all meant something very powerful to the Roman community, very powerful indeed. We would be remiss, it seems to me, if we just dismissed them all as utter fancy. But as I've repeated, we can't demonstrate the truth or validity of any of these stories. Tradition says that Peter was crucified in the circus of Nero on the Vatican Hill. One has to imagine the great area where the Basilica of Saint Peter's and Bernini's Piazza San Pietro and so forth, where all of that is located now, that was a "circus," a Roman horseracing course built by the emperor Nero. Tradition says that

Peter was crucified there. That's entirely possible. That would make a certain kind of sense.

Late in the 3rd century, Pope Caius, 283–296—we're at the end of the 3rd century, we're a long time now after Peter—referred to the "Trophies" of the apostles. What do we make of that? *Tropaion*, in Greek, can refer to a tomb, the tomb where a certain person is buried. But it can also refer to a cenotaph. A cenotaph is a monument erected at a place where oftentimes it's thought someone died—someone important, someone famous. Or, it can sometimes just be erected in honor of someone who died somewhere but not necessarily where the cenotaph itself is located, but the implication is that a tomb and a cenotaph are two different things. In other words, a gravestone is over a grave. A cenotaph is not necessarily over a grave. So was Caius referring to the very tomb of Peter and perhaps of others, or was he referring to a monument? It wouldn't matter too terribly much except for the fact that, as I said a moment ago, the Basilica of Saint Peter's was eventually built where the circus of Nero had been, and tradition has always held that the high altar of Saint Peter's is directly above the grave of Saint Peter.

If you go to Rome today and you go down the semicircular staircase in front of the high alter, you go down to the confessio of Saint Peter. You go down and there you see what is believed to be his tomb. Serious archaeology on Saint Peter's really only began in the 1930s. Remarkable excavations were carried out underneath the basilica. What was found was an enormous necropolis, a city of the dead, an enormous burial ground, a burial ground where a lot of elite high status Romans had been buried over a period of time. There are burial chambers there with beautiful paintings in them and exquisite stonework and so on. This was obviously a place where important people were buried. In the excavations there was found a red wall with a little niche in it, and it's been supposed that that might be the *tropaion* to which Pope Caius referred. Obviously, nobody had seen it in a long time.

We can just put in here kind of an amusing story, one of our little factoids about papal history. There was a German priest named Father Kaas, who was the head of the German Center Party in the early 1930s, a party that formed a very brief parliamentary alliance with the Nazis in the hope, not because they were Nazi sympathizers, but in the hope that they might be able to domesticate the Nazis politically. What happened is then that Pius XI signed a concordat with Nazi Germany—we'll get to that in a later lecture—and the German Center Party collapsed, Father Kaas then went to Rome. When he got to Rome, he became one of the principles of the excavations underneath Saint Peter's, he and a woman named Senora Guarducci.

Anyway, they began digging under Saint Peter's, one of the things they discovered was a series of sets of bones that were in about the right place, which on scientific testing proved to be from about the right date. In other words, it could have been the bones of Peter or someone like Peter. Anyway, these bones were brought upstairs while the archaeology continued. They were put in various boxes, and the story has it that the boxes weren't very carefully kept and they kind of got moved around from office to office, and pretty soon nobody quite knew which box had which bones in them, and so a story is wickedly, and not entirely fairly, told that poor Father Kaas first lost Germany to the Nazis and then lost Saint Peter. Well, anyway, in the 1970s, Pope Paul VI declared one set of those bones to be, in fact, the bones of Saint Peter. This is not impossible, but is it true? Those are the bones that are on display now in the confessio of Saint Peter, if you go to look. They are clearly the bones of a man who died at about the right time, and they are bones that were found in about the right place. Does it matter or not? We might say that in the grand scheme of things, it probably doesn't matter very much.

But this may be an appropriate point to add that when we talk about Saint Peter, when we talk about the story of the Petrine Office, when we talk about the emergence of the papacy, we are in some ways on contested ground. There is a way that this story is told in the Roman Catholic tradition and a way that the story is told in other traditions. The Roman Catholic Church, of course, is much more sympathetic to these legends, to these stories, to these traditions. Traditions are things handed down; that's what the word means. To others, they are mere legends, they are mere trifles, they're irrelevant, they're beside the point and they don't prove anything. So it's easy enough to see why one church tradition would place great emphasis on these traditions where other church traditions attempt rather to dismiss them. For our purposes, the crucial point is that the Roman community as early as the 2nd century placed great emphasis on these traditions, on these stories.

So we've met a man. We've met a story. We've met, well, some sort of an interesting connection to Peter and Peter as a leader. What we have to do now is try to explore how the historical Peter and a batch of traditions that surely have some foundation, even if they cannot be proved or disproved, and that's important—to reemphasize once more, you can't prove these traditions, but you can't disprove them either—how do we turn these raw materials into the papacy? Well, that's the subject to which we'll turn in our next lecture, when we look at the centuries between about 300 and 500, when this remarkable Roman church began to come out of hiding and very much visibly into the open.

Lecture Two
The Rise of the Petrine Idea

Scope:

Papal history changed dramatically in the period between about 300 and 500. Emperor Constantine made Christianity a legal religion. He ended almost two centuries of sporadic persecution and showered favors on the bishops of Rome, the popes. The sources available for the study of papal history expanded exponentially. From those sources, we can catch a first glimpse of an impressive institutional structure coming into being, refining itself to do its work, and assuming new and weighty responsibilities. From those sources, too, we can begin to observe the popes reflecting on the papal office itself. They began to stress Christ's words to Peter and to derive specific rights and obligations—their own and others'—from those words. Popes began to spell out a claim, a claim that was much contested, to primacy in the Church. And they began to define their relationships to the imperial regime and to secular authority more generally.

Outline

I. This lecture focuses on the crucial period from about 300 to 500.

   A. The Emperor Constantine (reigned [r.] 306–337) granted the Church legal status and permitted it to function openly.

   B. The importance and prestige of the popes rose dramatically in this period.

   C. A free and important papacy, however, encountered problems that would, in some cases, last for centuries.

   D. Slowly but surely, the popes began to define and reflect on the nature of their office and the powers it entailed.

II. Before we examine this history, however, we must say something about the extremely obscure 2nd and 3rd centuries.

   A. We have very few sources, and most of these are late and hard to evaluate.

   B. Tradition says that Peter and his successors were bishops of Rome.

C. Perhaps we should clarify what a bishop is: *Episcopus* (Επίσκοπος) means "overseer," "supervisor," "elder."
   1. Bishops emerged as the key Church officials in a particular town or area, with responsibilities for worship, teaching, and recruiting.
   2. By about 150, sources spoke of "monarchical bishops," suggesting that bishops had come to be significant figures in the cities of the Roman world.

D. Pope Clement (r. 88–97) encountered a controversy in Corinth—as had St. Paul!—and wrote to admonish and encourage the community there.

E. Pope Victor (r. 189–198) attempted to impose his will in the matter of the date for celebrating Easter. He had only limited success.

F. In 180, Irenaeus of Lyon spoke of Rome as "the great and illustrious church to which on account of its commanding position every church, that is, the faithful everywhere, must resort." To Irenaeus and others, Rome's "commanding position" derived from its "double apostolicity," the city's ties to Peter and Paul.

G. Pope Urban I (r. 222–230) met a contested election, and Hippolytus set himself up as the first antipope.
   1. This conflict hints at the emerging importance of the office.
   2. It also suggests the presence of factions, contending groups, and arguments.

H. A critical figure was Pope Stephen I (r. 254–257), who was the first, as far as we know, to assert vigorously the Petrine doctrine of Roman authority.
   1. He insisted that he held the "chair of Peter" (*cathedra Petri*) in succession to Peter.
   2. This assertion inaugurates the idea that each pope is Peter's successor.

I. Yet many early popes were martyred, the Roman community was frequently disrupted, and the Church could not function smoothly.

III. Things changed dramatically with Constantine.

    A. There can never be a satisfactory or definitive explanation of why Constantine decided to legalize Christianity, then to convert.

    B. Constantine issued the Edict of Milan in 313, making Christianity legal (*religio licita*).

    C. Constantine was not merely neutral.

        1. He ordered the construction of St. Peter's and St. Paul's basilicas, and he gave the Lateran Palace to Pope Sylvester.

        2. He initiated a long series of imperial decrees on behalf of the Church, conferring tax and military exemption, for example.

        3. Constantine also intervened in two doctrinal disputes, one involving Donatism and the other, Arianism.

            a. Donatism, named for Bishop Donatus, arose in Africa. When Constantine granted legal status to Christianity, most Christians wanted to welcome back those who knuckled under during times of persecution, but the Donatists objected to this forgiveness.

            b. Arianism was the great Trinitarian heresy of antiquity. Arius was a priest from Egypt who, in an attempt to preserve monotheism, taught that Jesus Christ was slightly subordinate to God the Father. Arians were declared heretics.

    D. Subsequent emperors regularly attempted to impose their will in doctrinal controversies.

        1. Emperor Constantius II (r. 337–361), an Arian, bullied Pope Liberius (r. 352–366); Emperor Zeno (r. 474–491) pressured Pope Felix III (r. 483–492) over Monophysitism, the belief that Jesus had only a divine nature.

        2. Popes and emperors alike wished to achieve unity in basic teachings but had different political perspectives.

        3. Pope Gelasius I (r. 492–496) wrote a famous letter to Emperor Zeno's successor, Anastasius (r. 491–518), explaining how and why priestly *auctoritas* was superior to kingly *potestas*.

IV. The rise of the papacy may be attributed to many causes.

    A. Amidst the chaos of the later Roman Empire, Christianity itself seemed more compelling, and the steadfastness of Rome's bishops seemed an attractive alternative to imperial inconsistency.

    B. In and around Rome, the popes became more visible and prominent.

        1. Popes built magnificent churches.

        2. Pope Innocent I (r. 401–417) ministered to Rome after the Gothic sack of 410, and Pope Leo I (r. 440–461) persuaded Attila the Hun (in 452) and Gaiseric the Vandal (in 455) not to sack the city.

        3. The popes began to be well connected to Roman society—for good or ill!

    C. But Rome's bishops were also playing on a larger stage before a bigger audience.

        1. The Council of Serdica in 343 decreed that appeals could go to Rome, and by the time of Innocent I, popes were claiming a prior right to make decisions.

        2. Pope Siricius (r. 384–399), the first Roman bishop to use *pope* as a title in the modern sense, issued the first *decretal* (a form of document and practice directly derived from Roman imperial procedure).

        3. When, at Church councils in 381 (Constantinople I) and 451 (Chalcedon), the clergy declared Constantinople to be the "New Rome," to be second in dignity and authority after "Old Rome," the popes objected fiercely, saying that their authority derived from Peter, not from Roman history.

    D. Indeed, there are many signs of the development of the Petrine argument first met in the pontificate of Stephen I.

        1. There was general agreement about the doctrine of apostolic succession and about Peter's leadership of the original community. There was, however, sharp disagreement about how these doctrines were to work in practice.

        2. Pope Damasus installed an inscription in San Sebastiano (the "Quo vadis?" church we discussed in Lecture One): "Whoever you may be that seek the names of Peter and

Paul, should know that here the saints once dwelt. The East sent the disciples—that we readily admit. But on account of the merit of their blood…Rome has gained the superior right to claim them as citizens."

3. The great exponent of the Petrine powers of the pope was Leo I, one of only two popes called "the Great."

    a. He imposed his will at the time of the Council of Chalcedon (451).

    b. He left behind some 150 letters and 96 sermons— vastly more than any of his predecessors.

4. Leo speaks as both pastor and lawyer. His claims are impressive but not more so than those of Gelasius a little later.

V. Withal, the Roman Church had emerged within the framework of the Roman Empire. What would happen when that empire vanished and Christianity conquered new geographies?

Recommended Reading:

Shotwell and Loomis, *The See of Peter*, pp. 211–715.

Ullmann, *The Growth of Papal Government*, chapter 1.

Questions to Consider:

1. What advantages and disadvantages did the bishops of Rome have in advancing their claims to authority?

2. Why did the doctrine of apostolic succession work particularly to the benefit of the bishops of Rome?

Lecture Two—Transcript
The Rise of the Petrine Idea

Hello, and welcome to the second of our lectures in this series of lectures on the history of the popes and of the papacy. This time we're going to talk about the rise of the Petrine idea, about the age of the emperor Constantine, and about the peace of the church. Essentially, we're going to talk about the period from about 300 to 500 A.D., which I think is really a crucial and formative period in lots of ways. Or, I'm going to suggest that, and in about 30 minutes time you can decide if I've made the case.

Let me enumerate some basic issues that we're going to talk about this time: First of all, the reign of the emperor Constantine, 306–337, who granted the church legal status, who permitted it to function open and publicly. Second, the importance and prestige of the popes grew dramatically in this period, as we'll see. Third, a free and important papacy, however, encountered problems that had never existed for a church that was small, persecuted and harassed. Fourth, slowly but surely, the popes began to define and to reflect on the nature of their office and the powers that it entailed. So those are the basic issues that we'll be tracing in this lecture. You may notice that there is some convergence between those issues and the ones I announced in Lecture One as being the issues that will run through the entire course.

Let's start off by saying something about the extremely obscure 2nd and 3rd centuries. I mean, last time, we kind of left the Roman world in the 2nd century making traditions about the 1st century, and I've just suggested this time we're going to look at the 4th and 5th centuries, so let's stick a little something, at least in the middle, in the 2nd and 3rd centuries. First of all, we just have to say we have very little evidence, and most of what we have is very late and hard to evaluate. For instance, we talked much about traditions last time. Tradition says that Peter and his successors were bishops of Rome. We'll have more to say in just a second about bishops. With respect to Peter, though, we can say this is possible. But we have no evidence for a functioning episcopal structure in Rome before the middle of the 2nd century, and even then the evidence is slim, and it doesn't start to come with any quantity and quality until the 4th century. Consequently, we know very little about what Rome's bishops actually did. What did it mean to be bishop of Rome in the year 150? That's a hard question to answer.

Bishops—maybe we ought to just pause here and say something about what exactly is a bishop. *Episcopus* in Latin, Επίσκοπος in Greek, means "overseer," "supervisor," "elder;" the word can be translated in various ways. The noun comes into English from Latin via old English, *biscop, episcope, biscop;* if you know German, you know the word *Bischof* in German. But all of the derivative forms come into English—episcopal, episcopate—straight from Latin and Greek. Words are wonderful things; they're designed as much to confuse us as to help us. What I'm really saying is we need the word *bishopal*, but we don't have that word in English. So when we're talking about "episcopal", we're not talking about the Episcopal Church, we're talking about things to do with bishops, with *episcopoi*.

Bishops emerged as key church officials in particular towns throughout the Mediterranean world—beginning in the Eastern Mediterranean world, gradually moving west—with responsibilities for leading worship, for teaching, and for recruiting both other members of the clergy, other people to assist them with these clerical responsibilities, and recruiting additional members of the Christian community. It appears that in many individual towns, individual Christian communities emerged. It would be anachronistic to think of parishes in this very early time, but just independent, sort of autonomous, Christian communities.

Probably each of these communities was led by a group of men called *presbyteroi*. The word *presbyter* comes from the Greek into the Latin through French into English as "priest". The word itself, again, means "elder," has something of the connotation of elder. In classical Greek, the word may actually also mean "ambassador." But anyway, it seems that most communities had a group of presbyters and that the senior presbyter was the overseer; he was the episcopus. About 150 A.D., plus or minus a little bit, we begin to find sources speaking of Monarchical bishops, *hoi monarchichoi episkopoi*. What this suggests is that somewhere in those towns, one of those bishops was beginning to become *the* bishop, that a town was beginning to have a variety of Christian communities, but over that town there was a bishop as the overseer, as the authority figure.

This also suggests to us that these bishops may have been—*may have been*—becoming fairly prominent figures in the cities of the Mediterranean world. Clement, pope ostensibly from 88 to 97, one of Peter's very early successors, encountered a controversy in Corinth. There's nothing new about that. You read Paul's letters to the Corinthians. How do they start? "Well, I'm so delighted to hear from you and to have news of you, and I'm praying for you and I hope you're praying for me and now I've got one or two things to talk to you about." Paul was always having problems with the Corinthians. In the 80s, Clement discovered that he had problems with the Corinthians, and he wrote them a letter. That letter survives, by the way. He doesn't say in this letter, "I'm writing to you because it's my job, because it's my duty, because I have the right to." He doesn't tell us anything about why he writes this letter; he simply offers them encouragement and admonishment. Was this a gesture of fraternal affection, or was it an assertion of a right or a duty to intervene? It's very hard to say.

Later in the 2nd century, Victor—189–198—attempted to impose his will in the matter of the date of celebrating Easter. What's that all about? Well, Easter, the feast of the commemoration of the resurrection of Christ. We know from the Gospels that the original last supper, crucifixion, resurrection took place during Passover. So in the early Christian community, a division arose fairly early from those who said that Easter, the resurrection, should always be commemorated at the time of Passover, and others who said it should *never* be commemorated at the time of Passover. Victor in Rome attempted to impose his will and had very limited success. People weren't willing to say "Victor says so; that must be it." Yet, a century before Victor—and I put these two events out of order precisely to give you a sense of the way things were and were not developing—in about 180, Irenaeus of Lyon spoke of Rome as "the great and illustrious church to which, on account of its commanding position, every church, that is the faithful everywhere, must resort." A hundred years later, they didn't all resort to Victor.

According to Irenaeus and others then, Rome's commanding position derived from its double apostolicity—two apostles, Peter and Paul. No other city could claim foundation. Remember, Rome claims foundation by Peter and Paul. We have reason to think probably they did not found that community, but the Roman tradition claimed foundation by Peter and Paul. In any case, no other city could claim two apostles, and no place could claim Peter and Paul, so that's a pretty big deal. But claiming links with the apostles—apostolic succession—was in and of itself ubiquitous. Every city that had the remotest claim for its community to have been established by apostles asserted that claim, so Rome was doing nothing more and nothing less than other cities.

Pope Urban I, 222–230, met a contested election when a fellow by the name of Hippolytus set himself up as the first antipope, the first of these individuals who tried to claim to be pope and who eventually was not, in fact, acknowledged as being legitimately a pope. I mention this case only because it hints at the emerging importance of the office and at the presence of factions, that there were contending groups, there were arguments; there were disagreements. What were they? It's pretty much buried in the mists of the past.

A very important figure is Stephen I, pope only three years, 254–257, but who was the first, so far as we know, to assert vigorously the Petrine document—there's that word again—of Roman authority. He insisted that he held the "Chair of Peter," the *cathedra Petri*. *Cathedra* in Greek is chair. Put an "L" on it, and it gives us our English word, cathedral. A cathedral is a bishop's church, and every cathedral has a bishop's throne in it. That's the chair of the bishop from which the bishop teaches, from which the bishop preaches to his community. So Stephen says he holds the *cathedra Petri* in succession to Peter. Here's one of our little fascinating fun facts about papal history. It inaugurates the notion that every pope succeeds Peter. Benedict XVI did not succeed John Paul II in April of 2005; Benedict XVI succeeded Saint Peter in April of 2005.

Many of the early popes were martyred. The Roman community was frequently disrupted, and the church could not function smoothly, publicly, visibly. That is certainly a big part of the reason that we know so little about it. These guys simply couldn't function in a way that left a lot of evidence on the record. Things changed dramatically with the emperor Constantine. If this were a course in Roman history or maybe even a course in the history of Christianity, we would probably want to go on at some length trying to figure out what made Constantine first favor, and then embrace, Christianity. Truthfully, there will never be a satisfactory explanation of that issue. I could go on at great length saying maybe this and this and this and this, and maybe that and that and that. The point is, for our purposes here, he did. He did first favor and then embrace Christianity.

Constantine and his co-ruler, whose name was Licinius, who's often forgotten, issued together the "Edict of Milan" in the year 313, which made Christianity licit. It made it a legal religion, *religio licita*, a legal religion in the Roman world. It was granted even status with all other religions. What this did is it put an end to the persecution and prosecution of Christians. Now Christians can function publicly. But Constantine was not neutral. He ordered the construction of Saint Peter's and Saint Paul's basilicas, that magnificent medieval basilica of Saint Peter's, which was replaced in the 16th century—we'll come to this in a later lecture—by the basilica that's there now. Constantine built Saint Peter's; he built Saint Paul's. These are staggeringly big buildings. You have some sense of the money that he spent on behalf of the church. He also granted to Pope Sylvester the Lateran Palace. The Laterani family had been a very wealthy family that had fallen afoul of the imperial authorities sometime earlier, and their lands in the southeast corner of Rome had come to the imperial family. So Constantine then gave these to Pope Sylvester, and eventually, of course, the Lateran Basilica emerged there. The Lateran Basilica, as you may know, is Rome's cathedral church. We always associate the pope with Saint Peter's. In a later lecture we'll talk about how all of Rome's churches kind of work, but the point is that the Lateran Basilica is given to the church by Constantine—well, the Lateran Palace, which evolves into the Lateran Basilica.

Constantine initiated a long series of imperial decrees on behalf of the church. He conferred tax exemptions, the tax exemptions churches enjoy to this day, reach back to Constantine. Military exemptions, the military exemptions the clergy enjoy, reach back to Constantine, and a variety of other things too. We could go through Roman law for the next two centuries and look at act after act after act on behalf of the Church. Constantine also—and this is important, and it's an issue that will be with us for many, many of our future lectures—he intervened in two doctrinal disputes. Again, if we were having a class in the history of Christianity, we would go into great length on these. I want just to say enough to make clear, sort of, what's at stake here without trying to dot every "i" and cross every "t". He intervened in a problem called Donatism and in a problem called Arianism.

Donatism was a problem. It's named for a bishop by the name of Donatus. It arose in North Africa. During the time of the persecution, there had been Christians, humanly enough, understandably enough, who knuckled under in the face of the persecutors. Once Christianity was granted legal status by Constantine, the people who had been brave throughout the curse of persecutions wanted nothing to do with these other guys who had sort of given up to the authorities during the period of persecution. In Rome and in many other places, a more conciliatory position was taken, "Let everyone back in. Bygones are bygones; we'll move on from here." So the Donatists didn't want these guys back, and it was really a quite brutal struggle in North Africa. So Constantine is faced with what he sees as a theological issue on the one hand, but he's faced also with real trouble in the North African provinces of the Empire.

Arianism—and it's worth mentioning this because it's going to occupy us again here a couple of times in the next few minutes— Arianism was the great Trinitarian heresy of antiquity. Let's unpack those words. Trinitarian theology is that branch of Christian theology that tries to explain how there can be one God—Father, Son and Holy Spirit. How can there be one God in three persons? Trinitarian theology tries to understand that subject. Eventually, the Arians were declared heretics. *Hairesis* in Greek means a choice; it means to choose. Essentially, it means you make the wrong choice. The heretics are the ones that the people in positions of power and responsibility eventually declare to be wrong. Arius was a priest from Alexandria, from Egypt, who, in an attempt to preserve strict monotheism, introduced what we call subordinationism. He said that Jesus was the firstborn of all creation, but not co-eternal with the Father. He made Jesus just that tiniest bit less than the Father by way of preserving pure monotheism. Of course, eventually Christian theologians said, "No, we don't believe that; Father, Son and Holy Spirit coequal, co-eternal."

So once again, it's a recondite theological problem that Constantine confronts, but he confronts battles in the streets in the cities of the Eastern Roman Empire. What's he going to do? Well, he attempted to impose his will, or he attempted to have the clergy decide what the correct theological interpretation should be. He would then impose that theological interpretation. So we find church and state—that's a little anachronistic—but we can say we find church and state beginning to be intertwined here in the early 4th century. And then, after all, we might say that a Roman emperor believes that everything to do with his Empire is his responsibility. It's his right and his duty to intervene, so he wouldn't have seen himself as crossing a line that might seem very clear to us, but that would have been invisible to him. Curiously enough, Constantine's successor, Emperor Constantius II, was an Arian himself. Constantius browbeat poor Pope Liberius, who was pope from 352–366, because he wanted to get Liberius to be a little more accommodating of the Arians. Liberius wouldn't have anything to do with it, but the emperor really leaned on him.

A century or a little bit more later, Pope Felix was bullied by the emperor Zeno over Monophysitism. Let's pause and talk about that for a second. Arianism was the great Trinitarian heresy. How do we understand Father, Son and Holy Spirit? Christology is that branch of theology that tries to understand the second person of the trinity—the Son, Jesus Christ—and in particular tries to understand that one being could be true God and true man. Monophysites—*mono physis*, one nature—Monophysites were people who, trying to preserve the unity of the second person of the trinity, said that Jesus had only a divine nature. He seemed to be human, as a man in the world, but he didn't have a perfect human nature; he had only a divine nature. Well, again, strict Christian theology said "No, not true; true God, true man."

The emperor in the East, however, was faced with a rather serious problem. There were lots of Monophysites. In fact, some of the cities in the Eastern Roman Empire probably had majority Monophysite populations, so the emperor Zeno is trying to gain a theological formula that will reconcile the Monophysites, and he's leaning on the pope in Rome, Felix III. Felix finally says "Enough, stop," and he would not accommodate the emperor. Popes and emperors, quite frankly, simply wanted to achieve unity: one faith, one emperor, one church, but they couldn't really quite get it. Now, Pope Gelasius I, who was pope from 492–496—only for a very brief time—spoke on this issue of the relation of emperors and popes in a rather decisive and, I think you'll agree, rather shocking way.

Our problems with the Monophysites continue. Zeno's successor Anastasius is still trying to lean on Rome to come to an agreement. By now actually, Rome and Constantinople are at loggerheads. The two churches have split; the pope in Rome has excommunicated the patriarch of Constantinople. Things are going badly, and Gelasius writes to the emperor Anastasius. He writes him a very famous letter, and he says there're two powers by which the world is governed, the *auctoritas* of priests and the *potestas* of kings. *Auctoritas* is a very rich word in Latin. It gives us our English word "authority," "dignity," "legitimacy," what's right. *Potestas* is a very different kind of word—"power," sheer power, the iron fist, police power. The pope says normally the two realms of priests and kings are distinct, but if they ever conflict, the rule of priests must take precedence because priests are responsible for men's souls, which are immortal, and kings rule men's bodies that are mortal. Four centuries earlier, a gang of rather petty Roman officials in a faraway province of the empire had executed a rabble rouser named Jesus, and now Gelasius in theory elevates the entire Christian establishment over the Roman Empire. That, I think you'll agree with me, is a pretty dramatic change.

Well, that's not the only change that we can observe in this period. The explanation for this change is, in lots of ways, attributable to the growing power of bishops, and from our point of view, given our interest, of Rome's bishops. In other words, let's talk a bit about the rise of the papacy—popes yes, but of the papacy, of an institution. Amidst the chaos of the later Roman Empire, Christianity probably began to see itself a lot more compelling, a lot more interesting, a lot more attractive than the changeability of the emperors. Rome's bishops, who had been very brave in the days of persecution—very steadfast, very theologically sound in the years after Christianity was granted freedom—were somehow attractive figures. In and around Rome, the popes began to become much more visible, much more prominent leaders, much more prominent figures in their city.

For instance, we saw that Constantine donated these great basilicas. Popes began building churches—San Marco by Pope Mark, Sant Anastasia by Damasus, Santa Sabina by Celestine I; Santa Maria Maggiore by Sixtus III. Those are just a few examples. They are not the only ones; those are just some of the really spectacular examples of papal churches. Innocent I, minister to Rome after the Gothic sack—the Visigoths sacked Rome in the year 410, sent a great shockwave through the Roman world—but it was Pope Innocent who really had the city back on its feet after this devastating blow, and it was Pope Leo I who persuaded Attila the Hun in 452 and Gaiseric the Vandal in 455 not to attack Rome, not to sack Rome. Who was papal Rome beginning to look to as their natural leader and protector?

The popes began to be very well connected to Roman society, Roman high society, for good or ill. Pope Damasus was called *matronarum auriscalpius*, "the ladies' ear-tickler." He apparently had a great gift at persuading women to join the church, and at persuading them to give lots of money and property to the church. The Roman government had to pass a law to try to put a stop to the latter practice. But mentioning Damasus, we might say that at his election, there were riots in Rome and 137 people died, so obviously being bishop of Rome was beginning to be a pretty big deal. The contemporary historian Ammianus Marcellinus, who was a pagan—very important source for the history of the Roman world, but a pagan, not sympathetic to the church at all—described the situation this way. "I don't deny that men who covet this office in order to fulfill their ambitions may well struggle for it with every resource at their disposal. For once they have obtained it they are ever after secure, enriched with offerings from the ladies, riding abroad seated in their carriages, splendidly arrayed giving banquets so lavish that they surpass the tables of royalty."

But Rome's bishops were also beginning to play on a larger stage and before a bigger audience than just the matrons of Rome. A church council, for example, in the year 343 in the city of Serdica in the Balkans, decreed that appeals from any controversy in a local church could be sent to Rome. By the time of Pope Innocent I, the pope was claiming that he had a prior right to make decisions in any areas where there was controversy. Siricius, who was pope at the end of the 4th century, was the first Roman bishop to use the title "Pope" in something like its modern sense, and he issued the first decretal. You can see the word "decree" hiding in decretal. A decretal is a papal letter basically commanding somebody to do something, for something to happen, some principle to be observed. It is making law; it is a policy, a procedure directly derived from Roman imperial chancellery practices. This is how the Roman emperors did things; they sent decrees. When church councils—for example, at

Constantinople in 381, and at Chalcedon in 451—declared Constantinople to be the "New Rome," second in dignity and authority after "Old Rome," the popes objected fiercely. They said "We're not important because the emperor says so. We're not important because the church council says so. We're important because we succeed Peter. Peter was the leader, we're the leader; end of case."

What we're seeing here, of course, are signs of the development of the Petrine argument. We first saw hints of this in the New Testament. We first saw an articulation of this in the pontificate of Stephen I, but now we're beginning to see something a little sharper, a little more precise. There was general agreement about the doctrine of apostolic succession. Even amongst Christian churches today, there's general agreement that the teaching of the apostles has been handed down. But is it the case that an office, a duty, a responsibility, a power, a jurisdiction has been handed down? That's where it gets sticky. Similarly, was this handed to Peter and, therefore, to Peter's successors, or to all of the apostles and therefore to all the successors of all the apostles? The Roman Catholic Church takes the Petrine view; other churches take a broader view of this succession. But the doctrine of succession isn't really disputed by anybody.

Pope Damasus—we've bumped into him a bunch of times—installed an inscription in the "Quo Vadis" church that we met in Lecture One, a big public inscription. If you've ever visited, really any place where Rome had ever been, but any of the Roman sites in Italy, you've seen these great inscriptions all over the place. It was kind of public relations Roman style in the old days. So he put up an inscription in the "Quo Vadis" church. "Whoever you may be that seeks the names of Peter and Paul, should know that here the saints once dwelt. The East sent the disciples; that we readily admit, on account of the merit of their blood. They all died in Rome, didn't they? Rome has gained the superior right to claim them as citizens."

The great exponent of the Petrine powers of the pope was Leo I, pope from 440–461, one of only two popes to be called "the Great". There is a movement now to call John Paul II John Paul the Great. We'll see; it'll take a while for that to stick, but so far, of 265, two are "the Great." We're going to meet the second one in our next lecture. We already met Leo as the man who defended Rome from the Huns and from the Vandals. Here is a pope who imposed his will at the time of the Council of Chalcedon, when all these issues about Monophysitism came up. He really put his foot down, made them heel to his message. He left behind some 150 letters and 96 sermons. We have no reason to suppose this is the entire corpus of letters and sermons that he ever composed, but it's interesting to say we have more material from Leo I than from all his predecessors put together. This is a substantial corpus of material. Now by the way, let me add, this material comes in a flood from then until now.

In his letter Number Eleven, he speaks this way. "It is certain that the only defense for us and our empire is the favor of the God of heaven; and to deserve it our first care is to support the Christian faith and its venerable religion. So, because the preeminence of the apostolic see is assured by the merit of the prince of bishops St. Peter, by the leading position of Rome, and also by the authority of a sacred synod, let none presume to attempt anything contrary to the authority of that see. For then at last the peace of the churches will be preserved everywhere if the whole body recognizes its ruler." I think you can see here that Leo is talking a bit like a pastor and a bit like a lawyer. His claims are impressive, but they are not more so than those of his successor, Gelasius, just a few years later. Leo is placing the pope at the head of the church. Gelasius placed the pope at the head of the world order.

Leo also used the word "see". I was translating there the Latin *sedes*, which means seat, literally the seat of authority. Do you know what a county seat is? It's the seat of authority. Well, when you bring that word into English straight out of the Latin, you have the Holy See, so it means the seat of authority, so it means something physical, concrete and geographical. It's there, and it's also something notional, so if in later lectures I use "Holy See," that's what we're talking about.

Well, the Roman Church had emerged within the framework of the Roman Empire. In our next lecture we're going to try to understand what would happen when that empire vanished and the pope had to deal with a very new geographical order.

Lecture Three
Popes, Byzantines, and Barbarians

Scope:

Roman authority around Rome had been weak throughout the 5th century and vanished in 476. From one point of view, the popes were left alone to deal with the new situation. From another point of view, the popes were hemmed in by real and potential enemies. If Rome no longer had emperors, then Constantinople certainly did. And those emperors were keen to impose doctrinal formulations on the popes and did not hesitate to kidnap and browbeat popes to impose their will. Popes had to contend with a series of views they regarded as heretical, from Monophysitism in the 6th century to Iconoclasm in the 8th. These struggles began to loosen papal Rome's ties to the Roman legacy. In Italy, the popes were hemmed in first by Ostrogoths, then by Lombards. The eastern and southern shores of the Mediterranean were lost to emergent Islam. But not all was bleak. The popes sent missionaries to England and supported missionaries in Germany. We can see the popes slowly reorienting their focus from the Mediterranean world to Western Europe. This period also witnessed the pontificate of Gregory I or Gregory the Great, one of the most remarkable of all Peter's successors.

Outline

I. The papacy faced a new world after the collapse of Roman order in the West.

    A. The eastern Roman Empire gradually evolved into the Byzantine Empire, and sharp conflicts on many levels separated Rome and Constantinople.

    B. Rome's former western provinces had been parceled out in a series of barbarian kingdoms with which the popes entered into varying relationships.

II. The papacy's dealings with imperial Constantinople wavered between hostility and reconciliation, only to end in estrangement.

    A. As we have seen, Arianism and Monophysitism had generated serious tension between popes and emperors, on the one hand, and between popes and prominent Eastern churchmen, on the other hand.

B. As the 6th century dawned, Rome and Constantinople were separated owing to the Acacian Schism: Pope Felix III (r. 483–492) had excommunicated Patriarch Acacius (r. 472–489).

C. Emperor Justin I (r. 518–527) was a devout Catholic who wished for religious peace and worked with Pope Hormisdas (r. 514–523) to achieve unity.

    1. More than 2,500 Eastern bishops signed the so-called "Formula of Hormisdas": "I consider the holy churches of God, that of Old Rome and that of New Rome, as one and the same church, the see of Peter the Apostle and the episcopal see of Constantinople as one and the same see...I agree with the pope's profession of doctrine and I censure all whom he censures."

    2. Within a few years, Popes John I (r. 523–526) and Agapitus (r. 535–536) were received in Constantinople with the highest honors.

D. But the unity was soon shattered.

    1. Emperor Justinian (r. 527–565) desired both religious unity in the East and firm union with papal Rome. He could not have both.

        a. His remarkable wife, Theodora (c. 497–548), was an avowed Monophysite, and Justinian wanted to find a formula that did not overtly violate Chalcedon while reconciling the Monophysites.

        b. His court theologians decided to condemn the writings of three relatively obscure Chalcedonians—the so-called "Three Chapters."

        c. Justinian was engaged in the reconquest of Italy and needed papal support, and he wanted papal acquiescence to the condemnation of the Three Chapters.

        d. Pope Silverius (r. 536–537) refused to budge and was arrested and deposed.

        e. Pope Vigilius (r. 537–555) was also arrested but then wavered, finally agreeing to the decisions of the Fifth Ecumenical Council in Constantinople (553).

2. Rome and most of the West were outraged, but much of the East did not think the condemnation of the Three Chapters went far enough.

E. As the 7th century progressed, the empire faced first Persian, then Muslim threats in the East, as well as Slavic, Avar, and Bulgar assaults in the Balkans.

    1. Unity was again imperative; thus, Emperor Heraclius (r. 610–641) looked for a formula of reconciliation.

    2. His theologians hit upon *Monoenergism*, which was soon refined into *Monothelitism.*

    3. Pope Honorius I (r. 625–638) accepted Monothelitism and was subsequently condemned in the East and West.

    4. When Pope Martin I (r. 649–655) called a Church council in Rome to refute Monothelite teachings, imperial agents arrested him, brutalized him, and led him in chains to Constantinople, where his mistreatment continued until he died.

F. In 680, Emperor Constantine IV (r. 668–685) held the Sixth Ecumenical Council, which repudiated Monothelitism. This move *might* have restored papal-imperial peace.

    1. Emperor Justinian II (r. 685–695, 705–711) called the Quinisext Council, which issued many decrees that were unacceptable in Rome.

    2. Pope Sergius I (r. 687–701) refused to accept the canons and responded in subtle ways, for instance, inserting the *Agnus Dei* in the Mass.

G. In the 8th century, the situation went from bad to worse.

    1. The imperial government repeatedly tried to raise tax revenues in Italy but would provide no help against the Lombards.

    2. In 726, Emperor Leo III (r. 717–741) began to campaign against icons, and some of his zealous followers—Iconoclasts—began to destroy them. The popes resolutely condemned Iconoclasm.

    3. In response, Leo stripped the papacy of critical revenues from southern Italy and the western Balkans and transferred the allegiance of bishops in those areas to Constantinople.

H. The papacy had arisen in the context of the Roman Empire but now had to think in new geographical and ideological terms.

III. What terms? The answer was gradually provided by the shifting political geography of the post-Roman West.

   A. Where there had once been a dense network of prefectures, dioceses, and provinces, there were now kingdoms.

   B. These kingdoms posed various problems for papal Rome.

      1. Several kingdoms were ruled by Arian kings: the Ostrogoths, the Visigoths until 589, and the Vandals.

      2. The popes had perforce to deal with the Ostrogoths in Italy, but the regime of King Theodoric (r. 496–526) was enlightened.

      3. Primarily, the popes had no experience in dealing with such peoples or their rulers.

   C. Circumstances began to change decisively with Pope Gregory I (r. 590–604).

      1. He struggled to achieve peace with the Lombards and tried hard, but unsuccessfully, to convert them from their Arianism.

      2. When the Visigothic King Reccared (r. 586–601) converted to Catholicism, Gregory entered into relations with him and encouraged him. Gregory also began an exchange of letters with Archbishop Leander of Seville.

      3. Gregory exchanged letters on a wide array of topics with Queen Brunhilde (d. 613) of the Franks, who was reigning as regent for her grandsons.

      4. Most famously, Gregory sent a mission to England in 596 that inaugurated the (re-)conversion of England.

   D. As the 7th century progressed and became the 8th, two issues were clear, while many were unclear.

      1. The Greek East and Latin West were drifting apart.

      2. The orientation of the papacy was increasingly Western.

IV. Gregory I or Gregory the Great is the first pope about whom a great deal is known and who can be treated in something like biographical fashion. Let us profile him.

   A. He was from a senatorial family and was the great-grandson of Pope Felix III.

B. His youth and upbringing are unknown, but from his voluminous writings, we can see that he was highly educated and widely read.

C. In 572, the emperor made him prefect of the city of Rome, the highest civil office in the city.

D. After serving only two years, Gregory resigned to become a monk.

    1. He turned his own house on the Caelian Hill into a monastery dedicated to St. Andrew and created six other monasteries on family lands in Sicily.

    2. In 578, the pope made him one of Rome's regionary deacons and, in 579, apocrisiarius to Constantinople. He held that office until 586.

    3. Gregory returned to Rome and to his monastic retreat, but on the death of Pelagius II in an attack of plague, Gregory was unanimously elected pope in 590.

E. Gregory's own writings reveal that he was dispirited by many concerns.

F. Yet, with a truly Roman sense of duty and responsibility, he took to his job energetically.

G. He also wrote voluminously, more originally and brilliantly than any pope before him and more than all but a few after him.

H. This remarkably attractive man, who called himself—as all his successors have done—"Servant of the Servants of God," is perhaps never more impressive than when we realize he was desperately ill his whole adult life.

Recommended Reading:

Markus, *Gregory the Great*.

Richards, *Popes and the Papacy*.

Questions to Consider:

1. What impact did the disappearance of Roman imperial rule from the West have on the emerging papacy?

2. In what ways was Gregory I an exemplary Roman and Christian?

Lecture Three—Transcript
Popes, Byzantines, and Barbarians

Hello, and welcome again to the third of our lectures in this series on the history of the popes and of the papacy. This time we're going to talk about popes and Byzantines and barbarians. You may recall that last time we discussed those dynamic centuries between about 300 and 500, when the popes asserted and began actually to exercise considerable leadership within the church, and when at least one pope, Gelasius, asserted a kind of primacy over the entire secular ruling apparatus. But as we know, late in the 5th century, the Roman Empire in the West came to an end. The Roman Empire in the East, of course, persisted for another millennium, but how would the pope—how would the papacy—deal with a very different world from the one that had given birth to it?

The Eastern Roman Empire, of course, gradually evolved into what we call the Byzantine Empire, and sharp conflicts on many levels separated Rome and Constantinople. In this lecture, as well as in some future ones, we're going to talk about the gradual separation of Eastern and Western, of Greek and Latin, of orthodox and Roman Catholicism. So that's one theme for this lecture, the emergence of a Byzantine world in the Eastern Mediterranean, and the papacy's relations with that world. The second theme that we're going to follow in this lecture, sort of pursuing this geographical idea, is that in the Western half of what had once been the Roman Empire, we find a series of barbarian kingdoms. How will the popes build relationships with these new barbarian kingdoms? So that will be a second issue that we'll talk about in this lecture. In some ways, we're watching, really, the forward march of Western civilization out of the Mediterranean basin and into the world of Western Europe, the papacy sometimes leading and sometimes following in that process.

So Byzantium, in the first place, then. The papacy's dealings with imperial Constantinople wavered between hostility and reconciliation, only to end in estrangement. As we've seen, Arianism and then Monophysitism had generated serious tensions between the popes and the emperors on the one hand, and between the popes and prominent Eastern clergymen on the other hand. As the 6th century dawned, Rome and Constantinople were separated, owing to what we call the Acacian Schism. You may remember that Emperor Zeno had tried to get Pope Felix III, and Emperor Anastasius had tried to get Pope Gelasius, to make some accommodations on the Monophysite question. The patriarch of Constantinople at that time—his name was Acacius—had also tried to find some accommodation on the Monophysite question, and as a result, the popes in Rome had simply cut off dealing with him. They had had schism—the word means split—so as the 6th century dawned the church is smack in the middle of what we call the "Acacian Schism." You notice that in Rome they named it the Acacian Schism. In Constantinople, of course, they didn't view it as the Acacian Schism. But anyway, Rome and the East are estranged as the 6th century opens.

Emperor Justin I, 518-527, was a devout Catholic. He wanted religious peace. He wanted to work with the pope. The pope was then named Hormisdas. We'll have a lot more to say about papal names in later lectures, but this guy is particularly interesting. Hormisdas is the Greek form of Ahura-Mazda. This guy obviously had pagans in his family tree—not himself, but he had some interesting pagans way back there somewhere. Anyway, Justin and Hormisdas want to work together to try to find unity. The emperor basically begged, wheedled and forced about 2,500 Eastern bishops to sign the so-called Formula of Hormisdas. Here's what they had to swear. "I consider the holy churches of God, that of Old Rome and that of New Rome, as one and the same church, the See of Peter the Apostle and the Episcopal See of Constantinople as one and the same see... I agree with the pope's profession of doctrine and I censure all whom he censures."

The next 15 centuries would have been a lot easier if the Formula of Hormisdas had stuck. It did not stick. What we can see is that the pope and the emperor were trying to find a way to accommodate all of these vast differences. Within just a few years, for instance, Pope John I and then Pope Agapitus were received in Constantinople with the highest honors. We're going to see in just a minute that in the next couple of generations, popes were received in Constantinople under very different circumstances. The unity so much sought for, and apparently achieved by Justin and Hormisdas, was soon shattered. Justinian came to the throne in 527. He ruled until 565, in many ways perhaps the greatest of the late antique emperors of the Eastern Roman Empire. Justinian, as did so many of his predecessors, wanted religious unity in the East and a firm union with papal Rome. That's basically what he wanted: religious unity in the East, union with Rome. He couldn't have both.

His remarkable wife Theodora—were this a course in Byzantine history or in other subjects, we would pursue her for a while; she's quite an interesting figure—was an avowed Monophysite. She may very well have exerted some influence on her husband. It isn't clear if Justinian was indifferent to matters of religion, if he was sort of willing to find a good deal, to find a good bargain. It's very hard to say. But one way or another, Justinian was trying to find a way to develop a religious formula that would not overtly violate the Council of Chalcedon. Remember, that's the Council in 451 that followed the teachings of Pope Leo I, which basically condemned the Monophysites, embracing the traditional Catholic, broadly Christian teachings of Diophysitism—that Christ has two natures, divine and human. Well, as I've pointed out, there were lots of Monophysites in the Eastern Roman world, so Justinian wants to find some formula that will reconcile the Monophysites but not violate Chalcedon. This is no easy trick.

Well, his court theologians hit upon the stratagem of condemning the writings of three rather obscure Chalcedonian—that means people who follow the teachings of Chalcedon—theologians. These are the so-called "Three Chapters," so if ever in your reading you've come across the Three Chapters controversy, it's because Justinian's theologians decided that what they would do was to condemn the teachings of three relatively obscure followers—adherents, I should say—of the Council of Chalcedon. Justinian at that very moment was engaged in the reconquest of Italy. He was re-conquering Italy from barbarian people called the Ostrogoths—we'll have more to say about them a little bit later—and he wanted papal support. He wanted good relations with the pope, and he wanted the pope to go along with his condemnation of the Three Chapters. Pope Sylverius simply refused; he refused to budge. He was arrested and deposed. The first time an emperor had done that.

Along comes Pope Virgilius. He refused, then he agreed, then he refused, then he agreed; he went back and forth, back and forth. Finally, Justinian called a great church council, the Fifth Ecumenical Council in Constantinople, in 553, and Virgilius signed on. We'll have occasion to see later on that this had consequences in the future. Rome and most of the West were outraged, but much of the East felt that the condemnation of the Three Chapters hadn't gone nearly far enough. There was no way, really, to compose these difficulties. As the 7th century progressed, the Roman Empire in the East faced a brutal series of wars with the Persians, only to exhaust the treasury and their physical resources as well, and then to face the onslaught of Islam. And, they faced in the Balkans repeated blows by Slavs, Avars and Bulgars. This was a very difficult time for the Eastern Roman Empire, for the emerging Byzantine Empire.

Still, the emperors want unity, so Emperor Heraclius, in the 7th century, begins to put his theologians to work trying to find a formula that will reconcile all these contending parties. They first hit on Monoenergism, so now they're off Monophysitism, one naturism. They're having Monoenergism; there's one energy in the second person of the Trinity, a divine energy. People said "No, that won't do." So he tries Monotheletism; there is one will in the second person of the Trinity, a divine will. No, that doesn't work either, except that Pope Honorius I, 625-638, accepted Monotheletism. Subsequently, Monotheletism was condemned in both the East and the West, and Honorius was condemned by name. In Dante's great poetry, the *Divina Commedia*, both of these popes wind up in the inferno. They wind up in Hell for not being very faithful to the Roman Church. But also, a subject that will occupy us much later in our course of lectures, papal infallibility—can the pope err? Two popes did. This will be a subject that will engage us in the future.

Martin I called a church council in Rome, for example, to refute the Monothelite teachings after Honorius. Imperial agents arrested him, brutalized him, led him to Constantinople in chains, imprisoned him and put him off in the Khersones way up in the Aegean Sea, where he was abused until he finally died. So this was the kind of treatment you got by the emperors in the East if you didn't go along with their teaching. In 680 Emperor Constantine IV held the Sixth Ecumenical Council of the Church. This council repudiated Monotheletism, returned, in other words, to the teaching of the Council of Chalcedon, which has remained the official teaching of the Orthodox Church, the Greek Church, ever since, as indeed it has always been the teaching of the Latin Church, the Roman Church. This might have restored imperial papal peace. Finally these guys were on the same page and there weren't any qualifications. The emperor had basically agreed that he was no longer going to try and find a formula to reconcile the Eastern provinces. It was a little bit easier for him not to try to reconcile those provinces now. He had lost them all; they were all in Islamic hands. The Muslims had conquered most of those cities in the East that the emperors had been trying to work with.

But then things get a little interesting. Emperor Justinian II, 685–695, was pulled off the throne, then he came back for a few years in the early 8th century—wanted his great church council too. But there was no big burning issue to have an ecumenical council, so he called a council that issued a bunch of disciplinary decrees—in other words, just rules about church organization and the conduct of business, that sort of thing—and added those to the decrees of the Fifth and the Sixth Councils, so tradition calls this the Quinisext Council. That means the Fifth-Sixth Council. This Fifth-Sixth Council passed a whole bunch of regulations on church government, and Rome immediately said "No, we don't like these rules. We're not going to obey these rules. We're not going along with these rules. We didn't have anything to do with formulating these rules. We disagree."

Here we have a very interesting case of the ways in which the resources the popes have to respond. One of those Quinisext rules forbade depictions of Christ as a lamb. Now, the image of the lamb of God, both as a literary and poetry and so on—the paschal sacrifice, the paschal lamb—but also in art, representations of a lamb—if you see a picture of a lamb in a Christian setting, you know that's a symbol for Christ—the Quinisext said, "No longer depict Christ as a lamb." Over in Rome, we've seen, they reject the Quinisext Council. Over in Rome, Pope Sergius I introduces in the mass, after the fraction rite—the fraction rite is when the priest breaks the host, breaks the bread—then in the mass, the next thing that happens, *Agnus Dei qui tollis peccata mundi*, "Lamb of God who takes away the sins of the world..." Sergius puts the Lamb of God prayer in the liturgy of the Catholic Church. Take that, Constantinople! And the Lamb of God prayer is still in the liturgy, in exactly the place that Sergius put it; very interesting, the ways that these guys have of sort of getting up each other's noses.

In the 8th century, alas, things went from bad to worse in relations between Greek East and Latin West, and I'll put a little bit of stress on that, Greek East and Latin West. For a long time, it had been possible to maintain the pretense that this was still one Roman world. But it was increasingly clear that these were two cultural worlds. In certain respects they always had been, and now in many ways this was simply coming to the surface in ways that could no longer be ignored or avoided. The imperial government, for instance, repeatedly tried to raise tax money in Italy. Why? Because they have to fight Muslims, they have to fight Avars, they have to fight Bulgars and they have to fight Slavs. In other words, they have battles in the East. They're trying to raise taxes in Italy. Italy is contending with people called the Lombards, who invade the peninsula in the middle of the 6th century. We'll have a little more to say about Lombards in a few minutes and a lot more to say about Lombards in our next lecture. For now let's just say the Lombards are giving the popes a lot of trouble in Italy. The people in Italy would like a little of that tax money spent In Italy. They'd like some of those Byzantine armies in Italy. Byzantium has no time for Italy.

In the 720s, Emperor Leo III began to campaign against icons. Emperor Leo was a man, he was a soldier, he was a man of fairly simple piety, and he came to the feeling that icons—we think of icons as the beautiful religious art of the East—that icons were idols, that they were offensive to God, that Byzantium's military defeats were owing to punishment by God, so he began to write against, his theologians began to write, against images. Then some of his more enthusiastic followers, we call them Iconoclasts—an iconoclast is an icon breaker—they began to destroy religious art. The pope jumped in and roundly condemned Iconoclasm, both as a theology and as a practice. Again, separation of East and West; how did Emperor Leo III respond? Well, he stripped the papacy of critical revenue from dioceses in southern Italy and in the Balkans, and he placed the bishops in those territories under the jurisdiction of Constantinople, whereas previously they had been under the jurisdiction of the Bishop of Rome. Those revenues and those bishoprics will engage our attention again in future lectures, but at this moment, what we see is simply more evidence of this very difficult struggle between East and West.

The papacy had arisen in the context of the Roman Empire. It now has to think in new geographical terms. This Roman Empire is, quite frankly, a big pain in the neck if you're in Rome and if you're the pope. The popes never threw it overboard, they never abandoned it and they never said at some moment, "That's it, we're not Roman anymore. We're having nothing to do with it anymore." But the facts were making the split between East and West clearer and clearer. In what terms would the popes learn to deal with this new geographical situation? This leads us then to talk a little bit about the shifting political geography of the post-Roman West. In the East, that Byzantine Empire may be shrinking all the time, but it can always make the claim until that year 1453, when Constantinople fell to the Turks, that the Roman Empire was alive and well. I don't know how well it was, but it was alive in some sense for a long time.

In the West, Rome was gone. There had once been a dense network of prefectures, dioceses, provinces; now there were kingdoms. These kingdoms posed various different problems for papal Rome. Several of them, for example, were ruled by Arian kings, and we could really kind of feel sorry for a number of these Germanic peoples. A number of them entered the Roman world or entered Roman military service in those decades in the middle of the 4th century, when Constantius II, Constantine's successor, was emperor and Arian. So a lot of these barbarians entered the Roman world and embraced the most up-to-date form of Christianity, only to find that that Christianity was then condemned. They wound up stuck with it, in a certain sense, so the pope is dealing with kingdoms whose rulers are heretics.

How do you do that? In Italy, things didn't work too badly, really. The Ostrogoths, who conquered Italy beginning in the 490s under their King Theodoric, were very enlightened. Theodoric was a very enlightened ruler, and the Ostrogoths generally speaking got along with the Catholic population of Italy, so things didn't go too badly. The popes learned that they could deal with these people. You didn't necessarily like them, you certainly didn't agree with them on religious stuff, but you could deal with them.

Things began to change pretty decisively in the West with Pope Gregory I, 590–604. The time that remains to us in this lecture, we're going to sort of be circling around Gregory almost all the time. Gregory struggled to achieve peace with the Lombards. There was really nobody else who could do this, so Gregory tried very hard to achieve peace with the Lombards. He also tried very hard, but unsuccessfully, to convert the Lombards from Arianism. They too, as a number of these other Germanic peoples, were Arians. When the Visigothic king Reccared—he reigned from 586–601—converted to

Catholicism, Gregory immediately entered into relations with him; moreover, Gregory began an exchange of letters with Archbishop Leander of Seville, so the great ecclesiastical leader of Spain, now Gregory enters into relationships with him. Those letters survive; they're really quite interesting.

Gregory, as another example, exchanged letters on a wide array of topics with Queen Brunhilde. She died in about 613. She was the queen of the Franks at this time as regent for her grandsons. The Franks would not have permitted a woman to rule them, but Queen Brunhilde was sort of functioning as regent, as I said, in place of her grandsons. Gregory entered into relations with her. Most famously however, Gregory sent a mission to England in 596 that inaugurated the conversion, or we might say really the re-conversion of England. There had been Christians in England going back to the last years of the third, the first years of the 4th century, at the very least; it may go back further than that. But in the tremendous chaos and tumult of the last years of the Roman Empire, the church just collapsed in England. There probably were pockets of Christians, for example, out in the West, in Wales, over a long period of time, but for the most part ecclesiastical organization had collapsed. There weren't many Christians in that part of the British Isles that that we now know as England, so Gregory launched the re-conversion of that part of the British Isles.

As the 7th century progressed and turned into the eighth, a couple of things were pretty clear, and a lot of things were very unclear. The Greek East and the Latin West were drifting apart. That's clear. How that drift was going to work, with what consequences? Might it be remedied? These are questions that will engage us in quite a number of our later lectures, but we can see by the year 700, we can see East and West drifting apart. Second, we can see that the papacy's future was no clearer than that of the West itself. Would the pope wind up as a kind of local bishop in a place called Rome that wasn't very important anymore? Would the pope be the head of some kind of universal church? But what would universal mean when certainly the Greek East didn't any longer think of itself as part of this universality, and where in the West, Franks and Anglo Saxon and Goths and Lombards and all of these people didn't think of themselves as heirs to, as parts of a Roman community in the way that people living in the Roman Empire a century, two, three, four, five centuries before had thought of themselves? What was this world going to be like? Well, it was very hard to say.

Some hints about what that future was going to look like emerged in the pontificate of Gregory I. Pontificate; we've talked about words here. *Pontifex* in Latin is the word for high priest. The word actually means bridge builder because the high priest in Rome was the one who watched the original bridge over the River Tiber. The ability to cross that river was a big deal, so *pontifex* in Latin is the word for a high priest, so a pontiff in England is a high priest. The pontificate is the rule of the high priest, so that's where those words come from. Gregory I, Gregory the Great, the second of the two popes ever called the Great, is the first pope about whom a great deal is known and who can be treated in something like biographical fashion.

Let's kind of pause and talk about Gregory for a little while. He's, in lots of ways, a quite interesting, quite compelling character. He came from a senatorial family. He came from the highest level of the Roman aristocracy. But he was also the great-grandson of Pope Felix III, so we can see that members of the Roman aristocracy had, at certain points at least, begun going into the clergy in the City of Rome. About Gregory's youth and upbringing, we know almost nothing. We could probably generalize from what we know about other prominent Romans and say he probably studied these books and learned these things, but we don't really know concretely very much about Gregory. We do know, however, from his writings—I'll have more to say about his writings in just a second, his voluminous writings—we know from his writings this was an extraordinarily well educated, well read man. He was a gifted Latin stylist, so this was a person who had a great deal of native ability, but he also was brilliantly educated.

In 572, the emperor over in Constantinople made Gregory prefect of the City of Rome. That was the highest civilian office in the city. This was the kind of office that would have culminated the career of a great individual. After serving only two years, Gregory resigned—to seek a higher office?—no, to become a monk. He turned his own house on the Caelian Hill in Rome into the Monastery of Saint Andrew, and he created six more monasteries on family properties in Sicily. It kind of reminds us that these powerful Roman families had lands scattered all over Italy, all over the West. These were some very wealthy, powerful people. In 578, the pope made Gregory one of Rome's regionary deacons. In a little bit later lecture, we're going to talk about how the Roman Church itself in the City of Rome was organized, and we'll see exactly who these deacons were. For right now, just trust me if I say this is a big job, this is a very important job.

So Gregory is made one of Rome's regionary deacons, and just a little while later, in 579 he's made Apocrisiarius. We would be more familiar in our times with the word *legate* or the word *nuncio* as the pope's representative to somebody. But in this time the pope's representative to the imperial court at Constantinople, to the emperor and to the church at Constantinople, is the Apocrisiarius, so the pope makes Gregory his man at Constantinople. That's a big job, too. Gregory held that position until 586, returned to Rome, returned to his monastic retreat. Four years later, on the death of Pope Pelagius II—he died in the plague—Gregory was unanimously, we're told unanimously, elected Pope in the year 590.

Gregory was dispirited. He was dispirited by the condition of his beloved Rome. Romans loved their city; they always have. Gregory said, "What is there now of delight in this world? Everywhere we observe strife; everywhere we hear groans. See what has befallen Rome, once mistress of the world. She is worn down by great sorrows, by the disappearance of her citizens, by the attacks of her enemies, by numerous ruins." He is dispirited as well by his own election as Pope. "Desiring nothing and fearing nothing on this earth, I felt as though I were standing on the summit of a high mountain," when he was in his monastery, he wrote, "but now this hurricane has thrown me down and I am dragged by the currents of problems and beaten about by the storm." This was not a man who sought out, craved high office; this was a man who thought he had been punished when he was elected Pope.

Indeed, shortly after this election, which he fervently asked the Emperor Maurice to forbid, he had this to say, "Under the pretense of being made a bishop, I have been brought back into the world, and I devote myself to the interest of secular things to a much greater extent than I recall even having done when I was a layman. I have lost the deep joy of my peace and quiet, and while I seem outwardly to have risen, inwardly I am in a state of collapse." Yet, with a truly Roman sense of duty and responsibility, he took his job as pope energetically. He protected the City of Rome from attacks by the

Lombards; there was no one else to do it. He negotiated with the imperial government on a wide array of issues. He intervened in ecclesiastical issues all over the Mediterranean world. He was very well informed on what was going on. He administered urban amenities and the food supply in the City of Rome. We're going to talk about the emergence of papal temporal rule in our next couple of lectures. For now just say there's no longer a functioning Roman government in Rome. Gregory put the papacy in the business of keeping the City of Rome going.

He also wrote voluminously, more originally and more brilliantly than any pope before him and more than all but a handful since his time. Intellectual brilliance has never been part of the job description of being pope, and I don't say that critically, I say that descriptively. Eight hundred and sixty-six of Gregory's letters survive as well as several dozen homilies. His book the *Pastoral Care* Christianized the Roman civic ethos. Cicero had written a great book, *De Officiis,* "On Duties," on how to do your business as a Roman. Gregory Christianized that ethos for bishops: how to be a bishop, how to be a pastor. Roman and Christian came together as one. His *Dialogues,* wonderful stories about the holy men of the Italian countryside, populated the Italian countryside with saints and with miracle workers and taught lots of simple little lessons. His *Moralia* are reflections on the Book of Job. The Book of Job, of course, is one of the most difficult and one of the most moving in the entire Hebrew Scriptures, what Christians call the Old Testament. Gregory's reflections on the Book of Job in the *Moralia* are among the most profound moral reflections in the Western literary tradition, alas, too little read, too little read indeed.

Gregory's books, we should say; this is a world of manuscripts, not of printing. Every book has to be copied by hand. His books were copied again and again and again and again and again throughout the Middle Ages. They survive in lots of manuscripts. This remarkably attractive man who called himself, as all his successors have done, "Servant of the Servants of God," is perhaps never more impressive than when we realize he was desperately ill his whole adult life. He said, "It is now a long time since I have had the strength to rise from my bed. For at one time the pain of the gout tortures me, and another a fire," of what kind I do not know, "spreads itself with pain throughout my whole body… it is a punishment for me to live, and I look longingly for death." Thus was Gregory the Great, this pope in this age of transition. In our next lecture we'll watch the popes become fully European.

Lecture Four
The Popes in the Age of Charlemagne

Scope:

The 8th and 9th centuries were decisive for the history of the papacy. As the popes loosened their historical ties to Constantinople, they turned to the Franks for protection from their Lombard foes in Italy. King Pippin III sealed an alliance with Pope Stephen II in 754, and Pippin's famous son, Charlemagne (Charles the Great), confirmed and strengthened that alliance. Pope Leo III crowned Charlemagne emperor in Rome on Christmas Day in 800, in the process laying the foundations for *Christendom*. The popes and the Carolingians—the family of Charles (Carolus) the Great—promoted missionary work, expanded the Church hierarchy, and reformed the Church in Western Europe. Although the popes and the Carolingians worked well together, their very collaboration planted seeds that grew into bitter contention in later centuries as people tried to define the boundary between the realm's royal and priestly power. Peace in Italy also afforded the popes the money and opportunity to rebuild Rome and to decorate its churches with impressive works of art, some of which are still there.

Outline

I. In one of the most famous events of world history, Pope Leo III crowned Charlemagne emperor in St. Peter's basilica on Christmas Day in 800. In this lecture, we shall try to discover why that happened and what it meant.

   A. The popes and the Franks—Charlemagne's people—had only sporadic contact before the middle years of the 8th century, but thereafter, their histories became inextricably intertwined.

   B. Freed from military and material threats, the papacy prospered.

   C. A Western veneration for St. Peter led to a focus on Rome and the popes that enabled a "second Romanization" of Europe.

II. The popes and the Franks first became involved as a result of the papacy's deteriorating relations with Byzantium, Lombard pressures on Rome in Italy, and missionary work in Germany.

    A. Theologically and culturally, Byzantium and Rome had been pulling apart for some time, and in the 8th century, Byzantium simply could not spare resources to counter the Lombards in Italy.

    B. The Lombard kings ruling from Pavia regarded the Byzantine presence in Italy as an irritant but particularly resented Byzantine control of Ravenna, Rome, and the strip of land connecting the two, because this territory prevented the kings from controlling the autonomous duchies of Spoleto and Benevento.

    C. The papacy did not initiate missionary work in the German lands of Central Europe but eagerly supported the labors of Englishmen, such as Willibrord and Boniface, as well as Franks, such as Emmeram and Corbinian, and Irishmen, such as Killian. As the Franks were attempting to expand their influence into this region, mutual interactions were inevitable.

III. Faced with Lombard threats and no help from Byzantium, Pope Gregory III (r. 731–741) wrote twice to Charles Martel, who was mayor of the palace in Francia, the Frankish kingdom.

    A. His appeal was without immediate effect, but Gregory began the process of emphasizing to the Franks that Peter was the keeper of the keys of the kingdom of heaven and that the Franks had a moral duty to come to Peter's aid.

    B. Gregory and his successor, Pope Zachary (r. 741–752), were in regular contact with Charles's sons, Pippin and Carloman, concerning the mission of St. Boniface and the reform of the Frankish Church.

    C. After Carloman retired to Monte Cassino in 747, Pippin, in 749, wrote to Zachary to ask if it were right that the person in Francia who had the royal title had no power, while the person who had all the power lacked the royal title.

        1. Zachary responded that this contravened the divine *ordo*, probably basing himself on Ecclesiastes and St. Augustine.

2. In 751, Pippin III (r. 751–768) became king of the Franks.

D. In 751, Aistulf, the Lombard king, conquered Ravenna, the primary Byzantine base in Italy, and began to threaten Rome.

    1. In 752, Pope Stephen II (r. 752–757) appealed in vain to Byzantium and Pavia. By 753, he turned to the Franks and, late in the year, set out to Francia—the first pope to cross the Alps.

    2. Pippin wanted to help the pope, desired further confirmation of his (usurped!) kingship, and had to persuade the Franks to exchange friendship with the Lombards for intervention in Italy.

E. In the end, Stephen crowned and anointed Pippin, and Pippin promised to help the pope in Italy.

    1. In 755 and 756, Pippin campaigned in Italy, defeated Aistulf, and forced him to hand over to Rome all lands he had conquered in Italy.

    2. The so-called "Donation of Pippin" created the first Papal State—the remote ancestor of today's Vatican City. For the first time, the pope was a temporal ruler.

F. For some years, the Franks were bogged down in frontier battles, and the Lombards were emboldened to refuse to hand over the lands they had sworn to relinquish.

    1. In 773, Charlemagne (r. 768–814), Pippin's son, headed for Italy, defeated Lombard King Desiderius (r. 757–774), and took the Lombard crown for himself.

    2. In 781 and 787, Charlemagne—Charles the Great—concluded pacts with the pope that settled the territorial shape of the Papal State as it would exist, at least in theory, for centuries.

IV. These dramatic changes in Rome and Italy, as well as the Frankish connection to Italy, had important consequences for papal Rome.

A. Members of the Roman nobility again sought the papal office and important positions in the papal government.

B. Factional squabbles among the Romans were imported into the Church.

1. The years 768 to 772, 799, 813, and 823, for example, were particularly violent and unstable.
2. In 799, Pope Leo III (r. 795–816) was attacked in a street by a mob led by disaffected relatives of his own predecessor, Hadrian.
3. Charlemagne wanted both to help and protect the pope and to keep a reasonable "hands-off" policy with respect to Rome.

C. Charlemagne himself had been campaigning successfully and brilliantly all over Europe, reforming the Church, and promoting scholarship.

D. In 797, at Byzantium, Irene, who had been serving as regent for her son, Constantine VI, since the death of her husband in 780, blinded and deposed her frivolous son and became *basilissa* (empress).

E. Many streams thus converged in the scene in St. Peter's when Leo crowned Charlemagne and the assembled Romans acclaimed him "Emperor and Augustus."

V. Although the popes were not always secure, the papacy was protected and empowered. But to do what? With what authority?

A. Charlemagne and Pope Hadrian I (r. 772–795) disagreed sharply on the question of the veneration of icons, and Charlemagne disagreed with Pope Leo III on the insertion of the word *filioque* (Latin for "and from the son") into the Creed.

B. Pope Gregory IV (r. 827–844) traveled to Francia to intervene in a quarrel between Charlemagne's son, King Louis the Pious (r. 814–840), and Louis's sons. He did so *ratione peccati* ("by reason of sin") as the chief priest of the Christian world. But the Franks paid scant attention to him.

C. The popes tried but failed to win Bulgaria away from Constantinople for Rome.

D. Popes quarreled with Byzantine rulers and churchmen over theology and Church practices.

VI. Let us profile one pope from this period, Hadrian I, on whose death Charlemagne wept "as if he had lost a friend or a brother."

    A. Hadrian was a Roman blueblood whose family lived in the tony Via Lata region.

    B. Hadrian served as one of Rome's notaries under Paul I (r. 757–768), and this pope brought Hadrian into the clergy. He rose through the ranks in about a decade and was elected pope in 772.

    C. At the time of his election, Hadrian found Rome in a state of political chaos, and he skillfully composed the situation.

    D. Hadrian successfully worked with Charlemagne—as noted—to secure the territories of the Papal State.

    E. Hadrian resolutely worked to defeat Iconoclasm and rejoiced at the Second Council of Nicaea (787) that condemned it.

    F. Most revealing of Hadrian's pontificate is the building boom that he initiated in Rome.

Recommended Reading:

Noble, *Republic of St. Peter*.

Schimmelpfennig, *Papacy*, chapter IV.

Questions to Consider:

1. How might the history of the papacy have been different if the Franks had not come to the pope's assistance?

2. Explain why collaboration and contention were both visible in the papacy's relations with the Carolingians.

Lecture Four—Transcript
The Popes in the Age of Charlemagne

Hello once again, and welcome to the fourth of our lectures in this series on the history of the popes and of the papacy. This time we're going to talk about the popes in the age of Charlemagne. I think it's fair to say that one of the most famous events of world history was when Pope Leo III crowned Charlemagne emperor in Saint Peter's Basilica on Christmas day in the year 800. In some respects, this lecture is really about: Why did that happen, and what did it mean? The popes and the Franks—Charlemagne's people were Franks—had had only sporadic contacts before the middle of the 8th century. From that point on, their histories became inextricably intertwined with one another. The popes, eventually freed from military threats in central Italy, prospered perhaps as never before. Moreover, a Western veneration for Saint Peter led gradually to a focus on Rome and the popes that enabled what we might call a second Romanization of Europe. The first Romanization, of course, had happened at the ends of the swords of the Roman legionaries. This one happened as a result of religion, of Rome and of the papacy.

The popes and the Franks first became involved with each other as the result of the papacy's deteriorating relations with Byzantium—we'll have more to say about that, and we've talked about that, actually, in our last couple of lectures—from Lombard pressures on the popes in central Italy and from missionary work in Germany. Let's look at these issues a little bit more in detail. Theologically and culturally, as we have seen, Byzantium and Rome had been pulling apart for some time. In the 8th century, Byzantium, facing Islamic threats in the east and Slavic and Avar and Bulgar threats in the Balkans, simply could not spare resources to counter the Lombards in Italy. The Lombards were a people who had entered Italy in some numbers in the middle of the 6th century and had, slowly but surely, from their capital at Pavia in the north, been spreading their authority southward through Italy. Eventually, they began to threaten the area immediately around Rome. Rome wanted help from Constantinople. Constantinople had other problems and simply couldn't really address the problem of the Lombards in Italy.

The Lombard kings regarded the Byzantine presence in Italy as something of a nuisance. Now, the Byzantine capital of Italy—we might call it that or the Byzantine administration of Italy—was the city of Ravenna in the northeast. Rome, of course, was an important outpost of Byzantine authority as well, and there was a strip of territory running from the northeast towards the southwest—from Ravenna to Rome—that connected these two centers, and from a Lombard point of view had this great disadvantage: they cut off the Lombard kingdom in the north from the two great Lombard duchies of Spoleto and Benevento in the south. The kings wanted to control those duchies. To control those duchies, they had to go across Byzantine papal land. Obviously, the Byzantines and the popes didn't want that, and that was in some fundamental ways the bone of contention.

With respect to this missionary work in Germany that I mentioned a moment ago, in the lands that we would now call Germany—it obviously wasn't Germany at that time—there had been a number of missionaries, some from the British Isles—for example, the Englishman Saint Willibrord and the Englishman Saint Boniface. There had been some Frankish missionaries who had come from the western Frankish lands, more or less what we would call France, people such as Emmeram and Corbinian. There had been Irishman such as, for example, Saint Killian, who had been working to spread Christianity in the German lands. These individuals often had very close ties to Rome. The missionary enterprise was not a Roman endeavor, but Willibrord went to Rome, Boniface went three times to Rome, and the popes were warmly encouraging of this missionary activity. This missionary activity, in turn, began to bring new lands—new because outside the former frontiers of the Roman Empire—began to bring new lands into the Roman and papal orbit. Here's part of that second Romanization that I alluded to before.

Faced with these Lombard threats, with the possibility—the popes complained that they might be turned into Lombard chaplains—faced with these Lombard threats, Pope Gregory III twice wrote to Charles Martel. Charles Martel was the mayor of the palace in the Frankish kingdom. That means, in effect, second to the king. He was sort of the king's—if it were modern times—we might call him the prime minister, or something like that. He was really, from 714 until his death in 741, the key player in the Frankish world. He wasn't more powerful than the kings were, and so Pope Gregory III wrote to Charles requesting assistance. Well, his request was without immediate effect, but Gregory began, in a lengthy correspondence that the popes would maintain with the Frankish rulers, to stress to the Franks that Saint Peter was the keeper of the keys of the kingdom of heaven, and that the Franks had a moral duty to come to Saint Peter's aid.

Gregory and his successor, Pope Zachary, were in regular contact with Charles's sons Pippin and Carloman. They succeeded him as joint mayors of the palace after the year 741. But also there was, as I mentioned just a moment ago, very close contact with the great missionary Saint Boniface; and Saint Boniface himself was in very close contact with Pippin and Carloman. So we can begin to see the knot tighten. In 747, Carloman, for reasons that we still can't really fully explain, retired from the world and went off to Monte Cassino in Italy to become a monk. Two years later, his brother Pippin wrote to Pope Zachary a very famous letter. The letter survives. Actually, his letter to Rome doesn't survive—we know about it from the chronicle—but we know the pope's answer. He asked if it was right that in the Frankish world, the person who had no power had the title of king while the person who had all the power lacked the title of king. Clearly, he was preparing a coup d'état.

The pope wrote back and said that this contravened the divine *ordo*—that's the Latin word that gives us our word "order," the grand scheme of things. The pope apparently was basing his opinion on the Biblical book of Ecclesiastes—"for everything there is a time and a purpose" —the Book of Ecclesiastes, this book of how to do things and when to do them and how to do them—and on Saint Augustine's commentary on Ecclesiastes. So the pope was suggesting, you see, that there was something wrong with the way things were in the Frankish world. He was clearly giving a nod to Pippin to become king of the Franks, and in 751, that's exactly what happened. Pippin was elevated to kingship in the Frankish world.

In 751, on the fourth of July, thus making that date historically significant, the Lombard king Aistulf captured the city of Ravenna, the primary Byzantine base in Italy, and he began to threaten Rome itself. In 752 Pope Stephen II first appealed to Constantinople, "Help". The Byzantines basically told him, "See to your own defense." Stephen then appealed to Pavia, to the Lombard kings, "Stop," to no effect. Late in the year 753, he made a fateful decision. He left Rome, crossed the Alps and went to see the new king of the Franks, Pippin. He was the first pope ever to cross the Alps. Stephen remained in Francia for a good many months. He negotiated with

Pippin, but Pippin also had to undertake serious negotiations with the Frankish elite. The pope wanted protection in Italy. He wanted a return, also, of the lands that had been seized from the area immediately around Rome by the Lombards.

Pippin, for his part, wanted to help the pope. All the evidence we have suggests that he sincerely wanted to help the pope, that he was outraged by the problems in which the pope then found himself. But Pippin also wanted additional papal confirmation for his, bear in mind, usurped kingship, to become king only in 751. His problem with the Franks, the Frankish elite anyway, was that for a long time the Franks and the Lombards had been allies. Pippin himself actually had spent some time as a young boy at the court, not of Aistulf, but one of Aistulf's predecessors as king of the Lombards, so he was asking the Franks, really, to exchange an old friendship for some sort of a new alliance that was unprecedented in Frankish history. Eventually all the right agreements were achieved, and before the assembled Franks Pope Stephen crowned and anointed Pippin, his wife and his sons—one of whom is Charlemagne—and forbade the Franks ever to choose a king from another family. Pippin in turn promised to help the pope in Italy secure the rights of Saint Peter, the pope's rights. He didn't say Rome's rights, he didn't say the Empire's rights; he said the rights of Saint Peter.

Well, there was some attempt on Pippin's part to negotiate with King Aistulf of the Lombards. Aistulf was having none of it. In 755 and 756, Pippin campaigned in Italy. He defeated King Aistulf twice, and he forced him to hand over to Rome not only the lands that he had seized in the immediate hinterland of the city of Rome itself, but also all of the lands in Italy that Aistulf had seized from the Byzantine Empire. This so-called "Donation of Pippin" created the first papal state, the remote ancestor basically of today's Vatican City. For the first time, it made the pope a temporal ruler. He had a state; it was a tiny state. How it would be ruled, how it would be defined, how it would be governed, all of these things were yet to be resolved, but the pope now has a state. We're going to be dealing with this papal state in lecture after lecture after lecture through the rest of this series.

Now, for some time, the Franks were bogged down in frontier battles in the north. They had lots of problems of their own. Italy was really in many ways the least of their concerns, and the Lombards—

actually, now Aistulf's successor, King Desiderius—were emboldened to try to refuse to hand over the lands they had promised in 756 to hand over, and even if they could, to seize additional lands. Pippin died in 768; he was succeeded by his two sons Charles and Carloman. Carloman died in 771, leaving sole kingship in the Frankish world to his son Charles, Carolus, who we know as Carolus Magnus, Charles the Great, but we usually call him after the French fashion of his name, Charlemagne.

Charlemagne was a decisive character. He recognized that Italy was likely to be a long-term provocation, just a long-term problem, and he didn't really need that. He had other things to do, so in 773, he headed for Italy. He defeated King Desiderius and then at Easter in 774 he went to Rome. He met with Pope Hadrian and began a process of negotiating how their mutual relationships would work out in Italy. He concluded a pact of "Peace, Love, and Friendship" with the pope, the first of the great Western arrangements with, treaties with, alliances with—in the 19th and 20th centuries we would call these concordats—with the papacy. But Charles had a lot of problems in the north, so having made himself king of the Lombards—his idea being that, that way the pope has nothing to fear—he has nothing to fear from him, from Charles—so Charles crossed the Alps and went back north to deal with his own problems.

In 781 and 787, after having some of his agents in Italy going around holding inquiries, sort of looking into the situation—he had conquered Italy, but he didn't really know what he had, so he had some of his agents studying the Italian scene. In 781 and in 787 Charlemagne concluded pacts with the pope, with Pope Hadrian I, which basically settled the territorial shape of the papal state as it would exist through most of the Middle Ages. Again, as I've said, we're going to come back to this papal state again and again and again, but in certain respects the agreements of the 750s between Pope Stephen II and Pippin had started the ball rolling. Charles basically defines the process in more or less definitive terms in the 780s.

These dramatic changes in Rome and in Italy, and the connection between the Franks and Italy, had very important consequences for papal Rome. Clearly, Byzantine rule in Italy was for all practical purposes at an end. What is the only game in town now—the papal government. And so in the mid-750s, for example, we find for the first time once again, after a long gap, members of the Roman nobility, of the local power elite, begin entering the papal government—begin holding offices in the Roman Church, and indeed even becoming popes. The Roman nobility, as anyone who has ever studied Roman history knows, was always a fractious group, and so interestingly, what began to happen now was that the battles, the struggles, the factional strife that always characterized the City of Rome—that's true today; that's been true for two and a half thousand years, so there's nothing new about this in the 8th century— it's just now the papal government becomes the prize in the battles of Roman politics. The struggles are imported into the church, where in certain respects they didn't leave for centuries.

We might just mention, for instance, that the years from 768–772, the year 799, the year 813, and the year 823 were all years of violent tumult in the City of Rome. In the year 799, in April, when he was celebrating one of the great processions through the city, Pope Leo III was attacked in a street by a Roman mob. Intriguingly, that Roman mob was led by two individuals who had been officers in the papal government under Leo's predecessor, Hadrian, and who, moreover, were relatives of Hadrian. They basically disliked Leo as a kind of newcomer, as a kind of *parvenu* in the papal government. Leo had not come up through the Roman aristocracy. He was not a Roman aristocrat, and so some of the aristocrats who had been prominent in the papal government for two or three decades now were kind of upset when the clergy elected Leo and that, in a way, left them sort of on the outside looking in.

Charles wanted to help. Leo fled; he came north—another pope crosses the Alps. Charles wants to help, but he has a couple of rather interesting problems. Once again, he has lots of other distractions in the north. He has wars with Saxons and all manner of things going on, doesn't really want to spare a lot of time for Italy. But also, Charles didn't see himself, somehow, as a successor to Roman emperors with the idea that Rome was his, Rome was his to rule. He wanted to keep a kind of hands-off policy if he possibly could. Now, over the last several decades—remember, Charles becomes king in 768, sole king in 771. We're now at the end of the 790s, the 8th century is turning into the 9th. Charles has been campaigning brilliantly and successfully all over Europe.

Charles had been carrying out massive reforms of the Frankish Church: restructuring its organization, improving the moral and intellectual life of the clergy, donating enormous sums of money for building churches, beautifying churches, rebuilding churches. He had been promoting scholarship all over Europe, gathering great minds from England, from Spain, from Italy, from all the lands of Europe. The so-called Carolingian Renaissance is in full bloom. Many of Charles's courtiers had begun to say that he ought to be emperor—that he deserved to be emperor. They wrote this back and forth in letters to themselves, they talked about it in treatises; they talked about it in poetry. Yes, they were in some ways evoking the ancient Roman past. Now they felt that here was a king who ruled many peoples, who ruled with great dignity, who ruled with great success. He should be an emperor.

At just about the same time, in 797, over in Byzantium, Irene, who had been ruling as regent for her son—her husband died in 780, leaving only a little boy as an heir—she had been ruling for some years as regent, sort of minding the store if you like, for her son, who it was thought would eventually succeed to the imperial office. That son, Constantine VI, was an utterly frivolous and useless character, and this seems awful to us, but in the year 797, in the very room in which she had given birth to him, Irene blinded her son. Let's put that in perspective. Among the Byzantines, as among the ancient Persians—as among many peoples—there was a notion that anybody who was physically imperfect couldn't rule. So blinding was actually thought, well, less unkind than killing; if you blind the boy, he can't rule.

The job was botched and he died, so Irene began to rule as *basilissa*. Now, *basileus* in Greek is the Greek word for "emperor," so a *basilissa* is an empress. Byzantium had never had a *basilissa* as a sole ruler. There had been wives who were consort to the emperor and sometimes called *basilissa*; now she rules alone as *basilissa*. She only lasted until 802, and she was deposed. But over in the Frankish world, some prominent thinkers began to say—partly because there was a woman on the throne and partly because of how she had come to the throne, blinding and then causing the death of her son—that the throne was vacant. So now we've had all of this discussion in the Frankish world for a decade or more that Charles ought to be an emperor, and now you've got very awkward, difficult circumstances in Constantinople leading some people to say the throne is vacant. So the idea of making Charles emperor percolates ever more vigorously to the surface.

Many streams converged on the scene in Saint Peter's, where Charles was made emperor in 800. What had happened is that, after the attack on Leo in April of 799, Charles had investigations undergoing in progress for about a year and a half and late in the autumn in 800 he headed for Rome. He was going to try to investigate the Roman situation, find out what had happened to Leo, and see if he could put things right. While Charles was praying before the high altar of Saint Peter's on Christmas day, the pope came up behind him, placed a crown on his head and the Romans in the building acclaimed him as "Emperor and Augustus." So now, for the first time since 476, there is an emperor in the Western portion of what had been the Roman Empire. But what on earth did it mean? One great scholar despaired of finding an explanation; he said, "It meant different things to different people." Indeed, it did. For good or ill, the idea and something now of the reality, of Christendom was born on that day—a Christian emperor for a Christian empire, made by a pope in the great basilica of Christendom.

But now a problem was raised in a particularly acute form. Did the emperor or the pope have final responsibility for leadership in this Christendom? That would be a thorny issue for centuries, as we'll see. We'll come back to that again and again and again. Can anyone on Christmas day in 800 have been aware of all of the problems that were going to follow from the acts that took place there at that time? The popes were not always secure in the City of Rome because of factional struggles there, but on the whole we could say the papacy now had a protector. The papacy had been empowered in ways that it never had been before—but to do what, with what authority? How would the pope deal with this completely new set of circumstances? Would relations with the new Carolingian—we call Charlemagne's family Carolingian, from Carolus; *Carolus* is Latin for Charles, so we call the family the Carolingians, the dynasty—so would the pope's relations with the Carolingians become like the old relations with Byzantium? Would they become like the old relations with the Roman emperors in antiquity? Would it be something new entirely?

Charlemagne and Pope Hadrian, for example, who reigned from 772–795, had disagreed sharply on a number of questions, for instance, the veneration of images. Remember, we talked in our last lecture about Emperor Leo III at Byzantium instituting Iconoclasm. Finally, Hadrian had the great pleasure of seeing in the Second Council of Nicaea in 787, Iconoclasm rejected, but that made it look as though the Byzantine veneration of images had been approved. Charles and his theologians believed that it was wrong to destroy religious art, but wrong to venerate religious art. Art, they said, was for decoration and commemoration, to remind you of things and to make places beautiful, but that's it. Art is not in any meaningful sense holy, so Charles and Hadrian, though great collaborators in many ways, were at loggerheads on that issue.

Charles disagreed with Pope Leo III on the insertion of the word *filioque* into the Creed. Now, this is one of those recondite theological issues that we mustn't let distract us. Let's just explain it this way; *filioque* in Latin means "and from the son", the words in the Creed. Does the Holy Spirit proceed from the Father through the Son or from the Father *and* the Son? Again, these are the kinds of problems that exercise theologians, more than ordinary people in their lives. *Filioque* is now in the Western Creed. The word had been inserted in the Western Creed in probably Spain, probably in the 7th century. That version had come to the Frankish court, and that's the way the Franks recited their creed, with the word *filioque* in it. The pope said, "Well, you're actually right on the theology, but you can't change the language of the Creed. The Byzantines went nuts. They said, "You're wrong on the theology *and* you can't insert words into the Creed." Anyway, Charles and Leo more or less agreed to disagree.

It's interesting if we notice that almost half of all surviving papal letters from the 9th century pertain to issues where the popes simply couldn't compel the Frankish clergy to do what they wanted them to do. On the one hand, all of those letters mean the popes are paying attention and they're really getting themselves involved with issues in the Frankish world. On the other hand, those letters prove to us, pretty convincingly, the pope couldn't simply speak and have things happen. Pope Gregory IV, 827–844, traveled to Francia, traveled to the Frankish world to intervene in a quarrel between Louis the Pious, who was Charlemagne's son and successor. Louis ruled from 814–840. Gregory IV went north to intervene in a great quarrel—civil war, in fact—between Louis and his sons. He said he did so *ratione peccati*, Latin for "by reason of sin". He saw himself as the chief priest of the Christian world. He saw political disruption in the Frankish world as sinful, and he sought to minister to these poor sinning Franks. They paid no attention to him. He couldn't change things.

The popes tried very hard but failed to win Bulgaria away from Constantinople, to win it for Latin Christendom instead of Greek Christendom. The popes continued to quarrel with Byzantine rulers and churchmen over both theology and church practices. Interestingly enough, these two realms, Roman and Byzantine, were constantly drifting apart but constantly in contact with one another—and almost never, in the period that concerns us now, cordially. Amidst one such quarrel, Pope Nicholas I, a very powerful and very interesting pope—he was pope from 858–867—made some of the loftiest statements of papal power ever expressed. Let's hear just a few of his words. He said on one occasion, "The judge, he means the pope, "shall be judged neither by Augustus," by the emperor, "nor by any cleric, nor by the people... The first see shall not be judged by any." In another letter, he said, "It is immediately clear that the judgments of the apostolic see, than which there is no greater authority, cannot be handled by any other tribunal, nor is it possible for any to sit in judgment on its decision. Appeals are to be made to that see from any part of the world. Such is the meaning of the canons." Canons are the laws of the church. "But no appeal is allowed from that see."

So in the age of Charlemagne, numerous fundamental issues were laid down that would be of importance for centuries. How would, in this new Christendom, leadership be arrayed? Where did final authority rest? In terms of practical power politics, it's easy to say that the emperors were vastly stronger than the popes. But in view of the words of Nicholas I, which I just quoted, it's clear that the popes have a sense that it is they to whom leadership and authority rest. Remember when we talked about Pope Gelasius's distinction between *auctoritas*, authority, and *potestas*, mere power—we can see that Nicholas stands very much in the tradition of Gelasius. The authority—the greater authority, the greater legitimacy—rests with the pope. How would the pope make such authority real? That is a problem which will engage us in a number of our later lectures.

In an earlier lecture, we profiled Pope Gregory I, Gregory the Great. Let's take one of the popes from this Carolingian period and talk about him a little bit, Hadrian I, a long-reigning pope, 772–795. He and Charlemagne disagreed on a few issues quite sharply, as I mentioned a moment ago, but they also worked together harmoniously on a wide variety of issues. Charlemagne's biographer, a man by the name of Einhard, said that when Charles learned of Hadrian's death, he wept "as if he had lost a friend or a brother." Hadrian was a Roman blueblood. He came from a very wealthy, influential, important Roman family. They had vest estates in the countryside outside Rome, but he lived in the tony Via Lata region of the city. *Via Lata* is Latin for "broad way." If you know Rome at all, the Via Lata was the great street that runs out of what is today the Piazza Venezia, just near the Victor Emmanuel monument, one of those broad streets running down in the direction of the Tiber.

Apparently, his parents died when he was quite young, and an uncle by the name of Theodotus saw to his upbringing. Theodotus was a very rich and influential man. He held offices both in the secular government of the City of Rome and also in the papal government. Now, Hadrian had served as one of Rome's notaries. Who these notaries were, we're going to learn about in one of our next lecture, so just hold your fire on that. Remember when we talked about Gregory I being a deacon, a regionary deacon, and I said hold your fire on that one, too. We're beginning to meet the officers of the papal government. The point is, Hadrian had risen to a very high position in the papal government rather quickly. He became a notary under Pope Paul I, 757–768. Paul, I might add, was the brother of Stephen II, who had been pope from 752–757. You're beginning to see these Roman families colonizing the papacy.

So Hadrian rose quite fast through the clerical ranks, and in 772, he was elected pope. At the time of his election, Hadrian had found Rome in a state of political chaos. He very skillfully composed the situation. Hadrian worked very successfully with Charlemagne, as I noted a moment ago, for example, giving form and definition to the first version, we might say, of the papal state. Hadrian worked resolutely with Byzantium to try to defeat Iconoclasm. He rejoiced when the Second Council of Nicaea, where he had representatives, condemned Iconoclasm. That got him in a bit of trouble with the

Franks, because, as I mentioned a moment ago, their theology of images was a little bit different.

In Rome itself, however, we can see, I think, the clearest monument to Hadrian's pontificate in the building boom, which he instituted in the city. It's important to say that for several decades, of course, central Italy had been ravaged by these Lombard deprivations. One of the things the Franks brought to Italy was peace. Hadrian spent from the papal treasury, enhanced as it was by Italy's newfound peace. He spent his own money. He restored Rome's city walls. He restored four of the city's aqueducts, those great water courses that were products of Roman engineering. The bond between the pope and the Romans couldn't have been clearer. He also refurbished a large number of churches that had fallen into disrepair over many years. He installed mosaics in churches. He installed artwork in churches. He built new churches as well.

The pope was now very much the spiritual and the temporal patron of Rome and its people, "Saint Peter's special flock," as the popes had begun to call them. In this new Christendom now, the time has come for us to pause and say what is this papacy like, and to that subject we'll turn in our next lecture.

Lecture Five
Rome, the Popes, and the Papal Government

Scope:

This lecture responds to some very basic questions: How did a man get to be pope? What was the pope's job and how did he do it? Who assisted him? What roles did the pope have in the secular administration of Rome and its region? What religious roles did the pope have in Rome and its region and in the world beyond Rome? In some ways, this lecture reaches back into the world of late antiquity, and in other ways, it prepares the ground for Lectures Eight and Nine on the papal monarchy. This lecture also introduces the major branches of the Lateran administration (this was before the Vatican!), the cardinals, the title churches and stational masses, the great liturgical processions—in short, the many features of papal life and work that still exist today, albeit sometimes in changed form.

Outline

I. Having situated the popes in their familiar European context, we may ask some basic questions about them and the papacy.

    A. How were popes elected?

    B. Who were the popes?

    C. By what means did the popes exercise their leadership of the Roman Church?

    D. How, after the emergence of the Papal State, did the popes exercise temporal rule?

II. This is also an opportune time to ask: How do we know about the history of the popes in these early centuries?

    A. The *Liber Pontificalis* (*LP*) is a series of papal biographies begun in the early 6th century and kept up more or less continuously until the end of the 9th century.

    B. Surviving papal letters from the period to the end of the 9th century number more than 3,500.

    C. Chronicles and histories often mention the popes, providing both valuable details and a gauge of the attention paid to papal Rome by outsiders.

D. Official records, court or financial documents, do not survive at all.

III. Like all bishops in early times, popes were elected "by clergy and people." It is hard to penetrate behind this formulation.

    A. Occasionally, there were factions, and sometimes, emperors intervened.

    B. From the mid-6th to the mid-8th centuries, the Byzantine emperors claimed a right to confirm papal elections, and the imperial administration in Italy routinely meddled in papal elections.

    C. The first major decree on papal elections came in a Roman synod—a meeting of bishops—in 769: Only the Roman clergy could serve as electors (the "people" were moved out of the process), and only the cardinal priests and deacons were eligible as candidates.

IV. Who were the popes in the early centuries?

    A. The majority of popes down to the 7th century were Romans.

    B. From the 7th century, a period of almost 150 years began when many popes were of Eastern extraction.

    C. When the popes began to liberate Italy from Byzantium, nobles began to enter the clergy and to become popes, beginning with Stephen II and his brother Paul I in the mid-8th century.

    D. Down to the 20th century, many popes then came from important Roman families.

V. Over several centuries' time, two parallel sets of administrative institutions emerged in papal Rome, one primarily for ecclesiastical administration and one for temporal rule.

    A. Rome's ecclesiastical structure was much like that of other cities except more elaborate. Everything focused on the bishop.

        1. Worship was provided by an elaborate system involving *suburbicarian bishops* and *title priests*.

        2. The pope (bishop) was always the principal liturgical celebrant, but obviously, he could not be everywhere.

　　　　a. Seven suburbicarian bishops could celebrate day by day at the main altar of St. John Lateran, Rome's cathedral church.

　　　　b. Twenty-eight title priests could celebrate day by day at the high altars of four *patriarchal basilicas*.

　　　　c. On a regular rotation, the pope celebrated at all these churches in *stational* masses.

　　3. Popes installed deacons into each of the seven regions of the city, and they oversaw charitable services and routine ecclesiastical administration.

　　4. The 7 suburbicarian bishops, 28 senior title priests, and 7 regionary deacons were the *cardinals* of the Roman Church. The origin of the word *cardinal*, by the way, is still unclear.

　　5. The archpriest and the archdeacon, along with the *primicerius* (head) of the notaries, ruled when there was a papal vacancy and served as key advisers to the pope.

B. Mention of the notaries brings us to the secular administration.

　　1. The notaries were among the first officials introduced by the popes with something other than strictly religious duties.

　　2. By the 5th century, the popes had introduced *defensores*, who possessed minor judicial authority.

　　3. The responsibility for feeding Rome's population and, increasingly, maintaining the city led to ever sharper administration of the Church's vast patrimonies.

　　4. In the 7th century, a system of *diaconiae* emerged as charitable institutions.

VI. As the 8th century became the 9th, the popes had made Rome into a papal city.

A. They governed the city.

B. They put huge numbers of people to work.

C. In complex liturgical arrangements, accompanied by massive processions, the papacy repeatedly put its leadership on visual display.

Recommended Reading:

Llewellyn, *Rome in the Dark Ages*, chapter 4.

Noble, *Republic of St. Peter*, chapters 6 and 7.

Questions to Consider:

1. What strengths and weaknesses do you perceive in the early papal government?

2. Was an ecclesiastical administration well placed to govern a secular entity?

Lecture Five—Transcript
Rome, the Popes, and the Papal Government

Welcome to the fifth of our lectures in this series on the popes and the papacy. This time we're going to talk about Rome, and the popes and the papal government. I've been dancing around this subject of a papal government and administration for several lectures now, so let's pause and take a look at it. Having situated the popes in their familiar European context—we've kind of moved them, in a sense in terms of their fundamental orientation, out of the Mediterranean world and towards Western Europe—we can begin to ask some very basic questions about the papacy. How were popes elected, for instance? Who were the popes? By what means did the popes exercise their leadership of the Roman Church? How, after the emergence of the papal state, did popes exercise temporal rule, rule in the world and rule in time?

This is an opportune time it seems to me to ask how do we know about the history of the popes in these early centuries. Let me mention some of the primary kinds of evidence that we historians have to work with. The *Liber Pontificalis*, the pontifical book, is a series of papal biographies composed in Latin, begun in the early 6th century and then kept more or less continuously until the year 891, until the very end of the 9th century. There were occasional continuations later on. Now, when the first set of biographies was written down in the early 6th century, they wrote up all the ones from Peter to that time, so not surprisingly, the early evidence is a little sketchy. But from the early 6th century until the late ninth, it is an absolutely contemporary record, and importantly, it reveals what we might call the papal eye view of what's going on in Rome, what was important to Rome, to the popes, what was important to the papal government.

Next, we have the papal correspondence. Surviving papal letters from the period of late antiquity in the early Middle Ages—the periods we've been talking about—number about 3,500. It's important to say, these are official letters—they're not private missives; it's not the pope writing to his friends or his family— official letters written by the popes in their capacity as pope. They're very unevenly distributed. None of the papal archives survive from the early Middle Ages. The popes' letters were kept in what are called *Registers*, that is to say, chronologically arranged sequences of letters. We have only fragments of some Registers from the early Middle Ages. From the 14th century on, we have virtually everything. Down to the 14th century, we have bits and pieces and fragments.

What we have are recipient copies. That's just a fancy term that historians use to say that we don't have the original archive version, exactly what was sent out from Rome. We have the versions that were received by people. They survive because getting a papal letter was a big deal, and there are, as I said, some 3,500 of these that patient scholarship over a long time has found in libraries and archives and monasteries and cathedrals and so forth all over Europe. These letters are very helpful to us, very, very important sources, but we have certainly only a fragment of what was once there.

Chronicles and histories, kept in some abundance all over Europe through this period, often mention the popes. These sources are valuable to us for two reasons, many reasons, but two in particular. One, they often provide facts we wouldn't otherwise have, just the odd detail about this, that or the other thing. Second, they show us people outside Rome reflecting on Rome and on the popes. They give us some sense of how the popes were seen by the people around Europe, or at any rate, at least by influential, intellectual types. Official records, let's say court documents, financial documents, we have nothing. This is unfortunate. This would tell us a great deal about how the government worked, but here we simply have nothing.

Let's go back to our popes with that brief summary of how we know about them. Like all bishops in early times, the sources tell us formulaically, popes were elected by clergy and people. That obviously means something; the problem is penetrating behind that formula. Who were the clergy? Exactly who could be involved? Who were the people? Exactly who could be involved? How did they do it? I mean, did they go drop ballots in a box or something? Did they poll people on the street? Was it more or less by acclamation? We really don't know. Only in a few instances do we have a lot of details about papal elections. We know, for instance, that there were factions on occasion. We know sometimes that emperors intervened. We know sometimes the Roman clergy was badly divided.

You may recall my mentioning a couple of lectures back that at the time of the election of Pope Damasus in 366, 137 people were reported to have been killed in the streets of Rome in consequence of that papal election. The papal election of 498 produced two violently opposed factions in the Roman clergy. The emperors had nothing to do with it; it wasn't outside interference and for a series of years, Rome was divided between two men claiming to be the legitimate pope. Well, eventually one won out, Symmachus; one failed, Laurence. Laurence is now an antipope. Symmachus became the pope, but it was a close-run thing.

From the mid-6th century to the mid-8th century, the Byzantine emperors—here they are again—claimed a right to confirm papal elections. This was a time-consuming process. It's a long way from Rome to Constantinople—a pope dies, the clergy and people choose a new pope. Emissaries have to be sent to Constantinople to inform the emperor of the election, the emperor then has to send back his approval that that person be installed as Pope. Now, the emperor would sometimes withhold his approval, he would sometimes withhold it just for a while as a way of kind of registering his disapproval about something, but in any case, this was time consuming. It's hard for us sometimes in the modern world to imagine what it was like before air mail letters, never mind e-mail and fax and telephones and this sort of thing. It took weeks or months for these confirmations to come back and forth. We also know that the imperial administration—remember the senate at Ravenna; we talked about that in our last lecture—that the imperial administration quite regularly meddled in papal elections. They found one candidate superior or better, from their point of view, than another, and they would often intervene.

The first major decree on papal elections of which we really have any knowledge came in a Roman synod. A synod means "running together"—a synod is a meeting. Typically, the word "synod" is used in an ecclesiastical context to mean a meeting of bishops. So there was a Roman synod in the year 769, and it was decided in this Roman synod—this synod, I might add, decided a lot of things; it was not just about papal elections—but in the course of its deliberations, it decided that only the Roman clergy could serve as electors. The "people," in other words, are moved out of the process explicitly. Then only the cardinal priests and deacons—we'll come to whom cardinals were in a few minutes—but only the cardinal priests and deacons were eligible as candidates. As we go through this lecture, you're going to see who the Roman clergy was exactly; therefore, we can figure out who these electors will have been. So 769, people are out, clergy are in, and only cardinal priests and deacons are henceforth to be eligible as candidates.

Who were the popes in the early centuries? What can we say about them? Well, the overwhelming majority, down to the 7th century, was Roman, but a few came from elsewhere in Italy, or from North Africa, or in a couple of instances from Greece. In terms of background, they had usually served some years in the Roman clergy. They had held one or another clerical office in and around the city of Rome before they were elected. Before the 4th century they almost never came from the Roman upper classes. That's not surprising; Christianity had been persecuted until Constantine granted it legal status early in the 4th century. From later on in the 4th century down to perhaps the early 7th, there was a notable rise in the status of the popes. Remember, we talked about Gregory I, this Roman blueblood who was elected Pope in 590.

Then in the 7th century, there began a period of almost 150 years when many of the popes were of Eastern extraction. How was this? In a way, they were fugitives or refugees from imperial religious policies. Remember our earlier discussions of Monophysitism, Monoenergism, Monotheism and Iconoclasm? Well, at various times, when the Eastern Empire took one position or another, members of the out group among the clergy would flee, and quite often they came to Rome. Some of these clergy were refugees or fugitives from the Muslim conquests of the eastern part of the Mediterranean.

Having said that, it's very important to say—and we can report this as a result of the *Liber Pontificalis*—that these men who were elected Pope, though of Eastern extraction, had usually themselves, or their families, been in Italy for a long time. They had often served five years, ten years or 20 years in the Roman clergy before they were elected as popes, so it would be a mistake really to think of this as a time when there were foreign popes, or to think of it as a time when sort of the Roman Church was swamped by Easterners. These were often people who had been rather "Romanized" and "clericalized" over a period of years, and in any case, it is important to bear in mind that the Roman Church always saw itself as universal, so there's a certain sense in which nobody is a foreigner.

Italy's countryside, which had been quite wealthy and productive in antiquity, had been ravaged in the Gothic wars, when the Emperor Justinian fought against the Ostrogoths in Italy for 20 years, 535–555, in the 6th century. They had been ravaged during the subsequent Lombard conquest and settlements, which occupied our attention in the last lecture, and as a result, wealthy landowners—for the most part, wealthy Romans were wealthy landowners; there were exceptions, but basically your money came from land—with the disruption of Italy, wealthy landowners were not much in evidence over a period of time 7th century, early eighth. Moreover, the plum jobs in Italy in the 7th and 8th century were in the Byzantine military administration of Italy. If you were a bright and ambitious person, you went to work for the Byzantine government in Ravenna. You didn't go down and work for the papal government in Rome.

It was when the popes began to liberate Italy from Byzantium—we talked about this in our last lecture—then the nobles began to enter the Roman clergy in some numbers. We talked last time about Pope Stephen II and his brother Paul I, two Roman nobles who are pope together from 752–757, then the great Roman nobleman Hadrian, 772–795. Here comes the Roman nobility into the church. As I said in the last lecture, this is now the only game in town. Down to the 20th century really, the majority of popes then came from important Roman families. There are exceptions, and we'll profile the popes again and again and again as we go through this series of lectures, but the point I want to leave you with here is that from the 8th century on, it is impossible to separate the history of the papacy from the history of the city of Rome. That's the point I want you to take away.

Now over several centuries of time, and often in circumstances that we don't know about, two parallel sets of administrative institutions developed in papal Rome: one primarily for ecclesiastical administration—that means running the church as an institution and organizing the worship of the church—and another administrative structure for exercising Rome's authority sort of in the wider world. Remember when we talked about Gregory I, we saw that he was concerned with urban amenities such as keeping the bathhouses up. We talked about Hadrian rebuilding Rome's walls and restoring the aqueducts, and then of course, from the middle of the 8th century on, the popes have the papal state, which they have to administer. So there are two parallel administrative structures that begin to emerge that are linked in the person of the pope. Sometimes we can point quite concretely to just where this institution, that office, this responsibility emerged. In the great majority of cases we don't know. We catch these things once they're already in place.

Rome's ecclesiastical structure was much like that of other cities. The central ecclesiastical officer in every city, as we saw in earlier lectures, was the bishop. In principle, everything revolved around the bishop. Rome differs from other cities in that its structure is a lot more complex. It was in antiquity; it remains so today. But basically, what we see in Rome is not something unique in that it's different from every place else. It's simply more complex. Let's start thinking about these two parallel administrative structures. Worship in Rome—and the church after all is fundamentally there to organize the worship of the faithful—worship was provided by an elaborate system involving individuals we call suburbicarian bishops and title priests. In the next minute or two we'll explain exactly who those folks are. The pope is the bishop. He is always the principal liturgical celebrant. The liturgy is the public work of the church, the public worship of the church.

But it's obvious that in a large city, the bishop, whether it's the pope in Rome or the bishop in any place else, whether it's the 8th century or the 21st, the pope can't be everywhere all the time. So he has to organize people to help him do his job, his job as principal officer for worship. Rome had seven suburbicarian bishops. The Romans divided Italy into *Italia suburbicaria*, Italy around Rome—you can hear the word suburb in there—Italy around Rome. The suburbicarian bishops are the seven bishops that are arrayed in small towns, really right around Rome. The other part of Italy to the Romans was *Italia annonaria*. *Annona* means grain. In other words, this is the farmland of Italy. This is "grainy" Italy, so we've got suburban Italy and cereal Italy. The bishops in suburban Italy, the suburbicarian bishops, celebrated day by day, seven suburbicarian bishops, seven days in a week, at the high altar of Saint John Lateran. That's Rome's Cathedral Church. So the suburbicarian bishops took it in turns to celebrate mass at the high altar of Saint John Lateran.

Rome had also, when the system was fully articulated—and it took centuries for the system to become fully articulated—28 title priests.

Near 800, there were probably 180 churches in the city of Rome of one kind or another. Twenty-eight of these are the title churches of Rome, and they constitute, along with the patriarchal basilicas—we'll come to them in just a second—they constitute the *santo Romana ecclesia*—the Holy Roman Church, the pope's church. The title churches take their name in this way. That's what *titulus* means; it means the name, it means the title. Early Roman worship communities met in people's houses, and gradually, as a church would grow up in that place. Sometimes the house was torn down and a church was actually built. Sometimes a house was expanded into a church. It took the name of the *titulus* and then a personal name, the *titulus* of somebody. Then gradually those churches came to be renamed after saints, so then we have Santa Cecelia, or Santa Sabina, or Santa Maria in Trastevere, or whatever it might be, but each one of these had begun as a *titulus* with a personal name attached to it. There were 28 of them, as I said, when the system was fully articulated.

Each of these churches would have had several priests serving at it, but the senior priest in each titulus—there're 28 of them—took it in turn to celebrate mass at the high altar of four of Rome's five patriarchal basilicas. We've met one of those basilicas already, Saint John Lateran, the pope's church, Rome's cathedral. The other four are Saint Mary Major, Saint Paul-Outside-the-Walls, Saint Lawrence-Outside-the-Walls, and Saint Peter's. Four patriarchal basilicas, 28 title priests, seven days in the week; do the math. There is the cycle of liturgical celebrations in Rome. Now, on a regular basis, the pope celebrated at all of these churches in what were called stational masses. The pope would go to the *stazio*, to the station of the day. When that system was fully articulated, there were some 180 stations, so about 180 times a year the pope went across the city to one or another of these churches giving symbolic and visible representation to the fact that it's all his church. He is the primary officer, but then worship can be provided, as it were, by the pope in all of these great churches every day of the week, right through the year.

Further on the ecclesiastical side of this administration, the pope installed deacons into each of the seven regions of the city. Seven regions of the city—well, what does that mean? Rome has throughout its history been divided into administrative districts. The

Emperor Augustus early in the 1st century, for example, created 14 districts. Ecclesiastically, Rome was divided into seven districts. They're actually marked down on a map. We know where these seven districts were. At some time, perhaps as early as the 3rd or 4th century, the popes instituted deacons in each one of these districts to do two things: to oversee basic ecclesiastical administration, to kind of keep the shop running; and to oversee charitable services. These were fairly important officers. Remember we talked about Pope Gregory I having been one of Rome's regionary deacons?

The seven suburbicarian bishops, the 28 senior title priests, and the seven regionary deacons were the cardinals of the Roman Church. Now, there's some mystery attending the emergence of this word "cardinal." We know who the cardinals were. The word *cardo* in Latin means "hinge," so some say that the word "cardinal" actually emerges from the notion that the cardinals were kind of the hinge or the pivot on which the whole thing turned, on which the whole thing depended. One can see metaphorically how that sort of works, but there's also a notion that comes over from Roman law into ecclesiastical law: that to be incardinated means that you have a primary seat of responsibility somewhere, but you are delegated to exercise responsibility somewhere else. Think of our cardinal clergy marching around the city all the time to carry out those liturgical celebrations. You can see how they are appointed in one church but incardinated to another. So as I said, there is some mystery over exactly where the term "cardinal" emerged and why, but it's very clear who the cardinals are: the seven suburbicarian bishops, the seven regionary deacons, and the 28 senior title priests.

Among these, there's a bit of a hierarchy: the arch priest, not necessarily the senior of the title priests in Rome, but one designated by the pope; the arch deacon, not necessarily the senior of the deacons—but he might be—but the one designated by the pope; and the *primicerius*, the prime guy of the notaries, and I will come to notaries in a second. So the arch priest, the arch deacon and the *primicerius* of the notaries were the three top officers under the pope in this administration. They had offices in the Lateran near the popes, and interestingly enough, when a pope died, these three ruled the Roman Church until a new pope was appointed. Think for a moment of that period under the Byzantines, when there could often be vacancies lasting quite a while, while you got approval from Constantinople. These three men kept the Roman Church functioning. They didn't function as pope, but they kept the basic administrative structures operating.

A second ago we mentioned notaries. That brings us to the secular administration. Scholars have long debated whether the papacy took over secular administration by delegation or by usurpation. In other words, how in the world did popes come to be responsible for the city of Rome? How did popes acquire a state? Did they usurp secular authority, or was it delegated to them by the imperial government? In a way the argument is sterile. Scholars have been debating this for a long, long time. It's a sterile argument. The pope stepped into a gap. After Roman imperial government in the West vanished in 476, there was no one there to do the job, so the popes took over.

In the secular administration, the first key officers were the notaries. Now, a legend says that Pope Fabian introduced a notary into each region of the city, so there were seven notaries—seven regions, seven deacons, seven notaries—to keep the records of the martyrs. That's possible, but it also has the whiff of legend about it. Essentially, the notaries were persons who kept ecclesiastical records, and at the very center of the notarial administration they wrote and prepared papal documents. They kept the library. They kept the archives in early days.

By the 5th century the popes had introduced officers called *Defensores*, defenders. These were basically judicial officers. While the imperial government was still up and running, the popes had introduced these *Defensores* to represent the little people, sort of ordinary people, people who didn't have a big voice, people who didn't have great patrons, to represent those people to the imperial authorities. Slowly but surely, as we've seen, the popes became the government of Rome, and the *Defensores*, then, were people who functioned, in a certain sense, as guardians of the interests of the poor. They were judicial officers. They were never really police officers, they weren't prosecutors. They were basically judicial officers intended to look out for the interests of ordinary people.

Now the responsibility for feeding Rome's population and increasingly maintaining the city—you think of any big city: you have to maintain the roads, you have got to maintain the sewers, you have to maintain the water supply, you have to maintain the food supply, you have to keep a fire brigade going—all of the things that you have to have in a city. All of these things together led to an ever-sharper administration of the church's vast patrimonies. The church had enormous stretches of land that simply belonged to it before the popes had a state over which they ruled, and the revenues from those lands came in and then were spent to keep Rome operating—to keep the church operating, but also to look out for the population of the city.

By the 7th century a system of *diaconiae* emerged as charitable institutions. The Greek *diakoneô* means "to serve;" a deacon is one who serves. The *diaconiae* are places that serve. What they were, and eventually there were more than 20 of these scattered around the city of Rome, on Fridays people from any given area of Rome would go to this place. There would then be a religious celebration, and then they would be given their food distribution, then they would go back to their homes, so the popes were organizing the agricultural produce of Italy, bringing it into the city and distributing it among the population.

As the papal state began to emerge, other financial and judicial officers began to attend the pope as well, some with military responsibilities, legal responsibilities, responsibilities for keeping records. Before the 12th and 13th centuries, basically those officers are pretty murky. It's pretty hard for us to see clearly who these people were and what they did. Generally speaking, we can say that owing to the preferences of Pope Gregory I, officers of the papal government were as far as possible members of the clergy. Gregory didn't like the idea of laypeople serving in key offices in the government, but once the popes assumed temporal rule in the 8th century, we find considerable numbers of laypeople holding responsibility as the heads, for example, of various blocks of land—which the Roman Church owns—holding responsibility for holding courts of law, holding responsibility for administering justice, holding military responsibility in the city, so that the papal government was never an exclusively clerical government, even though in certain respects it represented itself as a thoroughly clerical government.

How did people come into this service? Broadly speaking, in two ways—you knew somebody; that's the first way. Well, that's not a surprise. Is there any moment in history when that wasn't a way you kind of found your way into an institution, into a structure? But there was also the *scola cantorum*—the school for singers, the school for young boys who would sing in the liturgies in all these churches in Rome—and some of those boys then rose higher and higher and higher through the clergy. The vast majority of people who rose in the ecclesiastical administration of Rome came up through the *scola cantorum*. Could they all sing? Well, I don't know—maybe.

By the end of the 8th century then, the first years of the 9th, the popes had created a pretty impressive structure. They now clearly governed the City of Rome in a way that their predecessors had never been able to do, either to full effect or with full legal title. I mentioned in our last lecture that when Leo III was set upon in a Roman street in 799, one of the dilemmas for Charlemagne is he didn't want to really put his hand on Rome in a decisive sort of way. This was the pope's city. He wanted to help, but he didn't want to intrude where he didn't belong.

It's interesting too to see that the popes were clearly putting huge numbers of people to work. We mentioned Hadrian—remember we profiled Hadrian I in our last lecture. We talked about him restoring Rome's walls, restoring Rome's aqueducts, and also building and rebuilding and restoring churches all over the city. This carried on right down through the Middle Ages; it never stopped. We know, for example, that Pope Leo III in the year 807—the *Liber Pontificalis* tells us this—made a massive set of donations to churches all over the city—new chalices and patents and liturgical vessels, new lighting fixtures for the churches, great silken banners that hung in the churches, great altar cloths that went over the altars of the churches. We know that, for instance, Pope Paschal I, 817–824, put spectacular mosaics in Roman churches. Four of them survive, and in some of them Paschal's own picture is there to greet.

Well, what does that suggest to us? The people of Rome knew to whom they had to look for their income, for their livelihood, for their responsibilities, for their government. Pope and Rome are being stitched very tightly together. And as if all of that—the material side of it—weren't enough, let's think back just a moment to those stational liturgies. We have in *Ordo Romanus 1*—a liturgical document, an ecclesiastical document—the order of procession for those stational processions. Virtually the whole papal clergy lined up in a very set order, vested beautifully, carrying books, carrying censors, and they marched through the city up to 180 times a year, putting papal leadership very visibly on display. This was altogether quite a remarkable place, papal Rome in the early Middle Ages. It sounds as if everything is going very well indeed. Alas, the 10th century is going to see the papacy plunge to perhaps the lowest point in its entire history, and to that we'll turn in our next lecture.

Lecture Six
The "Age of Iron"

Scope:

With the decline of effective Carolingian power in Italy, the papacy sunk into depths perhaps unmatched in its long history. In 846, Muslim pirates brazenly sacked St. Peter's and St. Paul's. If Rome could not defend itself, neither could it avoid factional strife. John VIII was brutally murdered in 882 (the first pope to be assassinated). Nine months after his death (in 896), Formosus was subjected to a macabre ritual. His body was disinterred, dressed in papal garments, and "tried" by his enemies, who predictably, found him guilty and flung his corpse into the Tiber. The author of this deed, Stephen VI, was eventually arrested by Formosus's supporters, jailed, and strangled. The situation actually worsened. For two generations, the house of Theophylact, Alberic, and Marozia dominated Rome and the papacy. Marozia was mistress of one pope and mother of another. Later Protestant writers referred to this time as the "pornocracy," and the Catholic apologist Cesare Baronius could do no better than to call it the "Age of Iron." But positive developments took place, as well. The western empire was restored in 962 in the person of Otto I. The Papal State was restored to its Carolingian shape. Europe experienced wave after wave of spirited religious reform. German emperors dominated the papacy, but they were generally high-minded men and vastly better than the local Roman aristocrats.

Outline

I.   The 10th century, ridiculed as the "pornocracy" and lamented as the "Dark Age" or "Age of Iron," was perhaps the papacy's darkest hour.

    A. The collapse of the Carolingian system was primarily responsible for the troubles.

    B. Ironically, despite popes who were nonentities or moral wretches, some positive and important achievements did appear in this period.

II. Why did the Carolingian system collapse, and what were the consequences of that collapse?

    A. The Carolingian dynasty faced severe problems that precluded sustained attention to Rome.

        1. Dynastic squabbling set in at the time of King Louis the Pious (r. 814–840) and never really stopped until the dynasty itself disappeared.

        2. The Carolingians faced attacks from Vikings, Muslims, and Magyars that consumed their attention and resources.

    B. In Rome, no effective imperial presence existed to keep a lid on the aristocratic factions that became increasingly chaotic and brutal.

III. Three examples drawn from the history of the Age of Iron may suffice to reveal the general course of developments.

    A. One of the sorriest spectacles in papal history was the "Cadaver Synod."

        1. Pope Formosus (r. 891–896) was elected with the support of the pro-Carolingian party in Rome, whose opponents were centered in Spoleto and northern Italy.

        2. When Formosus died, his opponents secured the election of Stephen VI (r. 896–897), who hated Formosus with a passion.

        3. Formosus's body was exhumed, dressed in papal vestments, seated on a throne, and "tried" for treason and other crimes.

        4. The political worm turned within a year, and Stephen VI was, in turn, hounded by a mob, arrested, and murdered.

        5. John VIII had been brutally murdered less than 20 years before, the first pope to be assassinated.

    B. Throughout the first half of the 10th century, the family of Theophylact and Theodora dominated Rome.

        1. Theophylact was a duke and Master of the Soldiers, as well as *vestararius*—a financial officer of the Church.

        2. Marozia (892-937), Theophylact's daughter, was the lover of Pope Sergius III, by whom she had a son who was later elected pope as John XI.

3. Marozia also married in succession three powerful men who, in concert with her, named and removed popes at will.

C. Alberic II, a son of Marozia and Alberic I, insisted on his deathbed that his 18-year-old son, Octavian, be elected pope.

    1. Octavian changed his name to John (XII), only the second pope to do so, but with two exceptions, all later popes followed suit. The first pope to change his name, John II (r. 533–535), did so because he felt it unseemly for a pope to be called Mercurius.

    2. John XII forged a bond with the German king, Otto I (r. 936–962), who confirmed the Carolingian territorial privileges for Rome.

IV. The situation of the papacy in the 10th and early 11th centuries embodies paradoxes.

A. The papacy was dominated by powerful Roman or central Italian families.

B. The popes were surprisingly prestigious and effective outside Italy and sometimes within it.

    1. They continuously negotiated with the Byzantines.

    2. Popes secured Poland and Hungary for the Roman Catholic Church.

    3. They promoted monastic reform and worked closely with the great monastery of Cluny, founded in Burgundy in 909.

    4. In 993, John XV canonized Ulrich of Augsburg, the first papal canonization. Before that time, canonization was a local affair.

V. Instead of emphasizing all that is dreary, let us conclude by profiling one of the most interesting popes of the early Middle Ages: Sylvester II (r. 999–1003).

A. He was born Gerbert near Aurillac, France, circa 945, and he was educated there and in Vich, in the borderlands between France and Spain, where he had access to Arabic mathematical and scientific learning.

B. In 972, he went to Reims to study dialectic and soon became master of the school.

C. In 998, with Otto's influence, he was made archbishop of Ravenna and a year later, Otto engineered his election as pope.

D. Gerbert was the first French pope, and he took the name Sylvester to symbolize the ideal of papal-imperial cooperation between the Emperor Constantine and Pope Sylvester I.

Recommended Reading:

Mann, *Lives of the Popes*, vols. IV and V.

Schimmelpfennig, *Papacy*, chapter V.

Questions to Consider:

1. What weaknesses in the papacy's position permitted the institution to sink so low in the 10th century?

2. How did the relations between the German emperors and the popes differ from the earlier relations between the Carolingians and the popes?

Lecture Six—Transcript
The "Age of Iron"

Welcome to Lecture Six in our series on the history of the popes and of the papacy, this time the "Age of Iron," the tenth and the early 11th century—a period ridiculed as the "pornocracy," lamented as the Dark Age or the "Age of Iron." This was perhaps the papacy's darkest hour. We need to try to understand how things became so bad, and then we need to try to understand what resources for improvement persisted. You may recall in my very first lecture that there were moments when it seemed as though the papacy might just almost disappear. Boy! This is one of them, yet it didn't. So even though things became pretty bad, we're going to ask what was it that kept things going.

How did things become so bad? Well, we'll talk about this in a little bit more detail in a moment, but basically let's say the Carolingian system collapsed, the Carolingian system implying that there would be imperial protection for the pope, sometimes from themselves, sometimes from foreign threats. The Carolingian system collapsed. In its absence, things became pretty chaotic in Rome. But it's also true, and ironic, that despite popes who were nonentities, and despite popes who were moral wretches, there were some positive achievements, important achievements in this period. We'll have to ask too how that could be. How is it possible that such bad characters in such a bad time may also have accomplished good and positive things? In order to set up our discussion here, let's ask why did the Carolingian system collapse, and what were the consequences of that collapse? As we've had occasion to see, basically the Carolingian system implies nothing more than that the Frankish kings, and then emperors, would be the protectors of the popes in Rome.

The Carolingian dynasty faced severe problems across the course of the 9th century that gradually precluded any sustained attention to the City of Rome. In the first place there was dynastic squabbling. Pippin, you'll recall, left two sons in 768, Charles and Carloman. Carloman died in three years, and Charles ruled alone. Charles had several sons, but when he died in January of 814, only one legitimate son survived him. Charles's successor, Louis the Pious, had three sons; actually, he had four, but one of them died in 838, two years before his father did. Louis left three sons in the year 840, and these sons began battling with one another. In fact, they'd started battling each other as early as 828–829, when their father still reigned. From that point, the Carolingian world, except for one brief moment in the 880s, was never united again under a single ruler. Instead, rival families established their own dynasties. They were all relatives, they were all cousins and nephews and uncles and brothers and what have you, but they were fierce rivals of one another, and that was one great distraction in the Carolingian world that kept the Carolingians from paying much attention to Rome.

In the second place, the Carolingians faced attacks. For a long time the Franks basically had been on the offensive. They had been expanding their territorial holdings, but in the 9th century they faced attacks from Vikings, from Muslims and from Magyars, the ancestors of the Hungarians. Once again, valuable resources, human and material, were committed to meeting these new threats and could not, therefore, be committed to dealing with Rome. So the Carolingian system collapsed because the Carolingians were no longer there to keep that system up and running. In Rome, in the absence of an effective imperial presence to keep a lid on those aristocratic factions that we talked about in our last lecture, things became increasingly chaotic and also, as we'll see, brutal.

Italy also faced Muslim incursions. For example, in the year 846, Saint Paul's Outside-the-Walls and Saint Peter's—Saint Peter's in the Vatican region, of course, was outside the walls of the city of Rome in antiquity, and the great Basilica of Saint Paul's was also built outside the walls, so these places were particularly vulnerable—and were attacked in 846, and the fittings and furnishings of these two beautiful churches were all hauled away and had to be replaced. We might just add here as a kind of interesting footnote on papal resources and what these popes were capable of doing, in the 840s Pope Leo IV, in a period of slightly under three years, erected a massive set of walls to surround the whole Vatican region—the Leonine City so-called, or the Leonine Wall, long stretches of it are still there, and they are very, very impressive—so this was a city that could always recoil after a loss. But in any case, there had been serious losses to these same kinds of people who were threatening the Carolingians in the north.

In Italy, Carolingian factionalism had its Italian side as well as its northern side. There were petty descendants of the Carolingians who contested among themselves. They were sometimes counts and sometimes dukes, and sometimes struggling to become king of Italy, and sometimes even struggling to try to be made emperor. These people infuriated the popes, bullied the popes and interfered with the popes in all sorts of ways, the very Carolingians who were supposed to be protecting them. The heirs and successors to the Carolingians in Italy were sometimes, in point of fact, causing the popes no end of problems. We could tell lots of unsavory stories about the "Age of Iron," about the age of the "pornocracy"—why it was called that you'll learn in just a second—but let me just choose three, not because these are the three most interesting or most revealing, but because they will give us a good feeling for this period, so three developments from the "Age of Iron."

I think it's safe to say that one of the sorriest spectacles in papal history was the Cadaver Synod. Pope Formosus, the name means handsome. An interesting footnote here—in the 15th century a man was elected pope and he thought so well of himself, he was quite a vain fellow, that he was going to name himself Pope Formosus II—in other words, Pope Handsome II—and his advisers said, "You'd better not do that." If I remember correctly, he wound up being Paul II. But anyway, *this* Formosus, Formosus was his actual name. We're going to start changing popes' names in about 50 years or about 10 minutes, depending on your point of view.

Formosus, pope 891–896, was elected with the support of a pro-Carolingian party in Rome. The opponents of that party were centered in the Duchy of Spoleto and also in northern Italy. Again, this is the time when these various factions were sorting themselves out in kind of post-Carolingian Italy, and so the stakes in these battles became very high, indeed. When Formosus died, his opponents secured the election of Stephen VI, who was pope only for about a year, from 896–897, who hated Formosus with a passion. He was on the other side. He supported some of these local petty Italian despots and would have preferred to see them in positions of influence and authority. So after Steven VI was elected, Formosus' body was exhumed. It was dressed in papal vestments, seated on a papal throne and then tried for treason as well as various other crimes.

Predictably, Formosus was found guilty. His body was then stripped and the three fingers of his right hand—the fingers with which he conferred blessings—were cut off and cast away contemptuously, and his body—his cadaver, his mutilated corpse—was thrown into the Tiber. Legend says that it washed up on a bank a little way downstream and was found by a monk who solemnly reburied it. Be that as it may, the political worm turned. Within a year, a mob in the City of Rome arrested and then murdered Stephen VI. So getting involved in violent politics in Rome, in this time, was something that could come back to haunt you. I should add here that Steven was not the first pope to have been murdered. The first one to have been murdered was John VIII, who had been murdered only about 20 years before, so Rome was beginning to be a pretty nasty place. The Cadaver Synod then, one indication of what has gone wrong in Rome in this period.

The second example, actually the next two examples are related in a certain way, as you'll see, but we'll take slightly different focuses, on the family of Theophylact and Theodora, who through much of the first half of the 10th century dominated the City of Rome. Theophylact was a duke. He held military office, he was a master of the soldiers, *magister militum*—a title that actually went back to Roman imperial times, but basically the head of the local militia; you can think of him that way—but also *vestararius*. The *vestararius* was the official in the papal government who had—if you think of a vestiary, the place where you hang your coat, a place you put your vestments, let your mind work on that for a moment—the *vestararius* was the person who had charge of, responsibility for what we might think of as the movable capital wealth of the Roman Church. In other words, he wasn't concerned with the property of the Roman Church. He wasn't concerned with the buildings of the Roman Church. He was concerned with the books and the chalices and the patents, all of the, we might think of the treasure, in a way, of the Roman Church, and he was a key and very important officer.

There's something interesting and curious about Theophylact, however, being master of the soldiers and *vestararius*. Perhaps you'll recall that in the last lecture I had said that from the time of Gregory I on, the official view in Rome was that church offices should be held only by clerics, not by laymen. Theophylact was a layman. I would also emphasize that as the popes assumed temporal responsibility, there were more and more jobs that laymen were clearly going to fulfill. Well, the head of the militia was likely to be a layman and not a priest, after all. What's peculiar about Theophylact is that as a layman, he holds the office of *vestararius*, and he holds that office alongside the office of master of the soldiers, head of the local militia. This is something that back in the heyday of the Carolingian Age just wouldn't have happened. His wife, Theodora, was in, a lot of ways, quite a remarkable woman. She was a lover of the later Pope John X. John X, apparently because of this connection with Theodora, became a little bit too big for his britches, became a little bit too independent and was summarily murdered. This is the third time in recent years that a pope has been murdered.

Theophylact's daughter Marozia was one of the really quite remarkable figures of this period. She was the lover of Pope Sergius III, by whom she had a son, who was later elected as Pope John XI. Marozia married in succession three immensely powerful men, three people powerful in Rome and powerful more widely in Italy. In concert with her husbands, Marozia installed and removed popes at will over a period of some years. That, I don't think, is how anyone in the 8th or 9th century had expected this system to work. A pope like Gregory I must have been spinning in his grave at the very thought of what was happening in Rome in his time. As a third example, Alberic II—Alberic II was simply named for his father Alberic I, who was a prominent local Roman aristocrat and one of Marozia's husbands—so Alberic II was there, sort of followed on Marozia's period of dominance, and he himself rose to prominence in Rome. On his deathbed, he insisted that his 18-year-old son Octavian be elected pope—18 years old, not even a member of the clergy. Octavian was duly elected. That's not a very happy story, actually, but it has hiding in it a kind of interesting story.

There is no Pope Octavian. Octavian changed name to John. He became Pope John XII. It was felt that his name was offensive; Octavian was the name of Augustus Caesar—Gaius Julius Caesar Octavianus. He thought this was not an appropriate name for a pope. Prior to Octavian, only one pope, as far as we know, had changed his name. In the middle of the 6th century, a man named Mercurius, Mercury, was elected pope. He changed his name because it seemed not quite right for a pope to be called Mercury. Otherwise, however, from Peter—of course, Jesus changed Peter's name, but that's not quite the same thing—from Peter down to John XII, with the exception of Mercury, the popes' names as we know them were their names; if they were Paschal or Hadrian or Leo or Gregory, that was their name. From John XII on, with only one exception in the 16th

century—we'll talk about this; we'll mention the case several lectures down the road—so with that one exception in the 16th century, all popes have changed their names. One noticed in April of 2005 that Cardinal Ratzinger became Benedict XVI.

John XII, for all that he became pope at the age of 18, forged a bond with the German king Otto I and had Otto confirm the Carolingian territorial privileges for Rome. So things in central Italy had become pretty shaky after the collapse of the Carolingian system, and so Octavian, even though we might imagine that this character would have quite different interests in mind, did see that maintaining the territorial integrity of the papal state in Italy was an important objective for him, and he managed to work with the German king Otto I to secure confirmation of the old Carolingian territorial arrangements in Italy. So however bad the popes became, they could still sometimes attend to business. John XII, what happened to him? The story is that at the age of 27, he died. He suffered a stroke after spending a night in bed with a married woman. You can see why this period was ridiculed as the pornocracy.

When did it come to be called the pornocracy? In the 16th century, in the time of the emergence of Protestantism and when the great quarrels—the predictable quarrels—between Catholic and Protestant authorities in much of Europe occurred. History books, treatises, polemics were written back and forth on either side, and this was a period referred to by Protestant critics as the pornocracy, their basic point being, "Look at how terrible the Roman Church is, look how terrible the papacy is. How can anybody pay attention to it? How can anybody take seriously an institution such as this?" The great Catholic writer at that time, a man by the name of Cesare Baronius, was in a bit of a quandary because he couldn't actually dismiss the evidence, so what he did was to write and he called this the "Age of Iron" or the Dark Age, a lamentable period he said, but nevertheless one which the papacy survived. The papacy did survive, and that's interesting. So there are some paradoxes in the situation of papacy in the 10th and in the 11th centuries. All the bad stuff is there, and as I said, out of a rogues gallery I selected only a few for illustration here.

How might we describe the other side of papal achievements in this period, the Dark Age, the Iron Age, the age of the pornocracy? The papacy was dominated by powerful Roman or central Italian families. That's not new, is it? That has certainly been going on since at least the middle of the 8th century—Stephen II, Paul I, Hadrian, Paschal I, Gregory IV, the list goes on—people from important Roman aristocratic families. Well, we know that in the early 10th century it is the House of Theophylact that dominated the City of Rome. That house died out about mid-century, in the 10th century. But two sets of shirt-tail relatives—the Crescentii and the Tusculani—continued their dominance until the middle of the 11th century, so the City of Rome was being dominated by some very powerful local families. From one point of view, let me just ask you to sort of keep in mind that this is not new, and this is certainly not going to be unusual in later times in Roman history or in papal history. Again, I want just to stress a point that I've made a couple of times already—the history of the City of Rome and the history of the papacy cannot be separated from one another.

It's also true that a great deal that looks terrible to us in retrospect was actually part of a coherent policy. I don't mean that pornocracy was a coherent policy—murdering popes was not a coherent policy; sleeping with popes was not a coherent policy—but there was a coherent policy behind what I've been talking about. Here's what I mean. These important Roman families wanted to control Rome and central Italy, nothing unusual about that. Their mode of domination was control of the papal office and possession of key secular offices in the city, those offices also, and increasingly since the 8th century, themselves under the control of the popes. You see the point? The only game in town is the papal government. If you want to dominate Rome and central Italy, you have to dominate the papal government. The papal government has its ecclesiastical side and it has its secular side, given the Papal States. This puts into sharper relief somebody like John XII, making sure he gets together with Otto I to get the Papal States up and running again in good shape.

But this is what there is to run. We're going to see in a later lecture that in the middle of the 12th century, an attempt was made—it failed miserably—but an attempt was made to create an anti-papal secular administration in the city. But in the 10th century, there is no such possibility available. If you're going to control Rome and central Italy, you have to control the papal office. The Roman nobles had figured that out in the 8th century, but things in the 8th and early 9th century, when the Carolingian system was up and running, had not become as dreadful as they became in the 10th century, absent Carolingian rule. Now, another paradox in this period is that the popes were surprisingly prestigious and effective outside Italy and sometimes even inside Italy. We might say how could these monsters have any credibility? How could they have the temerity even to try to act as if there were the chief priests of the Christian world, as if they were those kinds of people referenced by Pope Nicholas I, who talked in such lofty terms about the authority of the pope? Could anybody have taken these men seriously in those ways?

Yes, they were taken seriously. They regularly arbitrated, with effect, ecclesiastical disputes in England, in France, in Germany, all around Europe. People still turned to the pope for decisions. They asked for hard cases to be decided by the popes in Rome. Pope John X sent representatives to the great German Synod at Hohenaltheim in 916. What was going on there was that the Carolingian family died out at the turn of the 9th and 10th century in Germany. A new dynasty came to the throne, and one of the things that it needed to do was to get its church reorganized, so they called a great synod of German bishops to come together to carry out church reform and to see to the organization of the church, and the popes sent representatives to that synod.

Popes struggled to return Croatia and Dalmatia. The Balkans had been a mess for several centuries historically. We've talked about Avars, Slavs and Bulgars, for example, moving into the Balkans, threatening the Byzantine frontier in the Balkans. Well, areas in the Balkans that had been Latin Christian for some time had been, temporarily at least, lost to the Latin Christian world and began to gravitate towards the Orthodox Christian world. You may recall my mentioning, for example, that in the 9th century, the popes lost Bulgaria. They tried very hard to win Bulgaria for Latin Christianity and failed to do so. In the 10th century, popes managed to return Croatia and Dalmatia, along the Adriatic coast, to Latin Christianity. But this is also a time when the popes managed to win Poland and Hungary for the Roman Catholic Church so that those two regions in Eastern Europe remain Roman Catholic to this day rather than Orthodox.

The popes promoted monastic reform. They promoted the reform of monasteries around Europe. They worked very closely with the great monastery of Cluny. We're going to talk about Cluny in a little bit more detail in our next lecture; suffice to say, a monastery founded in Burgundy in France in 909 with the idea of promoting a purer or a holier form of religious life. The popes worked very closely with Cluny.

In 993 Pope John XV canonized Ulrich of Augsburg. The reason I mention this, by the late 12th and early 13th century the popes had basically taken over control of the process of making saints, canonization. Prior, however, to the end of the 10th century, canonization was an utterly local affair. A holy man or a holy woman who came to be venerated by a particular community was a saint. There were no strict rules for making saints, for unmaking saints, for deciding who deserved to be a saint. So John XV actually jumpstarts the process of the popes taking charge of canonization by canonizing Ulrich of Augsburg in 993, the first papal canonization. Successive popes were able to raise money, for example, to stop Muslim raiding in central Italy. Muslims raided Rome, as we saw, in 846 but they continued to raid almost with impunity up and down the peninsula.

From one point of view then, the terrible history is invisible. If we go out around Europe, we would see a very different sense of Rome, of the popes and of the papacy than if we were in Europe. We can also see perhaps that a new or different kind of papacy may be emerging here, that the popes of the 10th century are not quite like those popes of the 8th and the 9th century. What I say to my students when I'm teaching is to say, "Let's imagine two visitors from a planet who plop themselves down on Earth, one in Washington and one in Topeka, Kansas. They spent a little time and talked to the natives and visited with everybody and collected information, and they went back to their planet and they tried to talk to each other. They would probably hardly understand anything they had to say to each other." I'm not trying to say anything about Washington or about Topeka. I'm saying that, just as in the United States there's the inside-the-beltway and outside-the-beltway way of thinking about the world. In Europe of the 10th century, things looked one way in Rome and quite a different way in other places.

By way of concluding this lecture, instead of emphasizing everything that's dreary, let's conclude by profiling one of the most interesting popes of the early Middle Ages, Sylvester II, pope for a very short time actually, 999–1003. His name was Gerbert. He was born in east central France in the town called Aurillac, about 945. He received his early education there, and then he went off to the dioceses of Vich, sort of in the borderlands between what we would call France and Spain. What was interesting about that area, of course, is that Spain had been conquered by Muslims in the early 8th century and a quite brilliant, flourishing culture had emerged in Spain. Gerbert, who was a precocious student, realized that he could learn in the areas of mathematics and science things in Spain that were not available to him in his native France, so he went along and advanced his education. In 970, he visited Rome. He enormously impressed Pope John XIII, but also Emperor Otto II, the German Emperor Otto II. They both tried to recruit him to get him to stay. He went back to France.

By 972, he was at Reims in France, where he studied dialectic. What's that about? The fundamental medieval school curriculum consisted of three subjects, grammar, rhetoric, and dialectic. Grammar was basically the study of the Latin language. Rhetoric in antiquity had been the art of speaking well, but gradually, as the Roman Empire became a despotic state, nobody got to speak much. The emperor did all the speaking, one might say, and rhetoric turned into the art of erudite textual criticism, sort of literary criticism, we might say. Dialectic was quite simply logic, right reasoning. We can imagine these medieval people as being backwards and living in the Dark Ages and so forth, but they actually believed that prominent people should have to make sense. What a shocking proposition that is! Anyway, Gerbert went to Reims for the purpose of studying dialectic. The great master of dialectic at this time was teaching in a school there.

Eventually, Gerbert himself became master of the school in Reims. He wanted to be Archbishop of Reims amid very complicated politics. This is one of those cases where a pope effectively intervened in a struggle in the north of Europe. Gerbert wanted to become Archbishop of Reims, and he wasn't given the job. The pope prevailed, and Gerbert's rival became Archbishop of Reims. At this time, it's interesting that Gerbert wrote violently objecting to the pope's right to interfere in the Diocese of Reims. We're going to see that he had to eat those words eventually. Having been vested in his quest to become Archbishop of Reims, Gerbert departed for the German court. He became tutor and friend to Otto III, the son of Otto II, whom he had met in Rome in 970. Otto III's mother was a Byzantine princess, Theophano, so Sylvester was working in what we might call a multicultural context, quite a lively and rich place. In 998 Otto had Gerbert made Archbishop of Ravenna—that's a very important position in the Italian Church—and a year later Otto III engineered Gerbert's election as pope.

Gerbert was the first French pope. He took the name Sylvester to symbolize the ideal of papal imperial cooperation represented by Pope Sylvester I and Emperor Constantine all the way back in the early 4th century. He had a keen sense of history, did Sylvester. As a pope, he was a champion of papal rights, and he, ironically now, demanded that his former opponent, who had meanwhile been bested himself, be made the Archbishop of Reims in France. He was a powerful force for the moral reform of the clergy in the Europe of his day. He was an able administrator. He saw to the creation of the new churches in Poland and Hungary. He was the one who really had to fold these new churches into the Roman scheme of things. But Gerbert had the kind of comeuppance that people who are brilliant sometimes do. He also introduced the abacus into northern Europe, that sort of proto-computer that scared the willies out of people just the way computers have continued to scare the willies out of people ever since. People said Gerbert must have made a pact with the devil because nobody could be so smart.

So the papacy came through the "Age of Iron" but, as we'll see in our next lecture, it moved from one crisis into an even bigger one, this time a great battle with the German Empire.

Lecture Seven
The Investiture Controversy

Scope:

From the 1060s to the 1120s, the papacy was constantly embroiled with the German emperors and often at odds with one or more of Europe's other rulers. Two broad sets of problems were at issue. On the one hand, generations of religious reformers had vigorously made the point that the Church could carry out its responsibilities effectively only if it were free of lay control. In other words, emperors, kings, dukes, and other rulers should cease appointing bishops, abbots, and priests and demanding secular services from them. On the other hand, supporters of the clergy and of the rulers sharply articulated very different views of how the world ought to be organized. Everyone agreed that God was the source of all power and authority. Disagreement arose from quarrels over who stood next to God, so to speak. Extreme clericalists insisted that the pope was God's vicar on Earth and the head of an ecclesiastical hierarchy that was to be served by all laymen—rulers first of all. Extreme imperialists argued that the emperor was the earthly reflection of the heavenly king and that the ecclesiastical hierarchy—and the pope first of all—were the emperor's "helpers." *Lay investiture*—the practice whereby a layman invested a cleric with his office—has given its name to an era and the controversy that animated it. But the struggle was over more than lay investiture in the strict sense.

Outline

I. Two vignettes will serve to frame the issues that are central to this lecture.

   A. In 1046, Emperor Henry III rode triumphantly into Italy and, at Sutri, deposed three rival contenders for the papacy and imposed a choice of his own.

   B. In January 1077, King Henry IV stood in the snow before Canossa castle, begging forgiveness and absolution from Pope Gregory VII.

II. The *Investiture Controversy* is the traditional name for the mighty battles between the popes and the German kings or emperors that lasted for nearly three-quarters of a century.

  A. Strictly speaking, *lay investiture* refers to the investing of a clergyman with both the symbols and the reality of his office by a layman.

  B. But as one historian put it, the controversy was really a "struggle for right order in the world."

III. *Reform* is a word commonly used to describe the developments of the 10th and 11th centuries, but it is a hard word to capture in its contemporary meaning.

  A. Gregory VII, who gave his name to the era, used the word *reform* only four times.

  B. There had been several powerful currents of "reform" in the 10th and 11th centuries in Europe, including those stemming from Cluny, Gorze, and other monasteries, as well as ascetic monks and rulers in the Carolingian tradition.

IV. The essential background to the Investiture Controversy is formed by the deplorable state of the papacy in the 10th and early 11th centuries.

  A. Emperor Henry III (r. 1039–1056) was a deeply pious man scandalized by conditions in Rome.

  1. In the 1040s, three men claimed to be the legitimate pope.

  2. Henry went to Italy, deposed the rival claimants, and engineered the election of Archbishop Suidger of Bamberg as Pope Clement II (r. 1046–1047); then, in rapid succession, he imposed the election of three more Germans (in 1048, 1049, and 1055).

  B. What made Henry think he could do this?

  1. Everyone agreed that the earthly realm should mirror the heavenly; that heaven was, in some sense, a monarchy; and that the problem was who on Earth reflected the heavenly monarch.

  2. Kings "by grace of God" had de facto filled the role of divine representatives since Charlemagne.

3. As a practical matter, kings (and other laymen at all levels) had ruled the Church and ruled through the Church.

V. Henry's popes were good men and ardent "reformers."

    A. Pope Leo IX (r. 1049–1054), in particular, traveled all over Europe, emphasized papal authority, and drew reformers to Rome.

    B. The reformers focused on two issues above all others:

        1. Clerical morality, in particular, clerical marriage and concubinage.

        2. Simony.

    C. In 1058, with Henry III dead and his heir a child, the Romans rose up against the reformers and elected a pope in opposition to the reformers' choice, Nicholas II, who nevertheless prevailed.

        1. Nicholas II (r. 1058-1061) called a Roman synod in 1059 that outlawed simony and clerical marriage, declared that clergy should not accept offices from laymen, and spoke only in vague terms about the emperor's rights in papal elections.

        2. Nicholas also allied with the Normans (of southern Italy), who helped him establish his authority.

VI. For a few years, relations between Rome and Germany were infrequent but cordial.

    A. Henry IV came of age in 1066, and between 1071 and 1073, he and Pope Alexander II quarreled over naming an archbishop in Milan.

    B. Alexander's resolve was stiffened by Cardinal Hildebrand, who had come to Rome with the reformers in the 1050s and who was later elected as Gregory VII (r. 1073–1085).

    C. Gregory is one of the most remarkable and important popes, but he is an enigma in many ways.

        1. The *Dictatus Papae*, found in Gregory's papal register, provides some insight into his thinking. It is not clear what this document actually represents—perhaps 27 headings for a treatise that was never written. Some provisions addressed rather routine ecclesiastical business, while a few might have raised eyebrows, and still others seemed startlingly new.

2. In Roman synods of 1074 and 1075, Gregory spoke vigorously against simony and clerical marriage, and he raised the issue of lay investiture clearly.

3. Henry put down a Saxon revolt and, to begin asserting his power, he started naming bishops, including one in Milan.

4. Sharply rebuked by Gregory, Henry summoned a council of German bishops that declared Gregory a false monk and deposed.

5. Gregory responded by excommunicating Henry and releasing his subjects from their oaths of allegiance.

6. By late 1076, German princes and some bishops were demanding that Henry reverse course. Some were concerned as a matter of principle, and some saw an opportunity to weaken the monarchy to the advantage of the landed princes.

7. A council under papal presidency was to meet in 1077 to pass judgment on Henry.

D. Henry stole a march on his foes by trekking through the snow to Canossa castle in north-central Italy, where he asked for forgiveness from the pope.

1. On one hand, Gregory could regard this as a capitulation.

2. On the other hand, Henry could regard this as a clever move that signaled his reconciliation with the pope and stripped his German foes of legitimacy.

3. Many Germans who opposed Henry—for whatever reason—felt that Gregory had abandoned them. Gregory continued to insist that he planned to come to Germany to judge between Henry and Rudolf of Rheinfelden.

4. In 1078, Gregory formally condemned lay investiture.

E. Some Germans elected Rudolf as ruler.

1. In 1080, Gregory again declared Henry excommunicated and deposed.

2. Henry marched on Rome, chased Gregory to the Castel Sant'Angelo, and installed Wibert of Ravenna as an antipope, Clement III.

      3. Gregory was rescued by his Norman allies, but they sacked the city and were, in turn, forced to depart.

      4. Gregory fled to Salerno, where he died in exile.

VII. For the next 30 years, the battle dragged on.

    A. Emperors wanted imperial coronation and sometimes tried to work with the popes and sometimes installed antipopes.

    B. Popes generally maintained the prohibition on lay investiture.

    C. Finally, Pope Calixtus II achieved a resolution in the Concordat of Worms (1122).

      1. Based on the thinking of some canon lawyers, *temporalia* and *spiritualia* were differentiated.

      2. The Concordat said that laymen could not invest with ring and crozier and that elections were to be free. But elections could take place in the emperor's presence, and after consecration, a cleric could be invested with *temporalia*.

    D. The popes had actually gained in prestige during the years of the Investiture Controversy, though not entirely because of the controversy itself.

    E. In a polity conceived as the medieval one was, it was hard to deny ultimate authority to religious authorities.

    F. Important, too, and fateful for the future, was the fact that the primary result of the Investiture Controversy was tremendously enhanced papal authority over the Church.

Recommended Reading:

Blumenthal, *Investiture Controversy*.

Tierney, *Crisis of Church and State, 1050–1300*, pp. 1–95.

Questions to Consider:

1. Of what practical and theoretical significance was lay investiture in the Investiture Controversy?

2. Who do you think had the better claim to ultimate authority, priestly kings or kingly priests?

Lecture Seven—Transcript
The Investiture Controversy

Hello and welcome to Lecture Seven in our series on the history of the popes and the papacy. This time we want to look at the Investiture Controversy, the great crisis primarily between the popes and the kings and emperors of Germany but, to some extent, rulers elsewhere in Europe as well. We saw in our last lecture that the 10th and early 11th centuries had been a very difficult time for the papacy. We're going to see that the second half of the 11th century was not any easier. Two vignettes, it seems to me, will serve to frame the issues that are central to this lecture. In the year 1046, Emperor Henry III rode triumphantly into Italy and its Sutri. He deposed three rival claimants for the papacy and imposed a choice of his own. In January of 1077, bitterly cold winter, Henry IV, king of Germany then, stood in the snow before Canossa Castle begging forgiveness and absolution from Pope Gregory VII. In a way, this lecture is about those two events, what they mean and why they happened and what their consequences were.

Investiture Controversy is the traditional name for these mighty battles waged between the popes and the German kings or emperors that lasted for about three-quarters of a century, from the middle of the 11th through about the first quarter of the 12th century. Strictly speaking, lay investiture refers to the investing by a layman of a clergyman with the symbols and the reality of his office. This was a factor in the "Investiture Controversy". You're wondering why in the world I would say that investiture was a factor in the Investiture Controversy; because, as one great historian put it, the controversy was really a struggle for right order in the world. Investiture—lay investiture—was in some ways the symbolic issue around which everything else turned. The controversy was in fundamental ways an affair that could only have happened in the Middle Ages, as we'll see.

The era of the Investiture Controversy has often also been called the Age of Church Reform, sometimes the Age of the Gregorian, so it may well be for us to pause and spend a little time reflecting on the word "reform". It's commonly used, as I say, to describe developments in the 10th and 11th century in the church and around Europe quite generally, but it's a word that's hard to capture in its contemporary meaning. For example, Pope Gregory VII, who gives his name to the whole era—you can find lots and lots of books about the Gregorian period, the Gregorian papacy, the Gregorian reform—in all of his writings he used the word "reform" four times. We can see what he was up to, but that wasn't exactly the word he used. Even where the word "reform" is used, however—and many of Gregory's contemporaries used it—the word can have two quite distinct meanings. This is true today.

To reform can mean to make better. To reform can mean to re-form, to make over. Historians and others have sometimes missed a rather interesting point here. That is to say, these reformers in the tenth and 11th, maybe early 12th century, never said they were innovating. They never said they were introducing something new, "I have a better idea." In fundamental ways, they thought they were restoring things that had been lost, that had failed or that had gone wrong. Sometimes, of course, they invented pasts that had never existed as they charted futures that no one had yet seen. But the point is that "reform" was a word that had very rich, but very multiple and very complex, meanings to people in the 11th and early 12th century.

The ideas that came to a head between about 1050 and 1080, the central moment in this great controversy, were all much older. That's the first key point to bear in mind. Everything that led up to this great crisis started much earlier. There had been several powerful currents of reform in tenth and 11th century Europe. None of them, in the first place, have anything to do with Rome itself. The Monastery of Cluny—I referred to this briefly in my last lecture—was founded in 909. It stood for reform outside the rule of laymen on one hand, and for the stateliness and elegance of worship and religious life on the other. It was founded by a French nobleman and then made utterly free of all lay control. His belief, and the belief of some reformers, was that one of the big problems with monasteries is too many of them were run by laymen and therefore distracted from, diverted from, the proper purposes. The Monastery of Gorze, which was founded in 933, and other monasteries founded about the same time also had it in mind to reform society, to make people holier, to make them better, to make the church better. But their view was not that the way to achieve this was to be independent of—separate from—laymen, but to work with them, to collaborate with them, to cooperate with them. You might see there something more like the old Carolingian model, where good rulers and good churchmen worked together.

This was also a time though, particularly in Italy but elsewhere as well, where ascetic monks wanted to avoid all worldly entanglements. They thought the church's business was best done when the church had as little to do as possible with the world around it. Here was a quite different kind of reform. This was also a time when there continued to be rulers, people such as German Henry III—with whom we started here—who, like the Carolingians before them, were sincerely interested in reform, wanted the world to be a better place, wanted the church to be a better institution, wanted the moral life of clergy and people to be better. So there were a lot of people interested in reform, and reform meant quite different things to different groups of these people. That's the very large-scale background.

Another essential background to the "Investiture Controversy" is formed, of course, by the deplorable state of the papacy in the 10th and the early 11th centuries. We talked about that in our last lecture; that is what brought Henry III to Sutri in 1046. Roman families had been controlling the papacy, controlling the church and controlling the city. Henry III, who ruled in Germany from 1039 until 1056, was a deeply pious man. He was truly scandalized by what was going on in Rome. There were three different men, each claiming to be the legitimate pope, and he was having none of this. He rode into Italy, deposed the rival claimants and then engineered the election of Suidger of Bamberg, a close associate of his from Germany, and then in rapid succession the election of three more Germans in a row, in 1048, 1049 and 1055. We'll have something to say about these folks in a few events.

For the moment, the question I want to put to you is what made Henry think he could do this. What made Henry think he could simply ride into Italy and start making and unmaking popes at will? Is this the same as the Houses of Theophylact and Marozia in the 10th century? Well, no. We must avoid anachronism. We are dealing with a Carolingian-style Christendom, not with a modern church-state clash. This is what I meant at the beginning when I said this is a problem that could only really have happened in the Middle Ages and not in modern times. People simply wouldn't have thought in our categories. What's at stake here? Everyone agreed that the Earthly realm should be, as nearly as possible, a reflection of the heavenly realm. Fair enough. What does that say about government?

Well, what's the constitution of heaven? It's a monarchy, not a democracy: no focus groups, no committees, no polling. It's a monarchy; Earth should be a monarchy, one ruler. In this Carolingian-style Christendom, and here is a problem that's been with us for several lectures or 250 years, depending on your point of view, who is this monarch on Earth? Is it the emperor or is it the pope?

For some time, kings by grace of God had de facto filled the role of divine representative on Earth ever since Charlemagne. The practical power, the real power of kings, but other laymen too—dukes and councilmen, barons and what have you—had ruled their kingdoms, had ruled the church and had ruled through the church. In many realms, after all, appointing bishops, appointing archbishops, appointing abbots of great monasteries, was a way of getting your work done, your programs. Very often the clergy was entirely willing to go along with that, with this policy, as long as those kings were themselves good and ardent men and ardent reformers and so on. So the church was, we might say, institutionally, a very important prop of the state, and the state was, we might say, institutionally, a very important prop of the church. But this is a world that we can notionally call Christendom.

Now, to come a little bit closer to the issues before us, I want to invite you to just think of two images. Let's imagine two political hierarchies. They all start with God; for medieval people, that was unquestionable. Authority came from God. It didn't come from the people. It didn't come from a constitution; it came from God. Who stood next after God—the pope, with emperors, kings, dukes, counts, barons, etc., the pope's assistants in carrying out God's work on Earth—or the emperor, with the pope and the archbishops and the bishops and the abbots and so on as the emperor's assistants in carrying out God's work? Each of these ways of thinking about the world was present, each was powerful and each was deeply and firmly held. But as I stressed a moment ago, as a practical matter, secular rulers, laymen, kings, emperors, etc., had been dominant for some two and a half centuries. That is now going to be questioned.

These popes that Henry III put into place were good men. They were ardent reformers. They brought these northern currents of reform to Rome itself, very important to see that this great papal reform of the 11th century started in northern Europe. Leo IX, for example, pope from 1049–1054, traveled all over Europe. He emphasized papal authority. He drew reformers to Rome. He also directed a campaign against the Normans in southern Italy. Normans in southern Italy, you say? Don't Normans belong in Normandy and in England? Yes, in 1066 Normans conquered England. A generation before that, Norman adventurers had conquered southern Italy. Pope Leo IX had mounted a campaign against them that ended in a military disaster but curiously enough resulted in the Roman Church for the first time in some centuries beginning once again to extend its religious influence over southern Italy.

You may just recall that these were the lands that, during the Iconoclastic Controversy, Emperor Leo III took away from the pope and assigned to the Patriarch of Constantinople. Now the pope is once again beginning to extend his authority over the Christians of southern Italy. This had the immediate result in Constantinople of leading to hysterical objections on the part of Patriarch Michael Kerularios, who was in turn excommunicated by the highhanded and pompous Cardinal Humbert in 1054, thus producing the schism, the great schism between the Orthodox and Catholic Church, which is only in our own times in the process of being healed. So sometimes these various reform currents in the 11th century had rather curious outcomes.

The reformers were focused on two issues above all others. They were focused on the issue of clerical morality, but in particular clerical marriage and concubinage, trying to put a stop to this. In the second place, on simony—simony the selling of the gifts of the Holy Spirit, named after Simon Magus. Selling the gifts of the Holy Spirit yes, but that came to be associated particularly with religious offices. Gradually, in the minds of at least some of the reformers, any lay involvement with religious offices, any trafficking in religious offices by a layman—be that layman an ordinary local nobleman, a local big shot or a king—is lay investiture and comes to be seen as simony. As we're going to see in a few minutes that's where the rub is, and that's why investiture does have a role in the "Investiture Controversy", paradoxical as it might seem to actually have to state that.

In 1058 Henry III was dead, his heir was a child, and the Romans rose up against the reformers and elected a Pope in opposition to the reformers' choice; that was Nicholas II. Nicholas did manage to prevail. He called a synod; he called a Roman synod in 1059. It outlawed simony. It outlawed clerical marriage, and it said that the clergy should not accept any offices from laymen. Finally, it spoke in only the vaguest terms about whether the emperor had any rights in papal elections. The reformers were then in Rome, and they were beginning to put their program into operation there. Nicholas also allied with the Romans of southern Italy, basically to try to create some kind of a counterweight to the Germans, who are unlikely to be well disposed towards his reform activities. The alliance that Nicholas II concluded with the Normans was roughly analogous to the alliance that Stephen II concluded with the Franks in the 8th century. For a few years relations between Germany and Rome were infrequent but cordial. There were no real problems, but there wasn't a lot of contact either.

In 1066 Henry IV of Germany came of age. Between about 1071 and 1073, he and Pope Alexander II quarreled over naming an archbishop to the city of Milan in northern Italy. The Germans had long exercised control over parts of northern Italy and Henry intruded himself there, assuming this was his right, his duty, his responsibility—the pope saying "No, stop, you can't do that." Alexander's resolve in opposing Henry in his attempt to name an Archbishop of Milan was stiffened by Cardinal Hildebrand, one of the real reformers who had come to Rome in the 1050s. In 1073 Hildebrand was elected pope and took the name of Gregory, Gregory VII. He was pope from 1073–1085.

Gregory is one of the most remarkable and one of the most important of all the popes, but he is an enigma in many ways. He's a very difficult man to grasp. It's hard to see him as a full-blooded human being. We don't know a lot about him personally, for example. He can seem austere. He can seem pompous. Certainly he was a man of conviction; certainly he was a man of conviction, a man of principle. He believed he was right, and so he acted with that kind of certainty that people who think they are right sometimes do. The *Dictatus Papae*, the "Dictate of the Pope," provides some insight into his thinking. This is a little document that survives amidst Gregory's papal registers. It's not at all clear what it represents. The prevailing view is that what we may have here is 27 titles for a treatise that was never written, 27 chapter headings, if you will, because each of the phrases really comes off like a kind of shorthand designation for a chapter, for an issue, for a question to be raised, a topic to be discussed.

Some of the provisions in the *Dictatus Papae* are rather routine ecclesiastical business. For instance, they say, "The pope alone can depose or reinstate bishops," "His legate takes precedence in a council," "He may transfer bishops from one see to another," "He has the power to ordain a cleric for any church," "No synod may be called general without his order." Well, fair enough. Those strike us as the kinds of things that have been being said for a very long time. Now, there were a few of the ecclesiastical provisions that might have raised eyebrows. "The Roman pontiff is alone to be called universal," "That he himself may be judged by no one," "That the Roman Church has never erred nor ever by witness of scripture shall err to eternity." Certain provisions, however, seemed startlingly new, "That he alone may use imperial insignia," "The pope is the only one whose feet are to be kissed by all princes," "That he may depose emperors," "That the pope may absolve subjects of unjust men from their fealty." These would have been seen as startlingly new observations.

How do we understand this Gregory, then? In Roman synods of 1074 and 1075, we mentioned earlier Roman synods—the one in 1059, we mentioned one in 769 that had passed a papal electoral decree, so Roman synods were very common—Gregory spoke vigorously against simony and clerical marriage, and he then raised the issue of lay investiture. He raised it very clearly, but there's some controversy among scholars over whether he formally forbade the practice at that moment or not, though he clearly pronounced it sinful. Henry IV, for his part, had just put down a Saxon revolt, and he'd begun asserting his power, so he began naming bishops in various places, including naming one in Milan. One has the sense that these men are feeling each other out. Sharply rebuked by Gregory, Henry summoned a council of German bishops and declared that Gregory was a false monk—he had been a monk before he was elected pope—and was deposed. In 1046 Henry III, Henry IV's father, had deposed three popes. Gregory responded by excommunicating Henry, putting him outside the church and releasing his subjects from their oath of allegiance to him.

By late 1076 some German princes and some bishops were demanding that Henry reverse course. They thought this was going too far too fast. Some were concerned as a matter of principle. They really saw big issues at stake. Some on the other hand, a bit cynically, saw this as an opportunity to reduce the power of a monarchy that was itself becoming very, very powerful, and they saw advantage for the local landed princes, the local landed powers in Germany if they weakened the king a little bit. Well, Gregory managed to establish the principle that a council under papal presidency would be held in Germany in 1077 to pass judgment on Henry. Henry then stole a march on his foes by trekking through the snow to Canossa Castle, where he appeared before the Pope and begged forgiveness.

Gregory was in a pickle. As a priest, he could not refuse absolution to a penitent sinner, and Henry had appeared as a penitent sinner. Gregory, of course, could regard this as capitulation; the king had given in to him. Henry could regard it as a very clever move that signaled his reconciliation with pope and that stripped his German foes of the legitimacy of their opposition to him. Many Germans, however, who had opposed Henry for a variety of reasons, felt Gregory had abandoned them because they really wanted to use the pope to weaken the king, so we're beginning to have a rather complicated situation here.

There was an individual called Rudolf of Rheinfelden in Germany, an utterly forgettable character in most respects except he was the German nobles' candidate to replace Henry IV. In 1078 Gregory formally condemned lay investiture. Some Germans, on the other hand, elected Rudolf as ruler of Germany. In 1080 Gregory again declared Henry excommunicated and deposed. Henry marched on Rome, chased Gregory to the Castel Sant'Angelo and eventually out of the city and installed Wibert of Ravenna as Clement III, as an antipope. He was going to put his own pope in. Gregory was rescued momentarily by his Norman allies who came into Rome, but they put the city to such a sack that the Normans and Gregory had to flee in disgrace. Gregory died in exile in Salerno.

It's very hard to drop a balance sheet on Gregory or on Henry, for that matter, not least because this battle dragged on for 30 more years. Emperors wanted what? Well, they wanted imperial coronation. One thing that had been established going back to the days of Charlemagne, if you're going to be emperor, you're going to be made emperor by the pope and probably in Rome. The emperors wanted to be able to work with the popes. They couldn't always do so, so they sometimes installed antipopes with whom they could work, but then there was always a question of the legitimacy of what was done. Popes, generally speaking, maintained the prohibition on lay investiture, which had now become the great symbolic sticking point in the whole controversy. On one occasion, Pope Paschal II, early in the 12th century, offered a radical solution. He said the clergy should simply give up all their temporal possessions, and there would be no problem. That satisfied nobody. There were rich luxuries; bishops who weren't about to give up all the goodies. There were kings who were not about to give up being able to name important officers of the church. There were others who felt this was simply an impractical solution.

Finally, Calixtus II, Pope Calixtus II in the Concordat of Worms in the year 1122, the agreement concluded between the pope and the German ruler, achieved a resolution. What form did that resolution take? What did that resolution look like? It's rather interesting in some ways. Based on the thinking of certain canon lawyers, a distinction was drawn between *temporalia* and *spiritualia*. Let's unpack those terms. Temporalia basically mean the temporal dimensions of the authority that a churchman might have. More concretely, what that means is that very often, when a king named a bishop that bishop would become also a vassal of the king, and he might be invested with administrative responsibility. He might be invested with military responsibility, he might be invested with legal responsibility, and he might be invested with financial responsibility. He might be called to serve the king in the king's court as an adviser, temporalia, temporal jobs, if you will, that a member of the clergy would get by dint of being invested with his religious office. Spiritualia, on the other hand, referred explicitly and directly to the spiritual side, to the sacramental side, to the holy side, to the purely clerical side of a churchman's office.

So some thinkers in the church, particularly church lawyers are beginning to say, "We can notionally divide these two things. We can think not all of this is one of bundle of rights, duties, obligations, responsibilities, etc. incumbent upon, let us say, a bishop. We can differentiate these, and if we differentiate them, then we can perhaps resolve this great controversy between the popes and the rulers of Germany." Though the popes had, we might say, almost minor-league controversies with the kings of France, with the king of England, and so on so that the big problem was always Germany, but there were other problems as well.

What would the compromise look like? The Concordat of Worms said that laymen could not invest with the ring and crozier. The ring, of course, is a bishop's ring. Originally it was his signet ring. It was what he used to seal documents and so on. It was the symbol of his authority and the right to pronounce his authority, to send out documents under his name or under his seal. The crozier is the hooked staff, a shepherd's crozier. Sometimes these things were gorgeous gold things with jewels on them and so forth. But they're meant to look like a shepherd's staff because the bishop is the shepherd of souls, the chief officer of the church, as we've seen, for example, when we talked about the ecclesiastical structure of the City of Rome. So no layman can any longer invest with ring and crozier. The spiritualia, the spiritual side of the ecclesiastical office, will be handled entirely by the church, and moreover, episcopal elections are to be completely free. In principle, in other words, the king can't simply call somebody in and say, "Hey you, you're the bishop now." The clergy of a cathedral church will elect its bishop.

But it was said in the Concordat that elections could take place in the emperor's presence. That, of course, gave the emperor considerable opportunity to bring pressure to bear, not to say outright intimidation. After a man has been freely elected and invested with the spiritualia by the church, the king—or the emperor, or a duke, or a count, or a baron, whom you please—could invest that person with the temporalia, could assign them temporal offices, could assign them temporal responsibilities, could make them accomplish other tasks. The idea was here, of course, that laymen, kings—and of course I want you to bear in mind that kings never saw themselves fully or exclusively as laymen; they thought they were God's special agents in a very powerful way—but from the church's point of view, laymen would no longer make clerical officers, but laymen would still get to draw these important, educated and influential people into their service and into their system. So appearances were preserved, and a compromise was affected.

We might say, actually, that in the long run, this was likely to be done more to the benefit of the church than of the secular states of Europe. The popes greatly gained immense prestige during the years of the "Investiture Controversy", not entirely because of the controversy itself, though it played a role.

We'll see in our next lecture some other ways in which the popes gained prestige in this period. But the fundamental point I want to make is that in a period such as the medieval one, where religion infused every aspect of life and where religion was seen as the end of life and the end of government, it was pretty hard to deny ultimate authority to religious authority. Let's again remember Gelasius in his authority and power. It's important, too—and interesting and fateful for the future—that in one of these great controversies over temporal rule, lay investiture, the popes vastly enhanced their control of the church, and it is that papal control of the church that we'll turn in our next lecture.

Lecture Eight
The Papal Monarchy—Institutions

Scope:

Although the popes were challenged in myriad ways during the Investiture Controversy, the papacy emerged from the battle stronger than ever. The 12th and 13th centuries marked the high-water point of papal power and influence, first in the Church, then in the wider world. In this first of two lectures on the papal monarchy, we will examine the papacy as an institution, focusing largely on the pope within the Church but also looking at new ways in which the papacy as an institution influenced the contemporary world.

We will begin by looking at the popes of this period from several different points of view. We will pay particular attention to important changes in papal elections. Then we will look at the Curia, the central government of the Church. We will examine law and law courts, financial offices, and the papacy's means for establishing contacts and effecting control across Europe. We will also examine important new ideological formulations by means of which the papacy defined its place at the summit of a hierarchically ordered society.

Outline

I. From the accession of Gregory VII in 1073 to the death of Boniface VIII in 1303, the papacy attained the height of its power, prestige, and influence.

    A. This dramatic surge was owed to the development of papal institutions and ideology and to a series of political encounters that usually brought the popes both short- and long-term gains.

    B. In this lecture, we shall focus on the papacy itself, and in the next one, we will turn to the papacy's complex dealings with Rome, Italy, and the wider world.

II. First, then, let us look at the period's 37 popes themselves from several points of view.

A. In terms of geographical origins, we may note that 19 were non-Roman Italians, 10 were Romans, 5 were French, and 1 each came from Savoy, Portugal, and England.

B. In terms of backgrounds, we may note that 8 were monks, 7 were canons, 16 were priests, 2 were deacons, 1 had been patriarch of Jerusalem, 1 held no clerical rank, and by the end of the 13th century, the new mendicant orders, Dominicans and Franciscans, had each contributed 1 pope.

C. Eight popes faced the effrontery of schism. Eleven antipopes disturbed the orderly papal succession.

D. Between schisms and Roman political turmoil, popes were absent from Rome for about 50 years in the 230 years under review here.

E. For various reasons, there were sometimes lengthy gaps between pontificates.

F. Some important changes took place in how popes were elected.

　　1. In 1179, Alexander III and the Lateran Council decreed that popes would be elected by the *sanior pars* (the "wiser part"; phraseology adopted from the *Rule of St. Benedict*), and a two-thirds majority was deemed necessary.

　　2. Because 13th-century cardinals had a habit of avoiding or fleeing Rome, in 1241, the Roman senator Matteo Rosso Orsini locked the cardinals in the old *Septizonium* and denied them food and drink until they elected a pope.

　　3. After several placid elections, Pope Clement IV died at Viterbo in 1268, and the locals locked the cardinals in a palace. The cardinals' prolonged deliberations prompted town authorities to rip the roof off the palace.

　　4. Gregory X, elected in Viterbo, formalized the *conclave*, indicating that the electors are locked in as they vote, a tradition that has been used with only minor modifications down to today.

III. The central government of the Church grew further and faster than ever before.

    A. Under Urban II, the term *curia* (or *Curia Romana*) began to appear. This could be a general reference to the papal court or to the Church's government, or it could refer quite specifically to the pope and the cardinals sitting in consistory. *Consistory* refers to times when the cardinals and the popes formally meet to discuss and make decisions about the affairs of the Church.

        1. In theory, there would have been 53 cardinals, but that number was almost never reached; at times in the 13th century, there were fewer than 10 cardinals.

        2. Sometimes politics suppressed the number of cardinals, but financial exigencies played a role, too. Cardinals were expensive and ate up a significant portion of the Church's budget.

        3. The Code of Canon Law expressed the cardinal's role this way: "The cardinals of the Holy Roman Church constitute the senate of the pontiff and assist him in ruling the church as his foremost counselors and helpers."

        4. By the late 13th century, policies were fairly well established that papal decretals required the signature of one or more cardinals and that *res ardua* (difficult cases) needed consultation.

    B. The writing and recordkeeping offices developed under the chancellor.

    C. Four times between 921 and 1062, the word *camera* appears in the papal sources; then, under Gregory VII, the financial machinery of the Church began to be put on firm footings.

        1. Urban II introduced the *camerarius* (chamberlain), several of whom went on to become pope.

            a. The Church needed money to maintain the papal court, wherever it might be; to keep Rome's churches in repair; to support the cardinals; and to bribe the Roman authorities.

            b. Revenues came from the Papal States, but these lands were in an almost constant state of turmoil.

  c. Funds also came from Peter's pence (an annual voluntary laymen's contribution), paid by England and Poland; feudal dues from princes; and annual fees from some 530 monasteries and canonical houses

  d. Shortly after their appointment, bishops usually paid taxes in the form of the equivalent of a year's diocesan income, then they paid set fees every year.

 2. In 1192, Cencius Savelli, as *camerarius*, drew up the *Liber Censuum*, a listing of virtually all revenues due to the papacy. No other government in Europe had any such listing.

D. Judicial institutions were refined, and the volume of business expanded exponentially. The *Rota Romana* gradually handled more and more business, and the Roman Church increasingly demanded that cases be brought to Rome for resolution.

IV. In matters great and small, we can see the papacy taking a leading position in Europe.

A. The Crusades were seen as a papal venture.

B. Rome took virtual control of the process of canonization of new saints.

C. For the first time, albeit with limited success, the popes began to demand liturgical uniformity.

D. Through papal provisions and expectancies, popes began to make more and more routine ecclesiastical appointments around Europe.

E. The popes steadily expanded the number and scope of legates.

F. Whereas popes had long used Roman synods as tools for governance, gathering central Italian clergy, now the consistory and the ecumenical council took over.

V. Papal ideology grew apace in sophistication and articulation.

A. The lawyer Hostiensis once said that the priestly dignity is exactly 7,644½ times greater than the royal. He obviously had Gelasius's letter to Anastasius in mind, as well as

Ptolemy, who had said that the Sun is 7,644½ times brighter than the Moon.

B. In the circles around Gregory VII—and later—thinkers interpreted Gelasius's letter as a commentary on Luke 22: 38: "They said, 'Lord, here are two swords.' He answered 'enough.'"

C. The hierarchical thought that undergirded the institutions of this papal monarchy is at once old and new.

D. We must now look to see how the popes could actually act in this world.

Recommended Reading:

Robinson, *The Papacy, 1073–1198.*

Morris, *The Papal Monarchy.*

Questions to Consider:

1. How did the basic institutions of the papacy change in the high Middle Ages?

2. In what ways is the term *monarchy* appropriate to the papacy between, say, 1100 and 1300?

Lecture Eight—Transcript
The Papal Monarchy—Institutions

Hello and welcome to the eighth of our lectures in this series on the history of the popes and of the papacy. This will be the first of two lectures on what I'm going to call—it's not my phrase—the papal monarchy. In this lecture we're going to look at the institutions of the Roman Church. In our next one we'll look at the interactions of the papacy with Rome, Italy and the wider world. From the accession of Gregory VII, about whom we spoke last time, in 1073, to the death of Boniface VIII in 1303, the papacy attained the height of its power, prestige and influence. This dramatic surge owed a great deal to the development of papal institutions and ideology, also, to be sure, to a series of political encounters, which usually brought the popes both short- and long-term gains. Those political encounters will be the subject of our next lecture. In this one we're going to focus on the papacy itself, then we'll turn to the papacy's complex dealings with the world around it.

First then, let's look for a bit at the 37 popes, and let's look at them from several different points of view. For instance, geographical origins: 19 were non-Roman Italians; ten were Romans; five were French; three came, one each, from Savoy, Portugal and England. Nicholas Breakspear was England's only pope. There was not a single German. Not again until 2005 would a German be elected Pope. In some ways that was one of the bequests of the Investiture Controversy. The predominance of Romans and Italians—these are not the same; one must never suppose that Italians and Romans are the same—is pretty obvious, but this is also a reasonably international period, perhaps since the very beginning the most international period in papal history.

In terms of the backgrounds of these popes, we can note, for instance, that eight of them had been monks; seven were canons—that means members of the clergy of a particular church; it might be a cathedral church or it might be a church designated a canonical church. You all know what monks are; monks live in a monastery. Canons are the clergy attached to a particular church, so seven of the popes were canons, usually a canon of a Roman or an Italian church. Sixteen were priests, two had been deacons, one had been Patriarch of Jerusalem and one held no clerical rank at the time he was elected. By the end of the 13th century, the new mendicant—that means begging, which means dedicated to poverty—orders, the Dominicans and the Franciscans, had each contributed one pope. These numbers, it seems to me, reveal some other patterns as well. Monks were prominent until the late 12th century and extremely rare thereafter. From the mid- to late-12th century right through the 13th, most popes were highly educated in law or theology, usually in Bologna or in Paris. It was an interesting period, too, when none of these popes was canonized a saint, what that might suggest to lawyers, I will leave it to you to decide for yourselves.

The average age at election grew. Most of the men elected had a long service in the church, often as legates. A legate is an envoy sent out by the pope to someplace. They could sometimes be sent to a particular place more or less permanently. When they settled in there, then they were really, for all the world, the same as ambassadors. A legate can also be sent out for a very specific reason, "Go and talk to somebody and find out something. Go and talk to somebody and tell him something." But anyway, legates were one important way in which the popes kept in touch with the world around them. So a considerable number of the popes elected in this period had been legates, which meant that they'd been outside Rome. They had some sense of what was going on in the wider world; they had a feel for the broader context.

Eight of our popes faced the effrontery of schism. That is to say, 11 antipopes were elected during this period. Between schisms and Roman political turmoil, popes were often absent from Rome. In this period of about 230 years, popes were outside Rome for a little over 50 years. That's important because later on in a future lecture, we're going to see the popes move down to Avignon in the south of France for nearly three-quarters of a century. But it's important to realize that before this, it was not so uncommon for the pope to be away from Rome. This actually produced the situation where 13th century papal lawyers formulated the doctrine "Ubi papa ibi Roma," which basically means, "Wherever the pope is, that's Rome".

In the 13th century, only two papal elections took place in Rome. For various reasons—politics, heaven knows all sorts of things—there were sometimes lengthy gaps between pontificates. In the turmoil of the Investiture Controversy, for example, in 1085 the gap was twelve months between the death of one pope, Gregory VII, and the election of his successor. Then a little later, 1087–1088, the gap was six months. Down to 1241, there were fairly rapid elections. Four popes, indeed, were elected on the very day of their predecessor's death. Eight were elected within a couple of days. After 1241 things got pretty bad. Let me just enumerate the gaps to give you a feel for how often the papal office was vacant: 1241, two months; 1243, 18 months; 1261, three months; 1265, four months; 1271, 34 months; 1277, six months; 1281, six months; 1288, 11 months; 1294, 27 months. So in addition to popes being away from Rome for about 50 years, the papal office was vacant for about ten years during this period.

There were some important changes in how popes were elected introduced during these years. You'll remember, perhaps, we talked about the electoral decree of 1059. Despite Nicholas's hopes, this did not prevent imperial interference. Moreover, whereas the electoral decree of 769 had privileged the position of the cardinal priests and deacons, the electoral decree of 1059 had privileged the position of the cardinal bishops. Consequently, Pope Urban II at the very end of the 11th century had to admit the priests and deacons alongside the cardinal bishops, or if you will, put them back to where they had been as early as 769, so even in the cardinal clergy there had been some jockeying for position. The decree of 1059 established in principle that the election was to be unanimous. It boggles the mind to think that anyone could have supposed papal elections would ever be unanimous, and it proved utterly impossible.

In 1179 Pope Alexander III, in the Lateran Council—we have seen that there were Roman synods for a very long time—the popes had been calling the Roman synods, very often the bishops of, the suburbicarian bishops of other bishops in Italy and occasionally of bishops more widely from around the European zone. In the 12th century those synods began to be held at the Lateran, so we begin to call them Lateran synods or Lateran councils, and they begin to have a much wider European representation as a matter of course. Earlier Roman synods only, extraordinarily, had people from all over the place. Now we begin to see a very wide representation of people, of churchmen—bishops in particular—coming to these synods. The Lateran Council decreed that popes would be elected by the *sanior pars*, the wiser part—literally the healthier part, but the wiser part. This was actually a rule adapted from the rule of Saint Benedict, which said that the abbot of a monastery was not to be elected by the *maior pars*—the greater part, the more part, the majority—but by the *sanior pars*, by the wiser part. Exactly how you decide who is *sanior*, or who is in *sanior*, not wiser, well, that was probably a little bit tricky. But for practical purposes it was decided that a two-thirds majority would henceforth be necessary for elections, so the pretense of unanimity was given up.

Thirteenth century cardinalate had a bad habit of avoiding or perhaps even of fleeing from Rome. In 1241 the Roman senator Matteo Rosso Orsini locked the cardinals in the old Septizonium, an old classical building in Rome. It had been a prison and various other things in antiquity. Anyway, he locked the cardinals up in there and denied them food and drink until they would agree to elect a pope. After several reasonably placid elections, Clement IV died at Viterbo, a city north of Rome, in 1268, and the locals locked the cardinals, who had been with the pope there, locked the cardinals in a palace. When their deliberations prolonged and they couldn't get around to electing anybody, the locals ripped the roof off the palace. They thought, "Well, if the bad weather comes in, it might stir them up and have them elect somebody."

Gregory X was finally elected in those awful conditions in Viterbo, went back to Rome, and formalized the conclave, which has been used with only minor modifications down to today—conclave with a key, shut in, So to this day, when a pope dies, the cardinals come to Rome. After the funeral for one pope and a certain number of preliminaries are settled, the cardinals are locked in until they elect somebody. Now, they don't live any longer in the rough conditions that they lived in in Viterbo in that nasty time in 1268, but in any case, they are still shut away, locked up with a key. They are still in a conclave.

The central government of the church grew further and faster than ever before. The range of business that it began to handle, and the sheer volume of business that it began to handle, was greater than ever before. We can and, as we go along, we'll see some roots in earlier time, some connections with issues that we've talked about and institutions we've talked about and practices that we've talked about in earlier lectures. But we're now going to see just a tremendous difference in the scale and quantity of business.

Under Pope Urban II at the very end of the 11th century, we first begin to see the term *curia* or *curia Romana*. A *curia* in Latin—

that's a court—a court in Latin always means a court of law, a place where judicial decisions are made, where legal business is handled. But curia can also be, a king can have a curia, an emperor can have a curia, a pope can have a curia. This can refer sort of to the court in the general sense—in other words, not to a court of law, but to the court of a king, to everybody who is there and to all the things that happen there and so on. Where the papacy is concerned, *curia* could mean court in this broad sort of cultural and ideological sense. It could mean court in a narrower sense of the court of law, and it could also need court in the sense of the pope and the cardinals sitting in Consistory.

There is still Consistory today. Consistory basically means when the pope and the cardinals sit down formally to deliberate on and to make decisions about the business of the church. We'll bump into Consistory one or two more times as we go along here in the next few minutes. So curia could mean various things, but the point that I'm really inviting you to keep in mind is that by the end of the 11th century, people have sort of conceptualized the papal government as the Roman curia. They now have a name for this beast. In earlier times, in the earlier Middle Ages, there never was really a single name like that for the papal government and all the activities that went on in that government.

Cardinals then, we've already met them. We have noted their role in papal elections, for example, just a few minutes ago. We saw that they emerged in late antiquity in the church, that already by 769 they had become key figures in the election of the pope. In theory, in the 12th century there would have been 53 cardinals, but that number was almost never reached. Sometimes indeed, in the 13th century there were fewer than ten at any given moment. Sometimes politics suppressed the number of cardinals, but financial exigencies played a role, too. Cardinals were expensive and they tended to spend a lot of money, so having a lot of cardinals ate up a big chunk of the budget of the church. So popes had an interest not in appointing too many cardinals because it gave them too many advisors and too many people they had to pay attention to, but they had an interest in not appointing too many cardinals because they were expensive, quite simply.

Now, canon law expressed the cardinals' role this way. "The Cardinals of the Holy Roman Church constitute the senate of the pontiff and assist him in ruling the church as his foremost counselors and helpers." Well, that's helpful in a way, but if you stop and think about it, that's not very precise. I mean, exactly what can they help? When can they give advice? Does their advice have to be listened to? What is their legal role? They are clearly the pope's key advisers; that's clear. But it's less clear exactly what their responsibilities are. Speaking to the cardinals when his own former pupil was reigning as Pope Eugenius III, so right in the middle of the 12th century, Saint Bernard—Saint Bernard of Clairvaux, one of the great ecclesiastical figures of 12th century Europe—he said, "God has put you in a high place so that the more useful your life is to his church, the more eminent will be your authority. There is no doubt that it behooves you especially to remove scandal from the kingdom of God, to cut down the thorns that grow, to bring an end to lamentation." So Bernard clearly sees the cardinals as people who have a responsibility, well, to continue the reform. We saw in our last lecture just how tricky that word "reform" is, but you'll notice he, Bernard, doesn't assign them specific legal roles. He gives them a kind of a moral role.

Early in the 13th century, a very important famous canon lawyer by the name of Hostiensis said this. "Today the Roman Church holds no greater dignity than that of the cardinalate, since the cardinals, together with the pope, judge all, but cannot themselves be judged by anyone other than by the pope and their colleagues." That's a little different from Bernard, isn't it? You see, that's a lawyer talking. Now, we get a little bit of language about what their responsibilities are, to whom they answer, who answers to them, and so on. Suffice it to say that in the 12th and 13th centuries, the period that engages us now, and indeed for many centuries thereafter, the role, the place, the power, the responsibility, the influence of the cardinals ebbed and flowed. It grew and diminished, it changed all the time. This was never something that was kind of fixed once and for all. We're going to talk about cardinals again and again and again and again, in this a little bit and also in later lectures. I don't want you to have a sense, though, that the cardinalate is a hard and fast office with a nice tidy agenda of duties and responsibilities and once settled it's settled forever.

By the late 13th century, it was pretty well established that papal decretals—we've talked about papal decretals before, those decrees issued by the pope when the pope makes new law—required the signature of one or more cardinals. This is a case where cardinals are actually able to impose this on the popes; popes don't willingly give that away. It was also decided that *res ardua*—that's Latin for "tough cases", so really tough, complicated cases that came to Rome—had be decided in consultation with the cardinals. Where did that consultation take place? It took place in meetings called Consistories. We're back to our Consistory. So sometimes the Consistory is kind of formally informal, a meeting of the cardinals around the pope just to discuss and take thought for the great issues of the day. But also, the Consistory can be where a hard case came to Rome and was discussed and settled.

The 12th and 13th century also represent a period when the writing and record keeping offices of the Roman Church, under an official called the chancellor, grew as never before. The volume of papal correspondence, for example, from this period that survives is many times greater than all the papal letters that survive from the first 1,000 years, and still we don't have the papal archives, so we know we have only a fraction of what was once there. You may recall that one of the great officers of the church in the early Middle Ages had been the primicerius of the notaries. The primicerius of the notaries is now a much less significant, a much less visible figure, and the chancellor of the Roman Church—who has responsibility, in a sense, for the record-keeping department, if you like, and the record-issuing department, if you like—is now one of the really important officers in the *curia Romana*, in the Roman curia, in the court of the pope.

Four times between 931 and 1062, the word *camera* appears—you know what a camera is, but a camera is a box; that's what a camera is. How does that work? Well, imagine a treasure chest, a box with the treasury in it, you see. So four times over a period of years, the word *camera* appears in papal sources, but then, under Gregory VII—so this very Pope who is carrying out this mortal struggle with the German emperors—reforms the financial machinery of the church and puts it on firmer footings. This will kind of remind us of the 10th century, when we've got these dreadful popes who are nevertheless able to carry on routine ecclesiastical business. By the end of the 11th century, Urban II introduced the *camerarius*, the chamberer. *Camera* really means chamber; by extension then, the chamber where the money is kept, the chamber where the treasury is kept. Several of these *camerarii* went on to become pope, so the chief financial officer of the Roman Church begins to be a much more prominent figure, a key adviser at the court, usually—not always, but usually—a cardinal, and as I said several times, the *camerarius* went on to be elected pope.

What did the pope need money for? What did he do with his money? Well, he needed money to maintain the papal court first of all, wherever it might be. Bear in mind that if the popes are something like 50 years outside Rome during this period, moving this big court around. It's not as though the pope and his private secretary are traveling alone. You have a substantial group of people going around, so somebody has to maintain the papal court outside Rome, and you have to maintain the papal court inside Rome. You have to feed them, you have to house them, you have to clothe them and you have to move them around.

They had to keep Rome's churches in repair. I want anybody who is listening to my words at this moment to think about this. Have you ever, in traveling, walked into a church that didn't have a box in the front asking you to drop in a few coins or a few bills in donation to keep the building up? Well, keeping up these old buildings is expensive. It's expensive in the 21st century; it was expensive in the 12th century. So one of the things that papal revenues had to do was to maintain the fabric of Rome's churches, and let's remember that the pope doesn't have one church. He has all those churches all over Rome that we talked about in an earlier lecture. The money had to support the cardinals. I've stressed on several occasions that the cardinals were great princes of the church and were not inexpensive figures. Then there could be other occasional expenses as, for instance, bribing the Roman authorities. Hadrian IV—Nicholas Breakspear, our Englishman—had to bribe the Rome authorities to the tune of 10,000 talents. That's a lot of money.

Where did popes get their revenue? Well, the revenues came from the Papal States; that was one important source of revenue. Money came from the Papal States in two ways. It came, on one hand, through the exercise of public power, collecting fines, judicial fees and that sort of thing; and from the papal patrimonies, from the farms, the lands that the Roman Church actually owned. But the Papal States were in almost constant state of turmoil, though the popes gradually built up a state that was actually the equal of virtually any in Europe in terms of its sophistication and the efficiency of its local government. That's another sense in which you may think of the popes as monarchs. They were monarchs of their own little state in the middle of Italy. Funds also came from Peter's Pence, pennies for Saint Peter that had been paid since the early Middle Ages from England, since the 10th century from Poland.

Feudal dues, there were various kings around Europe who were—more symbolically than practically—but nevertheless vassals of the pope, and one of the things they did was they sent in a certain amount of funds every year. There were annual fees from about 530 monasteries around Europe that sent in differing amounts of money to Rome. Cluny, for example—the great Monastery of Cluny—owed two solidi, two silver coins a year; in Rome, a pint of almonds; Reichenau, two white horses, a gospel book and a sacramentary. Woffenheim sent the golden rose that the pope carried on the procession on the fourth Sunday in Lent. So the kinds of things that people sent to Rome could vary enormously. There were also, of course, importantly, pilgrim offerings—the constant flow of pilgrims to Rome who left money in the city and who spent money in the city. Rome's tavern keepers and hoteliers loved those pilgrims.

Bishops usually paid taxes in the form, roughly, of the equivalent of a year's diocesan income right off the bat. When they were made a bishop, they basically have to send a year's diocesan income to Rome and then set fees thereafter. How do we know about these revenues? In 1192, Cencius Savelli—the Savelli were one of the great Roman families—was camerarius, so he's a chief financial officer. He drew up the *Liber Censuum*, the book of fees, the book of rents, the book of revenues, a remarkable listing of virtually all the revenues due to the papacy. No other government in Europe at that time had anything like this.

Judicial institutions were refined, and the volume of judicial business expanded exponentially. In 1140, the *Concordantia Discordantium Canonum*—the "Concordance of Discordant Canons"—which we usually happily call Gratian's *Decretum*—that's a little bit easier—was issued as a rationalized compendium of church law down to its time, down to the early 12th century. In other words, for the first time a real collection was made of the laws of the church. Subsequently, there were collections of papal decretals. Popes were now making laws much faster, much more frequently than their predecessors had ever done, and sometimes they issued decretals, which rule on a very specific subject. Sometimes they issued *constitutiones*, constitutions, where they ruled all at once on a whole variety of subjects. So the church was making a lot more laws.

Not surprisingly then, it also has to have a larger judiciary to handle the business generated by that law. The *Rota Romana*—broadly speaking, that means the judicial branch of the papal government— gradually handled more and more business, and the Roman Church increasingly demanded that cases of all kinds be brought to Rome for resolution. The *Penitentiaria* grew as a special court for dispensation. As an example, let's suppose you were of a mind to marry someone to whom, by ordinary church law, you were too closely related, you would appeal to the *Penitentiaria* for a dispensation from the law of the church so that you could marry that person. The *Penitentiaria* did lots of things, but that's a good example. Despite bribery and delays, the quality of papal justice was very high.

In a lot of ways, we can see the popes taking a leading position in Europe in this period, in the 12th and 13th century. The Crusades were seen widely as a great papal venture. Rome took virtual control of the process of canonizing saints. For the first time, albeit with limited success, the popes began to demand liturgical uniformity, uniformity in worship throughout Europe. Through papal provisions and expectancies, popes naming bishops; the popes took more and more control of routine ecclesiastical appointments. The popes steadily expanded the number and scope of legates, their connections to the European world. Indeed, of the 19 popes, for instance, between Gregory VII and Innocent III, 15 had been legates. Whereas the popes had long used Roman synods to gather the central Italian clergy to govern the church and the ecumenical council in the early church, now ecumenical councils called by the popes to Rome were taking over. The cardinalate was itself increasingly international, but these great councils in 1123, 1139, 1179, 1215, 1245 and 1274 were something like European parliaments, with the pope as the presiding officer.

Fittingly, at this time, when papal institutions were growing, so too, were definitions of the papal office growing in pace. Hostiensis, that lawyer we met a moment ago, once said, "The priestly dignity is exactly 7,644 ½ times greater than the royal dignity." Now you're thinking, "What on Earth was he talking about?" He had Gelasius in mind, didn't he, but also Ptolemy, who had said that the sun is 7,644 ½ times brighter than the moon. Across the 12th century, writers spoke of priestly and royal power in terms of sun-moon metaphors. Let's hear Innocent II.

Just as the founder of the universe established two great lights in the firmament of heaven, a greater one to preside over the day and a lesser one to preside over the night, so too in the firmament of the universal church he instituted two great dignities, a greater one to preside over souls, as if over day, and a lesser one to preside over bodies, as if over night. These are the pontifical authority and the royal power.

In the circles around Gregory VII, and later too, thinkers interpreted Gelasius's letter quite differently. They thought of it as a commentary on Luke 22:38: "They said, 'Lord, here are two swords.' He answered 'enough.'" Henry IV explicitly rejected this line of thought. Gregory, he said, "usurped the royal power and the priestly power and thereby shown contempt for the ordination of God who wished government to consist principally not in one but in two… as the savior made clear himself in the allegory of the two swords." But in the 12th century, the great English political thinker John of Salisbury wrote in his book the *Policraticus*—he's almost answering Henry here—"Since the prince receives the material sword from the hand of the church, since she herself does not hold the sword of blood… she uses the secular sword by means of the hand of the prince, on whom she has conferred the power of coercing men's bodies having reserved for herself this power of spiritual coercion." The hierarchical thought that has always under girded the institutions of this papal monarchy is at once old and new.

Lecture Nine
The Papal Monarchy—Politics

Scope:

The end of the Investiture Controversy did not bring an end to quarrels between the popes and Europe's rulers. Rulers lost a good deal of day-to-day influence over the Church but did not abandon their claim to a kind of sacred rule. Frederick Barbarossa of Germany referred to his *Sacrum Imperium Romanum* (his "Holy Roman Empire"; any use of that term before Frederick's time is anachronistic!). He meant to say that his empire was holy and that it derived from Rome but not from the Roman pope. Innocent III, on the contrary, calculated that the empire was like the Moon to the papal Sun: derivative. His meaning was lost on no one. In this lecture, we will examine some of the great battles of the day, emphasizing the struggles between the empire and the papacy.

Outline

I. We have seen the kinds of institutions and ideas that together made up the papal monarchy of the 12th and 13th centuries. Now we turn to the nuts-and-bolts history of that period to see what the popes could and could not do.

II. The Schism of 1130 was a portent of things to come in Rome and in the Church.

   A. In the last years of Pope Calixtus II (r. 1119–1124), the Pierleoni and Frangipani families began to contest for leadership of the city, and they inserted supporters into the College of Cardinals.

      1. When Calixtus died, the Pierleoni engineered the election of their candidate, who took the name Celestine II.

      2. Enraged, the Frangipani forcibly ejected Celestine and introduced Lambert, the bishop of Ostia, who took the name Honorius II (r. 1124–1130).

      3. Honorius managed to rule peacefully until his death in 1130.

   B. The international situation for Honorius was complex.

      1. The Salian dynasty was vanishing in Germany.

2. In the south, Duke Roger II of Sicily invaded and seized Apulia and Calabria.

3. Even in the countryside around Rome, Honorius found himself obliged to wage battles in support of Frangipani interests.

C. When Honorius died, 16 cardinals of the Frangipani faction elected Cardinal Gregory Papareschi, who took the name Innocent II.

1. The other 14 cardinals refused to accept the election and, in San Marco, elected cardinal Pietro Pierleoni, who took the name Anacletus II.

2. A few Frangipani cardinals agreed to accept Anacletus; thus, it appeared that he had a majority, and Innocent had to flee amidst questions about procedures.

D. France, Germany, England, much of Italy, the great religious orders, and key ecclesiastical figures, such as Bernard of Clairvaux, supported Innocent.

E. Anacletus had the support of the Romans and the Normans, whose allegiance he solidified by making Roger II king.

F. Only in 1133 was Innocent able to take control of Rome and then only because the German king, Lothar of Supplinburg, accompanied him into the city.

G. Lothar campaigned against Roger and weakened him sufficiently that he was no menace when Lothar died in 1137.

H. Anacletus's position was ruined, Innocent held a great council in 1139, and Roger was eventually recognized as king by Innocent.

I. What are the lessons here?

1. As the papacy and cardinalate became more international, they lost the loyalty of the Romans.

2. Great Roman families could still exercise dire influence over the papacy.

3. The popes could not protect themselves without having recourse to outside powers.

III. The Schism of 1159 to 1180 marked a return to papal-imperial tensions, complicated by problems in the city of Rome and urban dynamics in northern and central Italy.

    A. First, we must set the stage.

        1. The situation in Rome was intensely volatile and complicated.

            a. Angry with both popes and nobles, Roman craftsmen and merchants inaugurated a commune in 1143.

            b. Commune leaders and popes vied with each other to secure the support of both German and Sicilian kings, who were themselves bitter enemies.

            c. By 1159, Hadrian IV (Nicholas Breakspear, the only Englishman ever elected pope) had accepted Frederick Barbarossa as king, made peace with William I of Sicily, and patched up a peace with the Romans.

            d. But on Hadrian's death, the cardinals split into factions.

        2. The popes had generally supported and had been supported by Lothar of Supplinburg in Germany, but he declined to provide much help in Italy.

        3. We have already seen that the Normans in the south were a constant concern for the popes.

    B. One party of cardinals elected Orlando Bandinelli, a distinguished lawyer, who took the name Alexander III. He would eventually prevail.

        1. Another faction elected Cardinal Ottaviano, who took the name Victor IV and appealed to the emperor; Alexander had appealed to William of Sicily.

        2. Initially, Victor IV controlled Rome and Alexander was forced to remain away.

        3. Barbarossa came to Italy in 1160 to hold a council and decide between the rivals. When Alexander refused to appear, Barbarossa declared Victor the true pope, and most of Italy, Germany, and Europe opposed Barbarossa for going too far.

        4. There were three more antipopes down to 1180, but their cause was overtaken by other events. Suffice it to say that Alexander III was able to prevail because

Barbarossa was unable to provide continuous support to his antipopes in Rome.

   C. We learn here, once again, that the popes were always subject to the whims of other people's interests in Italy and that the Roman populace as a whole now added its troublemaking ability to that of the nobility.

IV. The first half of the 13th century was dominated by the papacy's battle with Frederick II of Hohenstaufen.

   A. Some background is crucial to understanding the inception, duration, and bitterness of this battle.

      1. The age-old desire of German rulers for dominion in Italy took a bizarre turn when Barbarossa married his son Henry to Constance of Sicily. The Norman male line had died out, and when Henry died young in 1197, the German and Sicilian inheritances were united in a 3-year-old child.

      2. When Constance herself died in 1198, young Frederick II became a ward of the pope.

   B. In Germany, two factions emerged. One, under Philip of Swabia, supported the Hohenstaufen, while the other, under Otto IV of Brunswick, supported noble privileges.

   C. Pope Innocent III intervened by supporting Otto, who renounced all claims in Italy.

      1. Then, in 1208, Philip was murdered, removing all restraints from Otto, who promptly invaded Italy and got himself excommunicated.

      2. In 1212, Innocent elevated Frederick II to the throne of Germany.

   D. Frederick was a remarkable character, more Sicilian by far than German, and determined to rule all of Italy and at least be recognized as ruler in Germany.

      1. Until his death in 1250, Frederick had almost entirely bad relations with the popes.

      2. Partly the troubles stemmed from Frederick's repeated failure to go on crusade, as he had sworn to do, and partly, Frederick's own morally dubious behavior was at issue.

    3. But the great issue, as so often, was Italy, where Frederick's policies threatened to surround the Papal States.

E. The whole struggle was unedifying in many ways and resulted in the demise of the Hohenstaufen family and a 60-year gap in the imperial succession (1250–1312), but this was an important period for the popes in other respects.
    1. Innocent III forced French and English kings to bow to his will and opened closer relations in Spain than had ever existed before.
    2. On the demise of the Hohenstaufen, the popes recruited first English, then French princes to reign in southern Italy and Sicily.
    3. New religious orders, especially the Franciscans and Dominicans, revitalized the Church.
    4. Under Gregory IX, the Roman Inquisition systematically pursued heretics.
    5. Laws were revised, the Papal States were administered effectively, and finances were carefully managed.

F. Two lessons here are clear.
    1. Temporal rule inevitably involved the popes in the great political issues of the day.
    2. However much it might seem that the popes were either dominated or distracted by secular concerns, the business of the Church went on apace.

G. But perhaps there is a third lesson: The papacy's secular rule and political actions were vulnerable to serious changes in thinking about the nature of society and the ends of government.

Recommended Reading:

Morris, *The Papal Monarchy.*

Sayers, *Innocent III.*

Questions to Consider:

1. How does the growth of papal institutions help in an understanding of papal politics?

2. What roles did Rome and Italy play in the papacy's battles with the empire?

Lecture Nine—Transcript
The Papal Monarchy—Politics

Hello and welcome to the ninth in our series of lectures on the history of the popes and of the papacy. Last time we talked about the papal monarchy of the high Middle Ages—really the 12th and 13th centuries—as an institutional and ideological proposition. This time we're going to sort of go through the nuts-and-bolts history of that same period to see what kinds of problems these popes encountered and how they were able to deal with them. As always in papal history, one of the things we've learned by now is that we'll have to take a good, close look at the Roman scene. We're also going to have to examine the papacy's gradually deteriorating relations with Germany. Relations with Germany had been difficult in the 11th century. They were going to get even worse in the 12th and 13th. We'll occasionally take a peek in other directions as well. If we had unlimited time, there would be lots of other stories to tell.

Through all of this we must observe the implications of a steady rise and fall of internationalism in Rome, the cardinalate and the papacy. Now, time just won't permit us the opportunity, really, of talking about everything we could talk about in this very busy 12th and 13th century period, so what we're going to do is focus on two papal schisms, two times the popes were challenged by antipopes, and then the great titanic struggle between the popes and the German Empire in the 13th century. The first, then, of these two schisms, in 1130; actually, this schism of 1130 was in lots of ways a portent of things to come in Rome and in the church. In the very last years of the pontificate of Calixtus II, who had been pope from 1119–1124, the Pierleoni and Frangipani families had begun to contest between themselves for leadership really of the City of Rome, and as we've learned, that's always going to mean trouble for the church. One of the things they were able to do is insert friendly cardinals into the College of Cardinals.

When Calixtus died, the Pierleoni engineered the election of their candidate, who took the name Celestine II. Enraged, the Frangipani ejected Celestine and introduced Lambert of Ostia, Bishop Lambert of Ostia, who took the name of Honorius II. Honorius managed to rule relatively peacefully until his death in 1130. In other words, he was able to overcome Celestine; he was able to overcome his opponent. But one has to wonder a little bit at least whether a removal of effective German protection in Rome—or German interference in Rome, if one wanted to look at it that way—was going to bring back the kind of aristocratic dominance that we talked about in the "Age of Iron" in the 10th century, when the Houses of Theophylact and Marozia and Alberic dominated Rome.

The international situation for Pope Honorius was very complex. The Salian dynasty, that is to say that family of rulers—Henry III, Henry IV, Henry V—who engaged our attention when we talked about the Investiture Controversy was beginning to die out in Germany. Lothar of Supplinburg, who was for a brief period of years, about 12 years 1125–1137, the king of Germany, was more or less favorably inclined toward the papacy, whereas his great rival Conrad of Hohenstaufen was not. Conrad had been excommunicated by the German bishops. He was in all sorts of trouble in Germany before he ever had any dealings with the pope, then he invaded northern Italy. We have seen, ever since the Carolingians, ever since the time of Charlemagne, these northern rulers have interests in northern Italy, and for a time Conrad was recognized as ruler in northern Italy. On Lothar's death, Conrad did manage to become king in Germany, but he never secured the imperial crown as he could never persuade a pope to crown him emperor.

In the south of Italy meanwhile, the duke Roger II of Sicily—remember, we've met these Normans in the south of Italy and in Sicily in the 11th century, allies from time to time of the popes—Roger II of Sicily invaded southern Italy and seized the lands of Apulia and Calabria. Now, these two territories in the south of Italy had for a long time been papal fiefs. The popes were not particularly keen on losing control of these lands. At the same time, after their very bitter experiences with the Normans in the 11th century, the popes didn't especially like them, but they really, in principle, didn't want a great power in the south of Italy, on the other side of the Papal States. Heaven knows they had been dealing with the Germans on the north side of the Papal States long enough. Honorius mounted a military expedition against Roger, but it was a dismal failure. So his situation internationally was, as I said, quite awkward. But even in the countryside around Rome, Honorius found himself obliged to wage battles on behalf of the familial interests of the Frangipani and their supporters. After all, he owed his election to them, so he was more or less beholden to them.

Well, now we really come to the schism proper. When Honorius died, 16 cardinals from the Frangipani faction elected Cardinal Gregory Papareschi, who took the name Innocent II. The other 14 cardinals, 30 at the moment—remember I mentioned last time there could be as many as 53, but usually weren't—so the other 14 cardinals went to the Church of San Marco, and in the Church of San Marco they elected Pietro Pierleoni, who took the name Anacletus II. The Pierleoni family itself is actually quite interesting. They were converts from Judaism, and since the middle of the 11th century they had actually been the pope's bankers. Well, a few cardinals from the original group now agreed to accept Anacletus, so it appeared that he had a majority, but there was a question about procedures. Could cardinals change their votes? Did it matter who was elected by more cardinals if someone else had been elected first? You'll recall perhaps from our last lecture that it was in 1179 that papal election procedures were regularized again, you see, so at this stage it was very much an open question who had actually been elected in 830.

It appears, moreover, that Anacletus had a good deal more support in and around Rome than Innocent did, so Innocent wound up having to flee the city. We saw last time popes were quite regularly away from Rome in the 12th and 13th centuries. France, Germany, England, most of Italy, the great religious orders, great ecclesiastical figures around Europe—such as Saint Bernard of Clairvaux, for example—pretty much all supported Innocent. So sort of everywhere outside Rome Innocent had the greater support, but temporarily at least, he couldn't gain control of Rome. Anacletus had the support of the Romans and also the support of the Normans in the south. Now, he had solidified his alliance with them by acknowledging Roger II as king. Remember, his predecessor, Honorius, had really tried to keep the Normans at arm's length. Only in 1133 was Innocent finally able to take control of Rome, and then only because Lothar of Supplinburg accompanied him into the city. In return for his support, Innocent crowned Lothar of Supplinburg emperor. Lothar, having received what he wanted, immediately left Rome, which left Innocent to the tender mercies of the Romans, which was not a particularly happy thing to have had happen to him.

Anacletus's main support, as I said, was the Normans, and Innocent—with help from Saint Bernard—persuaded Lothar of Supplinburg to come back to Italy now, because it was very clear that Innocent was not going to be able to maintain himself if he didn't have somebody's support. Insofar as Anacletus had the support of the Normans, the only person to whom Innocent could turn, actually, was the Germans. Lothar came to Italy, campaigned against Roger—he didn't really hound him to death; he weakened him sufficiently, but he was no longer a menace—and then Lothar died in 1137. Well, suffice it to say at this moment, Anacletus's position was ruined. His power base had really been kicked out from under him. Innocent managed to hold a great council of the Western church in 1139, which made everything look as though it were fine and everything was functioning effectively, and he even finally recognized Roger as king of Sicily. So it appeared that he had healed the breach between the popes and the Normans in the south.

So this is the first of our schisms. What lessons can we learn from this? Well, one interesting thing is that the papacy as an institution. The cardinalate, more particularly, had become more international; they were losing the loyalty of the Romans. The Romans didn't feel any longer as if these were their people, and the Romans felt themselves in some ways in opposition to the government of the church. We're seeing also that great Roman families could still exercise dire influence over the papacy. They could still treat the papacy as the prize in their own political contests. The popes, we see, again, cannot protect themselves without having recourse to powers outside Italy. The popes simply didn't have the means of imposing their will in contentious political circumstances. So that we think back to our last lecture, and the emergence of this spectacular papal government, we can see from the schism of 1130 that, in a very interesting way, the popes are at one and the same time becoming vastly more powerful and fragile. There is a paradox there, and it's not one that is readily resolved.

A second schism, this one in 1159, actually lasted from 1159 until 1180, and was a quite bitter and difficult and complicated quarrel. It marked a return once again to papal imperial tensions. You'll recall that actually the emperors had played a pretty small role in the difficulties of the 1130s. Now the German emperors are going to be front and center, but this time the schism is complicated by a whole new set of urban dynamics in Rome. As if Rome weren't complicated enough, we're going to make the Romans seem more complicated here in just a few minutes, and then also by new historical dynamics in central and northern Italy as well. Let's set the stage. The situation in Rome was intensely volatile and complicated. For a long time, there had been struggles, as we've seen, between and among great Roman aristocratic families.

Angry with both the popes and the papal government on the one hand and the great aristocratic families on the other hand, Roman craftsmen and merchants—it would be anachronistic; we might think of them as sort of the middle class in Rome—those kinds of people, who had really been on the outs in terms of having power and influence in previous times, now erected a commune, a secular government, a communal government, a government in which everybody was supposed to participate. Now, these weren't democrats. I mean ordinary kinds of people—poor people, day laborers and so forth—were not included here. The kind of craftsmen and merchants we're talking about were actually fairly prominent people, but theirs was a prominence of wealth; theirs was a prominence of business practices. It was not a prominence based on birth or based on hereditary nobility. So they created a commune, a communal government in 1143.

Now, the leaders of the commune sometimes focused on very specific political and economic issues. Sometimes, however, fired up by a real fire-and-brimstone preacher who had come to Rome from northern Italy—a man by the name of Arnold of Brescia—they demanded root-and-branch reform of the church itself. They demanded that the pope give up all temporal rule, and they of course promoted the idea of a secular government that would function, in certain respects, in opposition both to the papacy and to the nobility. Commune leaders and popes now began to vie with one another to gain the support of either the German kings or of the Sicilian kings as sort of weapons in their own battles. They were constantly trying to find alliances outside Rome that they could use against their foes inside the City of Rome itself. By 1159 Hadrian IV—we met him last time; remember Nicholas Breakspear, the only Englishman ever elected pope—anyway, so Hadrian IV had accepted Frederick Barbarossa as king, "Frederick with a red beard" in Germany. He had accepted him as king, he had made peace with William of Sicily, and he had patched up a peace with the Romans. So it looked, in a way, in 1159 as though the pope had pretty safely navigated these rocky waters in which he and his immediate predecessors had found themselves.

But on Hadrian's death—nothing surprising here—the cardinals split into factions. Now, the popes had generally supported and been supported by Lothar of Supplinburg. But as we saw, Lothar never really provided them with much help in Italy. He had his own problems in Germany. He only had so much time and attention to spare for the Italian scene, so he wasn't able to be continuously in presence there. Conrad of Hohenstaufen, remember 1138–1152, had been scheming to become the king in Germany and he did manage to succeed Lothar. He wanted very much to become emperor, and he wanted very much to dominate northern Italy, but of course he had been excommunicated by the German Church. The popes tried to get him, after he succeeded to Lothar, to help them against the commune. Interestingly enough, the commune appealed to him as well, so the question is which side was he going to jump in and support here?

In 1152 Conrad decided that actually, in the long term, his interests would be better served by an alliance with the popes, so he made a pact with the pope, but he died before it could be implemented, so in a way everything was up in the air. In 1152 Frederick Barbarossa—I mentioned him just a second ago—Frederick Barbarossa succeeded to the German crown. He honored Conrad's pact with the pope. In other words, he didn't make a deal with a commune. Moreover, he captured Arnold of Brescia and handed him over to the pope. He managed to secure his imperial coronation, something these German rulers always want, but once again he returned to Germany to leave the pope to deal with the Roman scene. That's then the situation we found ourselves in, in 1159.

We've also seen, of course—and we just have to remember because they're just offstage a little bit—that the Normans had been a problem for the popes over a long period of time, more than 100 years. The popes wanted help on their own terms. They didn't want the Normans dictating to them under what terms the Normans would help them. The popes simply wanted the Normans to help them, to more or less give them a blank check. What did the Normans want? They wanted recognition. They want to be acknowledged as kings. They wanted a removal of the bands of excommunication, which the popes had a way of laying on them every time the Normans abused papal trust, or at least that was the papal view of it.

So in 1159 one party of cardinals elected Orlando Bandinelli. He was a distinguished lawyer, and he took the name Alexander III. In the end he would prevail, but another faction of cardinals elected Cardinal Ottaviano, who took the name of Victor IV. He immediately appealed to the emperor; Alexander appealed to William of Sicily. This is kind of an interesting shift. The popes, generally speaking, had not been appealing to the Normans in recent years, though they had, you'll recall, in the middle of the 11th century. Initially, here again is something that we've seen play out again and again. Victor controlled the City of Rome, and Alexander was forced to remain away from the city. Again, we have the pope away from the city.

Barbarossa came to Italy in 1160 to hold a council to decide between the rivals. You may recall that in the middle of the 11th century, Henry IV of Germany had wanted to hold church councils and sit in judgment of popes. You'll recall that Henry III of Germany had marched into Italy in 1046, deposed three popes and then installed another one, so these German rulers loved the idea that they could come into Italy and dictate terms to the church. But as we've seen, this is not cynical politics. This was their own sense of the ideology of their imperial office. They believed they had every right, indeed a God-given responsibility, to act in this way. Well, not surprisingly Alexander refused to appear. He was having nothing of any court of law, as it were, where Frederick Barbarossa would sit in judgment on the papacy. So Barbarossa decided that Victor IV was the true pope, so then the empire supported the man who became in the end the antipope.

What's interesting here is that sort of informed opinion all over Europe just went nuts. They felt Barbarossa had simply gone too far. No one was prepared to accept his meddling in this way in deciding who was pope. What I would ask you to think about here is how very different this was from Henry III's going to Italy in 1046 to widespread acclaim, getting rid of three popes and installing a new one. Now Barbarossa went to Rome and people all over Europe said, "No, that's too much, that's going entirely too far." Well, down to 1180 there were three more antipopes, but their particular cause was overtaken by other events. In other words, Barbarossa was not in a position to provide continuous support to his antipopes in Rome, and that made it possible then for Alexander III and his successors finally to prevail.

Barbarossa's main problem was Italy, his constant efforts to try to control northern Italy. Now, the German emperors had been for a very long time trying to govern northern Italy for a variety of reasons. Inside Germany their power base was actually rather weak, so by controlling northern Italy they could raise taxes, they could raise troops, they could exercise authority in all sorts of ways they couldn't do inside Germany. But they could then apply those resources—particularly the human and material resources that they were able to gain in Italy—they could apply those resources in Germany to enhance their authority there. So in a paradoxical sort of way, Germany's Italian policy was a German policy. It was one way that the German rulers could gain power inside Germany. Well, if you're the pope, the last thing you want is a really powerful ruler in northern Italy right on the north side of the Papal States, particularly because now if you're the pope, from another point of view, to yourself you've got these Normans, so you don't want these powerful states on both sides of you.

Well, what Barbarossa's attempts to exercise authority in northern Italy did was call into being the Lombard League. In other words, the cities of Lombardi, the great cities of northern Italy, banded together in a league basically to reject domination by Frederick Barbarossa. Barbarossa marched his army into Italy and, somewhat surprisingly, was dealt a devastating military defeat at Legnano in 1176. That really brought Barbarossa's great plans crashing down, and for a moment at least it put the pope in a pretty strong position. As you can see, it put Barbarossa's antipopes in an extremely weak position, and the emperor was no longer in a position to be of much help to them. In 1177 Barbarossa and Alexander III concluded the Peace of Venice and essentially composed their difficulties.

What do we learn here? Well, we learn once again that the popes are always subject to the whims of other people's interest in Italy or to large-scale political movements in Italy over which they have virtually no control. We've also seen here, particularly in the erection of the Roman commune in 1143, that now the popes have not only to contend with the Roman nobility—that's been a problem since the 8th century, as we've seen in earlier lectures—they now have to contend with other elements of the local Roman social and political scene, mainly these craftsmen, merchants, etc. on the Roman scene who had previously not been particularly visible as players on the local scene. So as I've stressed again and again and again in earlier lectures, in certain respects papal history is a universal story. In other respects papacy is a very local story. Tip O'Neill always used to say, "All politics is local politics," and that is very, very true when one thinks about the popes. Thus far two schisms, two splits, two times when the pope was challenged by antipopes and other forces, other factors, other people entered the scene.

Now let's turn, as our third sort of case study for understanding this period, to the great battle between the popes and the Hohenstaufen family, in particular, and with Emperor Frederick II, in the 13th century. We need to fill in a little background here in order to understand how this big problem came about. In particular, we really have two pieces of background that are most important here. In the first place, Barbarossa had married his son to Constance of Sicily, who was the heiress of the rulers of Norman Sicily, and who had no brothers. The male line of rulers in Sicily had died out, so Barbarossa married his son Henry to Constance, and then after only six years Henry died and left a small child, three years old. A year later, Constance died, and that three-year-old child became a ward of the pope. That child was Frederick II. He'll be occupying us for the next 50 years, or about the next five minutes, depending on your point of view.

In Germany, immediately two factions arose. One, under Philip of Swabia, supported the Hohenstaufen. The other, under Otto IV or Otto of Brunswick, supported noble privileges. They regarded this as a very nice opportunity to slip away from the control that Frederick Barbarossa, in particular, had been able to impose in Germany. One of the interesting problems is that every time the rulers of Germany become very, very powerful, the secondary and tertiary powers in Germany start plotting together against the rulers to try to make them less powerful. Well, what could be a better situation for noble factions in Germany than a three-year-old heir off in Sicily? Well, this was a situation ripe with possibilities for trouble.

Innocent intervened in the first place and supported Otto of Brunswick, who agreed to renounce all claims to Italy. Well, that was a consistent papal policy for a long, long time, nothing novel in this, but in 1208 Philip of Swabia was murdered. This utterly removed all restraints from Otto who, guess what, invaded Italy. If you're a ruler in Germany in this period of time, somehow it's hard wired in your genes that you're going to invade Italy, so Otto invades Italy. For this, Otto gets himself excommunicated, so Innocent's former friend is now his foe, and in the year 1212, Innocent elevates Frederick II to the throne of Germany.

We might ask ourselves how was it that Innocent was able to intervene in this way. What gave the pope the idea that he could make and unmake German emperors in this fashion? Now, we have seen, on quite a number of occasions, that emperors had thought they could make and unmake popes, and we've talked in our last lecture, and a little bit in the one before that, about the theories on the basis of which those kings and emperors acted in making and unmaking popes. So what does Innocent think he's up to here? Well, we might say given those kinds of hierarchical thoughts that we talked about in our last lecture—the hierarchical thoughts, the sun-moon metaphors, the two swords metaphors giving the church this enormous kind of power—I would say generally speaking that, perhaps, explains things.

But in 1202 Innocent III issued a decretal, *Per venerabilem*. He said, "The right and authority to examine the person elected as king, who is to be promoted to the imperial dignity, belong to us who anoint, consecrate, and crown him for it is regularly and generally observed that the examination of a person belongs to the one to whom the laying on of hands belongs." He's equating making a king to making a priest. "If the princes elected as king a sacrilegious man or an excommunicate, a tyrant, a fool, or a heretic, and that not just by a divided vote but unanimously, ought we to anoint, consecrate, and crown such a man?"

Well, the answer was no. He was saying, "You see, we crown him; therefore we have a right to pass on the fitness of the person we will crown." He also said that the source of this authority, of this right and authority, he explained himself when he said, "No man of sound mind is unaware that it pertains to our office to rebuke any Christian for any mortal sin and to coerce him with ecclesiastical penalties if he spurns our correction." You may just recall a few lectures back Pope Gregory IV had gone to the Frankish world to intervene in a quarrel *ratione peccati,* "by reason of sin". Now we see Innocent articulating that doctrine, that these people are sinners, "I am the chief priest of the Christian world, of course it's my right and it's my duty to intervene in this situation."

Frederick was in lots of ways a remarkable character. He was more Sicilian by far than German. He was born in Sicily. He didn't like Germany. He thought Germany was cold and dark and dank, and he didn't like the language, and didn't like the people up there, didn't like the food as well as he liked the food in Sicily. He was a sensible man in lots of ways, we might say. He was also a person who managed to upset many people in his time. His contemporaries called him the *Stupor Mundi*, the wonder of the world. He had dancing girls at his court, he had Muslim advisers and he didn't seem, necessarily, to have taken his religious responsibilities as seriously as people might have wished he would have. Until his death in 1250, Frederick had almost entirely bad relations with the popes. In part, these bad relations with the popes stemmed from Frederick's repeated refusal to go on crusade. He kept promising he would lead a crusade and then he refused to go, promised to go, refused to go, promised to go and refused to go. But also, Frederick's sort of morally dubious behavior got himself in some troubles as well.

But the big issue, as so often in Italy, was Frederick's desire of ruling from the south—from Sicily and southern Italy—to control northern Italy and also Germany. What we have here is simply a reversal of what we have been watching for a century and a half or a couple of lectures in our series. Usually German rulers were trying to control northern Italy and to intrude any authority they could into the south. Now we had a ruler from southern Italy trying to control northern Italy and Germany above that. If you are the pope, that's the last thing in the world you could possibly tolerate, having one great power on both sides of you. The whole struggle was in a lot of ways unedifying. It resulted, finally, in the demise of the Hohenstaufen family. That itself resulted in a 60-year gap in the imperial succession between 1258 and 1312.

This was, in fact, an important period for the popes in other respects. Let's just recall a few of those respects by way of concluding here. Innocent III forced French and English kings to bow to his will. He opened up closer relations with Spain than any pope had ever done. Innocent was, if you take everything into consideration, the most powerful of all the popes who have ever reigned. On the demise of the Hohenstaufen, the popes recruited first English and finally French princes to reign in southern Italy and in Sicily. We're going to bump into those men in later lectures, too. This was a time when new religious orders, especially the Franciscans and the Dominicans, revitalized the church with papal support, with the explicit support of Pope Innocent III. This is a time when, under Pope Gregory IX, the Roman Inquisition proved signally capable of finding and suppressing heresy. What's interesting, too, is the Inquisition was handed to the Dominican fathers, the *Dominicani*, so humorists at the time called those at the head of the Inquisition the *Domini Canes*— the Lord's hounds—instead of the *Dominicani*—the Dominicans, the followers of Saint Dominic.

Laws were revised. The Papal States were managed effectively and very carefully. In a sense here, we can go back to our previous lecture, where we were watching the slow, steady growth of all those institutional structures in the papal monarchy. So today we see that we can had these two schisms, and we could have this great quarrel with the German emperors, and that didn't stop a lot of steady work in other realms. There are two lessons here, I think. Temporal rule inevitably involved the popes in the great political issues of the day. There was simply no way for them to escape them. Finally, second, however much it might seem that the popes were either dominated or distracted by secular concerns, the business of the church went on apace. Maybe we can add a third point, one that has been with us, in a way, for the last couple of lectures. In a medieval world, where all authority was believed to come from God and the end of government was religious, the papacy was perhaps inevitably at the top of such a world, but vulnerable to redefining that world in different—that is to say, secular—terms. Those are issues that will engage our attention in future lectures.

Lecture Ten
The Popes at Avignon

Scope:

The struggles between the popes and the empire foreshadowed an intense battle between King Philip IV of France and Pope Boniface VIII that did not end in such a way as to settle the fundamental issues. In one sense, it appeared that the signature event of the Investiture Controversy had been replayed in reverse. In the winter of 1077, a penitent Henry IV stood in the snow before Canossa castle begging forgiveness from Gregory VII. In 1303, Philip IV of France sent lawyers and thugs to Rome to seize Boniface and bring him to France for trial. By 1305, the cardinals—papal electors—were about evenly divided between those who wanted to seek reconciliation with France and those who, infuriated at Boniface's rough treatment, were intransigent. The former group managed to secure the election of Bertrand de Got, the archbishop of Bordeaux. As Clement V, he wandered for about four years in the south of France trying to compose the papacy's quarrel with Philip. In 1309, Clement and the papal court settled on papal territory at Avignon, with the idea of settling things with Philip, then returning to Rome. In fact, the popes remained at Avignon until 1378.

The Avignon papacy is difficult to evaluate. The Avignon popes were not saints, but they were not bad men either. Several were impressively pious. A few were superb administrators. They built the spectacular papal palace that dazzles tourists to this day. They tried hard to secure peace between France and England when the Hundred Years War broke out. When the popes returned to Rome, their reputation had suffered severely. St. Catherine of Siena referred bitterly to the papacy's "Babylonian Captivity."

Outline

I. We have seen that it was not uncommon for the popes to be absent from Rome; however, in the years 1309 to 1378, the popes were continuously resident in Avignon, a city in the south of what is now France but then safely on papal territory.

   A. Contemporaries, such as St. Catherine of Siena and Petrarch, condemned this "Babylonian Captivity" of the papacy.

B. We must ask how the popes came to be in Avignon and what they did while they were there.

II. The years at the turn of the 14th century saw a titanic struggle between King Philip IV of France (r. 1285–1314) and Pope Boniface VIII (r. 1294–1303), which is the fundamental background to the Avignon papacy.

A. Both Philip and Boniface were interesting, forceful personalities.

B. Two basic issues divided Boniface and Philip.

    1. Philip and King Edward I of England (r. 1272–1307) were continuously short of money and laid heavy taxes on their clergy.

        a. Boniface issued *Clericis laicos*, forbidding taxation of the clergy.

        b. England more or less capitulated, but Philip forbade the export of bullion from France, which severely crippled papal revenue collecting.

        c. In 1297, Boniface, needing revenue and battling the Colonna family in Rome, relented; he affirmed that kings could tax the clergy "in an emergency."

    2. In 1300, Philip attempted to haul Bernard Saisset, bishop of Pamiers, before the royal tribunal to answer charges of treason.

        a. In 1301, Boniface issued *Ausculta fili*, which put *Clericis laicos* back in force, insisted on the *Privilegium fori* for members of the clergy, and summoned the king of France and his bishops to answer for their conduct.

        b. In 1303, a troupe of Philip's supporters verbally and, perhaps, physically abused the 80-year-old Boniface at the papal summer residence at Anagni. Boniface died shortly thereafter.

C. This is nothing like the world of Innocent III; it is more like Canossa in reverse. What had happened?

    1. There had been searing criticisms for years of the wealth and secular preoccupations of the papacy.

    2. The rediscovery of Aristotle's *Politics*, along with the dissemination of Roman law and its dictates, including "What pleases the prince has the power of law," led writers as different as Dante and John of Paris to conclude that popes might possess property but should not have temporal political rule over people.

III. In the attempt to find some resolution to this bitter conflict, the popes wound up in Avignon.

    A. On Boniface's death, Benedict XI was elected, primarily as a non-Colonna, and he managed to achieve peace in Rome and with Sicily.

    B. On Benedict's death, the cardinals were hopelessly deadlocked for 11 months and finally settled on Bertrand de Got (Pope Clement V), the archbishop of Bordeaux, who was well connected to the French court.

        1. Clement V (r. 1305–1314) created numerous French cardinals and negotiated constantly with the French court. In his desire to achieve a settlement with France, Clement settled in 1309 in Avignon.

        2. When Clement died, Jacques Duèze, bishop of Cahors but formerly bishop of Avignon, was elected as John XXII. He moved into the bishop's palace in Avignon.

IV. Without anyone's having planned or desired it, the popes stayed in Avignon for the next 59 years.

V. How may we characterize the Avignon popes?

    A. All seven were French; three were monks. Average pontificates (about 10 years) were lengthy compared to those in the second half of the 13th century but similar to those of the preceding era.

    B. These popes had, for the most part, long and distinguished careers in the Church and were learned, thoughtful men. Their great gifts were in administration.

    C. Pope Innocent VI (r. 1352–1362) had to accept the first electoral "capitulation" in papal history, meaning that he would have to agree to accept certain conditions imposed by the cardinals in order to be elected pope. In this case, the agreement had to do with limiting the number of cardinals that Innocent could appoint.

    D. Without Rome as their natural stage, the popes developed a "palace style" more fitting for a secular court.

VI. As always, the international situation was complex and brought pressures to bear.

    A. The great issue of the age was the Hundred Years War (1337–1453) between France and England.

        1. Both the French and, especially, the English thought the popes were too sympathetic to their enemy.

        2. In reality, the popes were trying to free Europe's rulers (and money) for a new crusade.

    B. The papacy's relations with Germany were, on the whole, terrible.

    C. The south was now divided between Angevin princes in Naples and Aragonese princes in Sicily, all of whom got along poorly with one another and were often at odds with the popes.

    D. Maintaining the Papal States from Avignon was tricky.

VII. The Avignon popes always planned to return to Rome.

    A. In 1367, Urban V returned to Rome but went back to Avignon in 1370.

    B. Gregory XI left Avignon in 1376, arrived in Rome in 1377, and had just begun settling into the city when he died in 1378.

    C. In the election of 1378, the 16 cardinals in Rome (6 were still in Avignon) elected Bartolomeo Prignano, the archbishop of Bari, largely because a howling mob was demanding a Roman or, at least, an Italian pope.

    D. The new pope, Urban VI (r. 1378–1389), initially enjoyed the good will of the cardinals in Rome but then ruined his position by treating them terribly.

        1. The cardinals declared Urban deposed and elected Cardinal Robert of Geneva as Clement VII.

        2. Clement eventually returned to Avignon in 1381, and the West was plunged into the Great Schism, perhaps the greatest crisis in papal history.

Recommended Reading:

Mollat, *The Popes at Avignon*.

Renouard, *The Avignon Papacy, 1305–1403*.

Questions to Consider:

1. How would you account for the very different outcomes in the papacy's struggles with the empire and with France?

2. How would you rate the work of the Avignon popes?

Lecture Ten—Transcript
The Popes at Avignon

Hello and welcome to Lecture Ten in our series on the history of the popes and of the papacy. This time we're going to take the popes to Avignon in the south of France. Now, we've seen that it was not uncommon for the popes to be away from Rome in the 12th and 13th century, even a little bit in the 11th century. But in the years from 1309–1378, the popes were continuously resident in Avignon, a city in the south of what is today France. Then actually it was safely on papal territory. It was not then part of the kingdom of France, but it is geographically within what we would think of as France. Contemporaries—for example such as Saint Catherine of Siena, or the great Italian humanist scholar Petrarch—condemned this "Babylonian Captivity" of the papacy.

For our purposes, our job is not to condemn it or to praise it, but to try to understand it. In the first place, how did the popes wind up in Avignon in the south of France, and then to ask what did they do while they were there? How did you go about being pope if you were in Avignon? The years at the turn of the 13th and 14th century saw a mammoth struggle between Pope Boniface VIII and King Philip IV of France. As if it weren't bad enough that most of the 13th century had been taken up with these quarrels with Frederick II of the German Empire at the end of the 13th century, the great struggle was between the popes and the kings of France, and that struggle, in a way, was the background to how the popes wound up at Avignon.

The parties to this dispute were interesting and forceful personalities in lots of ways. Philip IV—Philip the Fair, Philip the Handsome—was an intense, intelligent, proud man. He was determined to enhance the power, the prestige and the authority of the French monarchy. As all rulers, he was perpetually short of money. Boniface, Benedetto Caetani, was a proud, maybe even arrogant Roman aristocrat, a learned lawyer, an experienced curialist, a patron of artists—not least the brilliant sculptor Arnolfo di Cambio, who left us a very famous sculpture of Boniface himself. Boniface certainly wasn't the moral wretch that his opponents believed him to be. He had a lofty sense of the papal office, but for his troubles he was cast into hell by Dante in Inferno 19. Some believed he was illegitimate because he had forced his predecessor Celestine V to resign. Celestine was the first and only pope ever to resign, though it isn't clear that Boniface made him resign. He was a monk, utterly ill-suited to the job, and seems to have abandoned the office on his own.

Two basic issues divided Boniface and Philip. Philip of France and his contemporary Edward I of England were continuously short of cash, not least because they were almost continuously at war with each other. In 1292, 1294 and again in 1296, both of these kings laid very heavy taxes on the clergy of their kingdom. Boniface responded with a ringing denunciation of this taxing of the clergy in a papal bull, *Clericis laicos*, which forbade taxation of the clergy, and it stood essentially on the legislation of Innocent III's great fourth Lateran Council that was held in 1215. So Boniface wasn't innovating there in denying kings the right to tax the clergy. He was basically reminding these kings that they had no such right. England more or less capitulated. It would be very complicated to get into the ins and outs of all of that, but Philip forbade the export of bullion from France. More papal revenue came from France than anyplace else, so Philip's prohibition of the export of bullion from France was terrible for papal finances and severely crippled papal revenue collecting.

In 1297, needing revenue—and because the Caetani family in Rome—Rome at this time was a kind of threesome of contending families—the Caetani, the Orsini and the Colonna—so Boniface has real problems with the Colonna family, and he has to deal with the Colonna in Rome—he needs money, so he decides he has to compose his problems with the king of France. He decides that the king of France could tax his clergy in an emergency, and the king even had to decide when it was an emergency. Boniface was trying to salvage the principle and to save face. You see, he was trying in a sense to have it both ways here.

A little bit later, King Philip attempted to haul Bernard Saisset—an otherwise forgettable character—he was bishop of the little bitty town of Pamiers in the south of France—not a terribly important person—but anyway, Philip tried to haul Bernard Saisset before his court for treason. In 1301 Boniface issued another ringing papal bull, *Ausculta fili*, which put *Clericis laicos* back in force—there he goes again, can't tax the clergy—then he demanded the *Privilegium fori*, the privilege of the court, the right of clerics not to be tried in secular courts, again an old longstanding right. He summoned the king of France and the French bishops to answer for their conduct. Can he honestly have thought that the king of France was going to say "Oh right" and just march on down to Rome and be judged by the pope? But anyway, Boniface's claims were pretty grand.

Philip's people publicly burned the papal bull, inaugurated a scurrilous propaganda campaign—in French, interestingly enough; they were clearly trying to reach the French public with this—and they forbade any French clergy from attending any council that Boniface might call. Moreover, in 1303 a troupe of Philip's supporters went down to the pope's summer residence in Anagni. They verbally abused the pope, and they may even actually have roughed the old guy up—Boniface was 80, for heaven's sakes—and a short time later, disgraced, saddened and a failure in many ways, Boniface died. Don't you almost see here that scene before Canossa castle, when Henry IV stood in the snow begging absolution from Gregory VII, being played in reverse? Now the agents of the French king go to Rome and hound the pope.

This is nothing like the world of Innocent III. What on earth had happened here? How had things changed so dramatically, apparently so quickly? Well, in the first place, there had been searing criticisms for years of the wealth and secular preoccupations of the papacy. That's part of why Dante wound up putting popes like Boniface VIII in Inferno, in his great *Commedia*. A 12th century satirist already had pilloried, in a wonderful work, the bogus relics of Saints Albinus, silver, and Rufinus, gold, that had been reverently installed, he said, in "the treasury of St. Cupidity, next to the confession of her sister, Extreme Avidity, not far from the basilica of their mother, Avarice." Saint Bernard, writing to his former pupil, who became Pope Eugenius III, warned him against secular preoccupations. But Innocent III, rather like Gregory I—remember those quotations that we had from Gregory I a few lectures back, where he lamented the fact that he's drawn into all of these cares and concerns as pope—Innocent III also wrote *De Contemptu Mundi*, "On the Contempt of the World," about how awful that world is and how distracting.

It's also true, however, that the 13th century saw, for instance, the rediscovery of Aristotle's work the *Politics*, which laid out a very different sense of what a state is, what a society is, what a government is and what the ends of each might be. This was also a time when Roman law began to disseminate further and more rapidly than ever before. When people picked up Roman law books, they found things such as, "What pleases the prince has the power of law," not what pleases the pope, but what pleases the prince, has the power of law. We find that writers as different as the great Italian poet Dante and the French ecclesiastical scholar John of Paris could agree that popes should not possess temporal political rule over people.

The first faint sounds of the ideology of the secular state—and perhaps the beginning of a ringing of the death knell for Christendom—are audible in this controversy between Philip and Boniface, and so it appears to us that Boniface's position was untenable. Yet, at the very end of his pontificate, he issued the bull *Unam Sanctam*, the most powerful statement of ecclesiastical right and papal privilege ever issued by any pope. Was he not aware of how difficult his world was? Be that as it may, the bull was without effect. What's a papal bull? It's a papal letter signed with a bullum. A lead bullum is the great lead seal that goes on a bull, so a bull is a document that has been bulled, that has been sealed with a lead bull. That's where the word comes from. Well, it was in an attempt to find some resolution to this bitter conflict that the popes wound up in Avignon. All of that is my way of saying "How in the world did we get the popes up there to Avignon?"

On Boniface's death Benedict XI was elected, primarily because he was a non-Colonna. The politics in Rome, they were looking for anybody who wasn't a Colonna. Anyway, so they fixed upon Benedict XI. He managed to achieve a measure of peace in the city of Rome. He managed to achieve a measure of peace with Sicily, which had once again been a thorn in the pope's side in just recent years, and Benedict wanted very much to find a way to achieve peace with Philip in France, but Philip was demanding a great church council be called to condemn Pope Boniface. Benedict was not prepared to do that. Now, Benedict did withdraw many of Boniface's anti-French measures, but nothing he did would appease Philip. Philip wanted Boniface condemned. On Benedict's death—he was pope only a couple of years—the cardinals were hopelessly deadlocked for 11 months, and finally the Bonifatian faction itself split down, the faction that really wanted to maintain a hard line against the French, and the cardinals settled on the Archbishop of Bordeaux in France, Bertrand de Got.

He had a lot to recommend him. He was French, and he had very good relations with the French Court. Maybe there was somebody who could compose these difficulties with the king of France. As Clement V, Bertrand created numerous French cardinals, and he negotiated consistently, continuously with the French Court. He managed to avoid a complete condemnation of Boniface, but he paid some prices. He had to rehabilitate the Colonna family, Boniface's great enemies. He had to forgive Philip's agents for the attack on Boniface at Anagni in 1303, and he had to acquiesce in Philip's destruction of the Knights Templar. The Knights Templar was one of the military orders, sort of quasi-monks, quasi-warriors that had formed during the crusading period. The Templars, as a matter of fact, ran a very substantial banking operation that extended all the way from the Holy Land back to Europe. Philip trumped up awful charges against these guys and wanted to crush them because he wanted to seize their money, so the pope was finally forced to acquiesce in the destruction of the Knights Templar.

In his desire to achieve a settlement with France, Clement settled in 1309 in Avignon. Remember, the city in the south of France that is not in the kingdom of France, but is obviously just next door. When Clement died, the majority of the cardinals were French. He had been pope for a few years, from 1305–1309; the majority of the cardinals were French. The Italians, however, managed to hold out for almost two years, but finally Jacques Duèze, who was the bishop of Cahors—a small city in the center of France—formerly, however, the bishop of Avignon, was elected as Pope John XXII. He moved into the bishop's palace in Avignon and immediately began expanding it quite substantially because he had to accommodate his enormous papal entourage. We've seen that a pope is in some respects exactly like all other bishops, but that he runs a much larger, more sophisticated, complicated operation. So the Episcopal palace in Avignon simply wasn't big enough, and they began building the spectacular papal palace in Avignon, most of which is still there today and can be visited.

Without anyone's having planned it or desired it, the popes wound up in Avignon until 1378, for a long time. Avignon was preferable to Rome in certain ways. There was no Roman nobility to contend with, there were no Roman merchants, there were no Roman traders, financial people to contend with. It was a long way from Sicily, you didn't have to contend with the kings of Sicily; a long way from

Naples, you didn't have to mess with them. It was comfortably far from the French Court, but it was not too far from Germany—there always are going to be complications with the Germans. This is also a period, as we'll see in just a moment, when the Hundred Years' War between France and England was raging, so you were reasonably close to be able to, perhaps, have some influence on that situation, and there were also excellent communications. Avignon sits astride the river Rhone, so travel up and down the river Rhone was fine. There was also a great bridge at Avignon, the Pont Bénézet. If you know the children's song, "Sur le pont d'Avignon on y danse, on y danse..." that's the bridge. It was there over the river Rhone, so there was excellent communications in this particular site.

Ironically, the Avignon popes built a continuously effective government precisely because they were continuously resident in Avignon, something they had not been in Rome for two centuries, paradox upon paradox upon paradox. How might we characterize these Avignon popes? There were seven of them; they were all French. The average pontificate was about 10 years. That's lengthy compared to the second half of the 13th century, but about in line with the length of pontificates in earlier centuries. Most of the elections went very smoothly. Only John XXII faced an antipope, Nicholas V, for a couple of years, 1328–1330, who was utterly the creature of Louis IV of Germany and really a nonentity, and not anybody we really need to contend with here.

These popes had for the most part had long and distinguished careers in the church. They were for the most part learned and thoughtful men, but interestingly their great gifts were as administrators. These were not in a sense holy men. They were not great religious leaders in a sense, not great reformers, but they were great governors. They were great administrators, hardheaded, practical types. So they don't exactly command respect in the way that some historical popes have done, but there is something. We owe them a kind of a grudging respect, I think, for the work which they did. They refined, for instance, the record keeping, the judicial and the financial machinery of the papacy, as never before.

In part, we know a great deal about these Avignon popes because the papal registers from this period on—I mentioned this on an earlier day, when we talked about how we actually know about the papacy—the papal registers, the great collections of papal letters.

The official archives, if you will, survive from this period on down to the present, so we have an enormous amount of information about these men. We really do know, day in and day out, in detail what they were doing. For the most part, they weren't so much innovators as improvers. They were always tinkering with things and refining things and making things work a little bit more smoothly. Their relentlessly bureaucratic style engendered criticism among their contemporaries and, as I said, leaves us looking back at them, not finding much to praise, not finding much that inspires us, and yet they were sort of good, competent, workaday popes.

Innocent VI, who was pope from 1352–1362, interestingly, had to accept the first electoral capitulation in papal history. We're going to bump into electoral capitulations quite a few times in later lectures, so we'll pause and just reflect on the capitulation that Innocent had to accept as a price of election. What it meant was that the candidate—the cardinals agreed—that whoever was elected would have to capitulate to a particular agreement. The terms of these agreements will change a lot over the years. In Innocent's case, the cardinals were particularly concerned about the fact that if the pope kept making new cardinals, it would cost those cardinals already in office power, and it would also cost them money because the revenues and funds available to the cardinals would be carved into smaller pieces.

So the cardinals said before the election in 1352 that whoever was elected pope had to agree that no new cardinals would be appointed unless the number fell below 16, and that there would never be more than 20. Moreover, all newly appointed cardinals had to be agreed to by the assent of two-thirds of the sitting cardinals, so the cardinals basically said—amongst themselves, they made this deal—whoever was elected has to agree to this, so they all agree. They capitulate to this bargain, and Innocent was elected and was, therefore, required to observe this electoral capitulation. So as I say, we're going to see electoral capitulations on a number of occasions in the centuries just ahead, but this is the first instance of this having happened.

Not being in Rome, and not having the city and its churches as their natural environment, led the popes to develop what we could call a "palace style," much more fitting, really, for a secular court, and this style would actually characterize the papal court for the next several centuries. What do I mean? Remember when we talked about the stational liturgies of the City of Rome, those up to, finally, some 180 times a year, when the vast papal entourage went from the Lateran to one or another of Rome's churches in these glorious processions around the city, the pope in a sense going out to his church, being visibly on display before all the people of Rome?

Well, in a palace style, the popes of Avignon were basically shut up in the palace. They didn't have Rome before them. They didn't have all of those churches before them, so they weren't going out in great processions, stational processions, to the churches of Rome. They were having, like caged monkeys, great displays inside the palace. The people came to the pope as the people would go to a king or the people would go to an emperor. So it is a palace style of rule, and we're going to see, as we go through the Renaissance period and then into the Age of the Baroque in the 17th century, that this palace style became more and more and more a fixture and feature of the way the popes represented themselves to the world—how they behaved, how they acted—than had been the case in earlier times, when the stational liturgy was really the great representation of the way the popes went about their business.

Well, as always, the international situation was immensely complex, and as always, the popes found themselves mixed up in it all. The great issue of the age was the Hundred Years' War. The Hundred Years' War is one of those wonderful anomalies. It lasted from 1337–1453—I'm not very good at math, but I think that's 116 years—but anyway, the Hundred Years' War. France and England had been, in certain respects, fighting ever since a French regional potentate, William the Bastard, the Duke of Normandy, had conquered England in 1066. So a French prince had a purchase on England. He became the king of England, and he still retained interest in France. So, for the next centuries, the English and the French had multiple, conflicting interests. The Hundred Years' War was actually one slice out of that long struggle, out of that long ancient rivalry between the French and the English. One is inclined to think in the course of the 20th century that because the English and the French were allied against the Germans in two World Wars that somehow there's some inevitably of an Anglo-French friendship. The world changed pretty dramatically on the eve of World War I, when English and the French allied with one another.

So we're in one moment of this longstanding controversy. The popes wanted the war to end. Popes were opposed to wars, generally speaking, and the popes wanted to be honest brokers of a just peace. We're going to see in the course of this Hundred Years' War—and then in a good many wars right down through World War II in the 20th century—that the popes always took a position of neutrality—or as they often said, of impartiality—in great international conflicts, particularly in conflicts which pit Catholics against Catholics. They said, "We simply cannot take sides here. We don't like the war at all, we want the war to stop, but we're not going to choose up sides and decide who we favor or who we oppose."

It won't surprise you to learn that both the French and, especially, the English thought the popes were too sympathetic to their enemies. The English, of course, thought the popes were too sympathetic to the French because the popes are at Avignon in the south of France. The French thought the popes were too sympathetic to the English because the popes wouldn't overtly support them. Honestly, the popes tried to stay above the fray. The popes had another project; they really wanted the English and the French to stop fighting with each other so that there would be sufficient revenues available to mount a great crusade against the Muslim powers in the East. The popes had still not given up on the dream of crusade.

The pope's relations with Germany were on the whole terrible. We don't need to say too much more than that about it. In Germany itself, the Hapsburg family who would, of course, rule in Germany until the First World War—or, at least they ruled the Austrian Empire, which was the successor to the Holy Roman Empire, which was the successor to the rule in Germany, but that's not our story here—anyway, the Hapsburg family had emerged in the 13th century and was prominent from then to the 20th. They were contesting authority with the Witteslbach family, so there was controversy inside Germany. What do the Germans want from the pope—coronation as Holy Roman Emperor. What does the pope want from the Germans—various kinds of concessions before they would agree to crown anybody. Well, that was a recipe for disaster, so papal relations with Germany were, as I said, pretty routinely awful.

The south was divided. You have Angevin princes in Naples and Aragonese princes in Sicily. Who are Angevins? They were a cadet branch of the French Royal Family, centered in Anjou, the region called Anjou, sort of in west central France. Who was the Aragonese? Well, they came from Argonne, the kingdom in the northwest corner of the Iberian Peninsula. So the popes had Angevin and Aragonese characters to deal with in the south of Italy. Again and again and again, the Papal States have engaged our attention here. It won't surprise you to learn that when the popes were off in Avignon, in the south of France, it was very difficult for them to maintain the Papal States. It had been hard enough for them to maintain the Papal States when they were in Rome. What were they able to do? How would they deal with the Papal States?

Well, for a while they used legates. They simply sent legates down to try to look after papal affairs, and this didn't work very well until, in 1353, Cardinal Gil Albornoz was sent to Italy. He was there for about 12 years, from 1353–1365, and this man was really an administrative genius in a lot of ways. He's oftentimes called the "Second Founder" of the Papal States. He really put things back in good operating conditions. But Albornoz and the popes faced two problems, many problems but among these let's just mention two. Rome itself continued to be politically volatile, and in the 14th century a new communal movement in Rome emerged under a leader, a quite interesting character by the name of Cola di Rienzo.

The commune in Rome was itself in an interesting kind of predicament. In some respects they opposed the popes, the papacy and the papal government. In other respects they wanted the pope back. That is to say, if you were in Rome, the popes being in Avignon was really bad for business. You didn't have pilgrims—tourists. Lots of important things didn't happen. All that revenue that flowed through the papacy was not being spent in Rome. It was being spent there in Avignon. So the commune in Rome wanted the pope back, didn't want the pope back, wanted the pope back, didn't want the pope back, a very awkward situation. In addition to that, up in northern Italy, the Visconti dukes of Milan were trying very hard to establish hegemony in Italy. They really wanted to try to dominate Italy as much as they possibly could. Now, they were trying to thwart the popes. They were trying to thwart the Germans too, but that's another side of the story. So any efforts by the popes to consolidate their positions in central Italy, while the popes themselves were in the south of France, was being thwarted by the

Visconti in Milan, so the situation down there was pretty tricky, the situation down there in Italy.

The Avignon popes always planned to return to Rome. Their aim, their intention, their desire was to return to Rome; they knew they didn't belong in Avignon. In 1365, Urban V actually did return to Rome, but he felt very insecure there. He was French, most of the cardinals were French, he had never ruled from Rome, and in 1368 he left for northern Italy. By 1370 he was back in Avignon; that didn't work. Gregory XI left Avignon in 1376. He arrived in Rome in 1377. He began settling in a little bit, and just as he began settling in, he died, in 1378. Interestingly enough, when he began settling in, he began settling in over in the Vatican region because the Lateran had fallen into terrible disrepair while the popes had been at Avignon. The popes were going to move into the Vatican temporarily. They're still there.

In the election of 1378, the 16 cardinals in Rome, six of whom were still in Avignon, elected Bartolomeo Prignano, who was the Archbishop of Bari, largely because of the howling mob outside the door demanding that a Roman, or at the very least, an Italian, be elected pope. Bartolomeo, Urban VI, who was pope from 1378–1389, initially enjoyed the goodwill of the cardinals in Rome, but then he utterly ruined his relationship with them by treating them wretchedly. He was well intentioned, Urban was, and I think he would have been a sincere church reformer had he been given an opportunity to act as he might have wished. But he was totally inept and probably delusional. Apparently he went around talking to pictures. Other historical characters have done such things, too. In July the cardinals declared that the April election had been illegal because it was conducted under restraint and fear. Now, that's perfectly true. Elections were not supposed to be conducted in such conditions, with a howling mob outside the door.

So the cardinals decided that Urban was to be deposed. He wasn't the legitimate pope, and they left Rome momentarily for Neapolitan territory to the south, and they elected Cardinal Robert of Geneva, who took the name Clement VII. Clement slowly but surely worked his way back to Avignon. He arrived there in about 1381. When Clement arrived in Avignon—mind you, Urban VI was still down in Rome—the cardinals have declared him deposed, but he didn't sort of pack his bags and leave. He claimed the cardinals had no right to declare him deposed. As a result, there were two men, each elected in some sense by the same College of Cardinals a few months apart—one in Avignon, where the popes had been for a long time and one in Rome, where the popes had always been—both claiming to be the legitimate pope.

This inaugurated what we call the Great Schism, the great split, perhaps in certain respects the greatest of all the crises in papal history. Just as a footnote, occasionally there is a misconception that the Great Schism is the schism of 1054, when Michael Kerularios, the Patriarch of Constantinople, and Humbert of Silva Candida, the pope's legate, excommunicated each other, separating the Greek and Latin churches. No, that was not supposed to be a schism at all. Officially, it never was a schism, so the Great Schism is this period in the 14th and early 15th century, when more than one man claimed to be the pope, claimed to be the successor of Saint Peter. To this Great Schism we will turn our attention in the next lecture.

Lecture Eleven
The Great Schism

Scope:

The Great Schism (1378–1417) constituted the greatest crisis in the papacy's long history. For four decades, two and, sometimes, three men each claimed to be the legitimate pope. By the time the schism ended, the papacy's prestige had taken a beating and the monarchical theory of Church government had been dealt a blow.

The schism grew out of the papacy's period of residence in Avignon. There was always a basic assumption that the papacy belonged in Rome, yet Rome and Italy presented real challenges. The Lateran was dilapidated, the Papal States were in open rebellion, and enemies threatened. Still, Urban V did return to Rome in 1367, but less than three years later, he returned to Avignon. Finally, Gregory XI returned to Rome in 1377 and died there the next year. In the first conclave held in Rome since 1303, the archbishop of Bari was elected. He proved so high-handed, however, that several cardinals deposed him. They returned to Avignon, joined the cardinals Gregory XI had left there to administer Church business, and elected Clement VII. Two men claimed to be pope, and Europe split down the middle in its allegiance. In 1409, a council at Pisa tried to resolve the dispute but only succeeded in adding a third claimant. Finally, the Council of Constance (1414–1418) accepted the resignation of two "popes," declared a third one deposed, and elected a new pope, Martin V. Constance also declared that a general council was superior in authority to the pope, a dramatic reversal of trends in place for four centuries. For the next 30 years, the popes struggled resolutely to defeat *conciliarism*.

Note: The dates mentioned in this lecture may be confusing because of the complications with popes and antipopes who refused to leave even after they had officially resigned or were deposed.

Outline

I. To understand the Great Schism, we need to review just a few of the details pertaining to the last days of Gregory XI and the election of Urban VI.

   A. When Gregory XI died, it is not clear what the cardinals might have done had they felt completely free.

   1. They were inclining toward Prignano of Bari but panicked and elected the aged Roman Francesco de' Tebaldeschi, only to have Prignano rally them to his cause; he was elected pope (Urban VI).

   2. Through the summer of 1378, delegations of cardinals went to Urban VI to express doubts about the election and to call for a new one in which Urban could be a legitimate candidate.

   B. Europe soon split down the middle, and it is only hindsight that makes it so clear that the line of Urban VI was uniquely "legitimate."

Popes during the Great Schism

Rome	Avignon	Pisa
Urban VI (r. 1378–1389)	Clement VII (r. 1378–1394)	Alexander V (r. 1409–1410)
Boniface XI (r. 1389–1404)	Benedict XIII (r. 1394–1409)	John XXIII (r. 1410–1415)
Innocent VII (r. 1404–1406)	Clement VIII (r. 1409–1417)	
Gregory XII (r. 1406–1415)	Benedict XIV (r. 1425–1430)	
Martin V (r. 1417–1431)		

II. The lines across Europe changed somewhat as the schism dragged on, but the basic contours may be identified for the first 20 years or so.

   A. Among major states, the support divided as follows:

1. **France, Scotland, Castile, Aragon, and Navarre** supported Clement and, initially at least, his successor, Benedict XIII.
2. **Germany, Scandinavia, the (Catholic) Slavic world, England, Portugal, and most of Italy** supported Urban.

B. The great religious orders—Franciscans, Dominicans, Cistercians—were divided as well, not one from another but internally.

C. The old curialists and cardinals supported Clement, whereas Urban created new curialists and cardinals.

III. At this point, we will turn to an account of the basic course of the schism, then look at some of the concepts implemented to bring it to a shaky resolution.

A. Down to 1395, Urban and his two successors (Boniface and Innocent) and Clement, plus his successor (Benedict), tried hard to win or maintain supporters.

B. In 1395, the French crown and the University of Paris chose the *via cessionis*: They withdrew their support from Benedict XIII.

C. In 1403, Benedict escaped, won back his cardinals, and achieved renewed French backing because he had the support of the duke of Orléans, who was dominant at the French court.

D. Benedict made some effort to come to an understanding with his Roman rivals, but it is not clear if this was because or in spite of their troubles with the kingdom of Naples (always the Italian territorial situation!).

E. In 1408, the duke of Orléans was murdered, and France again withdrew its support from Benedict.

F. The majority of Avignonese and Roman cardinals, however, desired a council and called for it to meet in Pisa in 1409.
1. The council's main goal was to remove both the contending popes and elect a new one recognized by everyone.
2. In June 1409, the council declared Benedict XIII and Gregory XII excommunicated and deposed as heretics and schismatics. Both popes ignored the council.

3. A conclave elected Peter Philarghi as Alexander V. There were now three popes!

4. Alexander called for a new council to meet in 1412 to address general issues needing reform.

G. Germany at first maintained its allegiance to Rome, but when Sigismund of Bohemia was elected king of Germany in 1411, he opened negotiations with Pisa's John XXIII. Sigismund and John called for a new council to meet at Constance in 1414.

H. The Council of Constance (1414–1418) was at once successful and problematic.

1. John XXIII convened the council but was immediately asked to resign; he then fled to Vienna. He was captured, brought back, tried, and deposed.

2. In July 1415, news came that Gregory XII had resigned.

3. Sigismund never could get Benedict XIII to resign, and Benedict had successors down to 1430 claiming, of course, to be the only legitimate popes.

4. On November 11, 1417, Oddo Colonna was elected as Martin V, and the schism appeared to be over in all important respects.

5. Martin agreed to undertake a broad program of Church reform, and he accepted, under duress, two critical decrees of Constance.

   a. *Haec Sancta* (1415) declared that the authority of councils was superior to that of popes.

   b. *Frequens* (1417) called for a new council in 5 years, then another in 7 years, followed by councils every 10 years.

I. Martin could not get to Rome until 1420 and faced military anarchy in central Italy, along with the hostility of Naples.

J. Clerics began assembling in Basel by late 1431, but only a few of them; thus, Martin's successor, Eugenius IV (r. 1431–1447), declared the council dissolved.

1. In 1439, radicals at Basel declared Eugenius deposed and elected Amadeus VIII of Savoy as Felix V, who earned little recognition except as history's last antipope.

2. To everyone's great relief, the Great Schism did not open again.

IV. The kind of papacy that emerged from the schism will be a prominent feature of later lectures, but first, we must address all these councils.

    A. The papal monarchy of the high Middle Ages did not leave much room for shared governance of the Church.

    B. Already in the 12th and 13th centuries, writers were trying to understand the implications of the papal "fullness of power" (*plenitudo potestatis*).

    C. The increasing study of Roman law led to reflections on the doctrine of corporations and its principle, "What touches all ought to be approved by all" (*Quod omnes tangit approbetur ab omnibus*).

    D. The schism raised problems to which a *conciliar* ecclesiology emerged as an answer.

    E. The fact that Pisa tried to solve the schism and that Constance did so conferred legitimacy and prestige on conciliarism.

    F. The combination of Avignon and the Great Schism sent the papacy into the epoch we dub the Renaissance in a very different posture than the papacy had enjoyed in its high medieval heyday.

Recommended Reading:

Smith, *The Great Schism*.

Tierney, *Foundations of the Conciliar Theory*.

Questions to Consider:

1. What central flaws in the papacy's governing structure permitted the Great Schism to occur?

2. How, exactly, did conciliar theory counter the hierarchical thought of the high Middle Ages?

Lecture Eleven—Transcript
The Great Schism

Hello once again, and welcome to the eleventh lecture in our series on the history of the popes and of the papacy. This time we're going to talk about the Great Schism, the great split of the Western Church in the late 14th and the early 15th century, a very great grave crisis for the church. To understand the Great Schism, we need to review just a few details pertaining to the last days of Gregory XI and Urban VI, the popes with whom we left off in our previous lecture. It appears that Gregory XI, as was Urban, was planning a return to Avignon. He prepared a decree invalidating the electoral decrees of Alexander III and Gregory X. You remember Alexander's decree in 1179, Gregory X's in 1270—the latter regulating conclave; the former setting two-thirds majority, saying that the wiser part should be the electors, and so on. His subordinates never released the document, so what exactly his intentions were is hard to say. What would have been its force? Well, it would have permitted a small number—a minority, to be sure—of French cardinals themselves almost all from the Limousin, from the area around the city of Limoges, to carry an election. It's hard to say exactly what was going on there.

When Gregory XI died, it's not quite clear what the cardinals would have done had they been completely free to act as they wished. You'll remember, perhaps, our saying at the very end of the last lecture that there was a howling mob outside demanding the election of a Roman—or at the very least, of an Italian. Well, the cardinals were inclining in the direction of Cardinal Prignano of Bari when the Romans basically burst in the doors. For the moment, the cardinals, having elected Prignano, then regretted their choice and decided they would instead elect Francesco de' Tebaldeschi, who was an old Roman, only then to have Prignano stiffen their resolve and rally them back to his cause, so he then was elected and became Urban VI.

Throughout the summer of 1378, delegations of cardinals kept going to Urban VI to express doubts about the election and to call for a new one in which they said Urban could be a candidate. This poses interesting questions, doesn't it? Were the cardinals being entirely self-serving, or did they have some real legitimate doubts about this election in the spring of 1378? Had Urban VI—we characterized him a little bit last time—had Urban VI been a different sort of character, might things have turned out differently? Well, one thing we do know; Europe split right down the middle. It's only in hindsight, only in retrospect that we can see that Urban VI is the legitimate pope and not Clement VII, elected by the cardinals, who then went back to Avignon making, therefore, the Avignon line illegitimate.

Over the next few minutes here in our lecture and over the next 20 or 30 years in the history that we're recounting, the names and the numbers are going to become powerfully confusing. Those listening to these words might wish at some point to have a look at the chart of the Avignon popes that you'll find in the booklet for this course. Those of you are watching the course will have, from time to time, an opportunity to see the chart before your very eyes. If I tried to keep track of it in end detail, it would take us the rest of the month in order to do that, so what we'll try to do, instead, is move along with some dispatch through what is, in fact, a very complicated story. There were a number of popes during this Great Schism.

What are the basic issues? What are the kinds of things that we need to talk about here? Well, the basic lines across Europe changed a little as the schism dragged on, but the basic contours can be identified for the first 20 or so years of the period. Among the major states of Europe, for example, the division looked like this: France, Scotland, Castile, Aragon, Navarre supported Clement, supported the pope at Avignon and his successor Benedict XIII; Germany, Scandinavia, the Catholic Slavic World, England, Portugal, and most of Italy supported Urban and his successors at Rome. The great religious orders were badly divided, not one from another, but internally. The Franciscans, the Dominicans, the Cistercians, the Benedictines, they were divided. Some supported one; some supported the other. The old curialists and cardinals, generally speaking, supported Clement, supported the Avignon line. They went back with him to Avignon. But Urban, of course, at Rome and his successors at Rome named new cardinals and a new curia and, therefore, they had their supporters in Rome.

This was a period that produced characters like the amusing Pileus of Prata, "the cardinal with three hats." He was made a cardinal at Rome in 1378, then he became a cardinal at Avignon in 1387, then he became a cardinal again at Rome in 1381. The red hats, the lingo of the church is that when a man gets a red hat, he's made a cardinal, so one always speaks of the red hats, or when he received his hat. So the point is that Pileus had three hats, you see, so he was "cardinalized" three times.

Politics was one issue. The division between France and England—they're still at war—that was always a big problem. But there were also very real, deep, authentic concerns about the validity of sacraments and ordination. One of the things, of course, that is central to the ecclesiology of the Catholic Church is that the apostles laid hands on their successors, who laid hands on their successors, who laid hands on their successors—an unbroken line today, not only under the pope in Rome, but every parish priest in the Catholic world. Which of these lines represented the unbroken chain and which the broken chain? That was a serious problem.

To sort out what comes next, what we're going to do here is to proceed this way. Right now I'm going to turn to an account of the basic course of the schism itself, kind of what happened with these various people claiming to be legitimate pope, and eventually the resolution of the synod. Then what I want to do is go back and look at some of the theories on which the various actors in this drama acted, and then offer just a few reflections at the very end on the implications of the schism for the longer-term history of the papacy. Some of these implications, of course, will be with us in future lectures, and we'll have occasion to refer to them. Down to 1395, Urban and his two successors, whose names were Boniface and Innocent, and Clement, plus his immediate successor, whose name was Benedict, tried very hard to win or to maintain supporters, not surprisingly. They tried very hard around Europe to win support for themselves. You'll remember in those schisms of the 12th century that various popes tried to gain support in Italy, in Rome, and in the wider world. Same thing is going on now, nothing surprising here.

In 1395 the French crown and the University of Paris chose what they called the *via cessionis*, the way of ceding, the way of cession. They withdrew their support from Benedict XIII, the Avignon pope. They wanted him to cede; they wanted him to yield his position. Castile followed the policy of its ally, France. This is a big deal now because France had been the great supporter of Avignon, so now the French court says, "We want the Avignon pope to step down." Castile follows the policy of its ally, and in July of this year, 18 cardinals departed from Avignon, apparently following France's lead as well. That wasn't all the cardinals, but that was a significant number of them. In 1399, to kind of nudge the pope, the Avignon pope, along toward this cession, the French actually bombarded the papal palace, to no avail. In 1403, Benedict escaped. He managed to win back his cardinals, and then he gained French backing again because the Duke of Orléans, who was very, very influential with the French court at that particular moment, supported him.

Well, Benedict made some efforts to come to an understanding with his Roman rivals. There was negotiation back and forth. There were exchanges of correspondence and messengers sent back and forth. It's not clear, however, that this was out of a sincere desire to heel the schism, or rather, if this was because of threats in Italy, particularly owing to problems being raised then by the kingdom of Naples. In other words, it really wasn't in anybody's interest for Naples to exercise too much authority over Rome. There were attempts to arrange meetings between the contending popes in 1407 and 1408. They didn't occur, mainly because Gregory XII, who was now the pope at Rome, simply refused to appear. He would not go and meet with the Avignon pope. The pope in Rome felt that the Avignon popes were illegitimate, and that going to talk to them would, in a sense, legitimize, you see, their position.

Well, at this point Gregory's cardinals began to desert him. They felt that he should go and negotiate and meet and talk and see if a resolution could be found, and they began to say, "We need a church council. We have to have a great church council to settle this problem. This problem is scandalous; it's gone on long enough." In 1408 the Duke of Orléans was murdered. That has nothing to do with our story except that France again withdrew its support from Benedict, withdrew its support from the Avignon pope so that the greatest single supporter of the Avignon popes now, once again, no longer supported them. Benedict, the pope at Avignon, called for a council to meet at Perpignan in the south of France, sort of basically under his watchful eye and also under the watchful eye of the kingdom of Aragon, who also followed him. The majority of the Avignonese and virtually all of the Roman cardinals, however, desired a council, but they wanted it to meet in Pisa, in Italy, and so it did in 1409.

The Council of Pisa met under the presidency of Simon de Cramaud, who was the Patriarch of Alexandria, and Peter Philarghi, who was the Archbishop of Milan. In all, the council met in 22 sessions. It did a lot of work and, interestingly, it was organized by nations. What that means is that the clergy, for example in the Lateran councils that we've discussed in earlier lectures, didn't simply all come together as the clergy of the universal church and deal with issues. They came and sat as French, English, German, Italian and Provençal. They sat as nations, they sat as groups, and they worked, they deliberated, and they voted in a sense as blocs. It's the first time that that policy had appeared in a significant way in church history, and we're going to see that it remained in force for quite some time. The cardinals represented in a sense another group at the Council of Pisa.

The council's main goal, the fundamental thing they wanted to accomplish, was to remove the contending popes and elect a new one. Interestingly, they didn't want to try to decide which of these men was the right pope. They wanted to get rid of both of them and elect a new pope who would be recognized by everybody. So in June of 1409 the council declared Benedict XIII, the Avignon pope, and Gregory XII, the Roman pope, both excommunicated and deposed as heretics and "schismatics". Both popes ignored the Council of Pisa. So we have an interesting thing here. If you look at long lists of the popes, you will see, for example, that Gregory XII on the official Roman list ceases being pope in 1409, and yet in just a few minutes we're going to see that he doesn't actually resign until 1412. The dates, the names and so forth get terribly complicated in this period.

Anyway, Pisa now calls a conclave, which elected Peter Philarghi, the Archbishop of Milan, as Alexander V. Alexander called for a new council to meet in 1412 to deal with a whole host of broad ecclesiastical issues needing reform in the church. Nothing unusual about a pope calling for church reform, except now you have to understand there are not two, there are three popes. There's one in Pisa, there's one in Avignon and there's one in Rome. The Council at Pisa has deposed and excommunicated the one in Rome and the one in Avignon, but they said, "Baloney, we're not going anywhere." So there were three popes.

Germany at first maintained its allegiance to Rome. Pretty much right through the period, Germany had been loyal to Rome. But when Sigismund, who actually was the king of Bohemia—Bohemia was one of the electoral principalities of the German kingdom of the Holy Roman Empire—so Sigismund of Bohemia was elected king in 1411. He opened negotiations with the pope at Pisa, who was John

XXIII. We see also here that some of these names are going to get recycled. There was another John XXIII, Cardinal Roncalli, who was elected in 1958, so this poor John XXIII was moved off the official list and his number was taken away from him.

Anyway, Sigismund and John called a new council to meet at Constance in 1414, a city basically in the German part of what is today Switzerland. Sigismund worked tirelessly to get the Spanish monarchs to abandon Benedict XIII and participate in their council. He also managed to affect a truce. France and England are still at war. He affected a truce between France and England for the duration of the council so that they could send representatives to the council. He managed to compose the struggles of the Burgundians, who were generally participating, also, in the Hundred Years' War. This is quite interesting in some ways because it's the first time since late antiquity that an emperor has acted in these ways to compose these kinds of difficulties.

The Council of Constance, which sat from 1414 to 1418, was at once problematic and successful. Let's pursue that a little bit. What do I mean, problematic and successful? Well, John XXIII convened the council. What did the council do? It no sooner opened than it asked him to resign. He fled, fled to Vienna. He was eventually captured, brought back, tried and deposed, so now this John XXIII was declared illegitimate. In July news came from Rome that Gregory XII had resigned. Sigismund never could manage to get Benedict XIII to resign, and he had successors right down to about 1430 claiming, of course, to be the only legitimate popes. I mean, they wound up even being down in Aragon in Spain, still holding out and claiming to be the legitimate popes. One of the things that Sigismund was able to accomplish, however, once he persuaded the Spanish to abandon their allegiance to the pope at Avignon, was they sent their own representatives and added another nation to the council of Constance. So now in lots of ways this really was a European-wide council of the most important and most prominent—each of the most important and prominent—political units in Europe was now represented at Constance.

Virtually everyone supported Constance's decisions and the very fact of its existence. There was really no questioning the legitimacy of this church council. But if we look back, we could say there is something a little bit interesting here. It was called by a German ruler and a pope who was himself deposed. Of course the popes had long been claiming that it wasn't the emperor's business to call councils; it was the pope's business to call a council. So if you said, "Well, John XXIII actually called the council," you would also say, "Yeah, but we fired John XXIII," and "Well, the emperor called the council." "Yeah, but emperors aren't supposed to call councils." So the council was viewed as legitimate, but remember I said this is a successful but problematic council. On the 11th of November in 1417, Oddo Colonna was elected. He took the name Martin V, and it appeared that the schism was over, at least in all important respects.

At the very least, there's now only one person who had any plausible claim on being pope. Yes, the Avignon line was still there, but no longer did anybody pay any attention to them, really. So there was basically then one pope, and his legitimacy was unquestioned. Incidentally too, this was the only Colonna pope. From the 13th century, maybe even in the late 12th, down into the 19th century the Colonna family was very powerful in Rome and very influential in Rome, and they only managed to produce one pope—Oddo Colonna—who became Martin V as a way of healing the Great Schism. Martin agreed to undertake a broad program of church reform, and he accepted, under some duress, we may say, he accepted two great decrees of the Council of Constance.

The first of these—1415, *Haec Sancta*—declared that the authority of councils was superior to that of popes. This decree is going to be a constant companion of ours over the next several lectures. Then in 1417 the council issued the decree *Frequens*, and Martin had to accept this as well. This said that there would be another council in five years, and then one in seven years, and then one every 10 years after that. It was now that the church was basically going to be ruled on a regular basis by church councils. Owing to—surprise—political complications in Italy, it was 1420 before Martin could get back to Rome. Anyway, he finally did arrive in Rome. He faced military anarchy in central Italy and in the Papal State. He had the hostility of Naples to his south to contend with and, as always, there were struggles in the city itself.

These serious complications and problems actually delayed the implementation of the decree of *Frequens*, the one calling for a new council in five years then seven years then ten—although this was a kind of a blessing in disguise for Martin, who wouldn't have wanted to call another council anyway. Martin and his successor, Eugenius IV (1431–1447) tried various strategies to avoid calling another council. The popes basically don't want to call councils. Let's remember that spectacularly hierarchical thought of the papal monarchs of the 12th and 13th century—the idea that councils run the church, not popes. That's anathema to these men, but they are in somewhat straitened circumstances in the 1430s.

Finally however, they did have to agree that there would be a council that would meet at Basel in 1431. You remember Constance had concluded its work in 1418. There should have been a council in 1423, another one in 1430, 1440, 1450, 1460 and so on. Well, it was 1431 before another council assembled, and it met in Basel. Only a very few people showed up, so Eugenius declares the council dissolved. Well, supported by Sigismund, those in Basel refused to depart. They said, "Excuse me, this is a council, we're not going anywhere," then gradually a few more people began to show up in Basel. In February of 1432, Eugenius retreated; he acknowledged the council. He said, "Alright, I accept this council." Over the next several years, the council actually accomplished a good deal of worthwhile ecclesiastical reform. We'll meet some of this reform in our next lecture.

For the present purposes, what we want to notice is that the pope was all the while dubious about what was happening in Basel and carrying on negotiations with the Byzantines. He was trying to affect a reunion of the Greek and Latin churches. In 1437 Eugenius declared the council moved to the city of Ferrara. This had a number of interesting results. On the one hand, it was a whole lot closer to Rome than Basel up in Switzerland, a whole lot closer to Rome, therefore, easier for the pope to exercise influence, and it was a more agreeable site to the Byzantines. This is a very important thing for the pope, to try to be able to effect a healing of this schism with the Greek Church that's been going on since the 11th century.

But moving the council from Basel to Ferrara effectively stripped anything then going on in Basel of legitimacy. So in 1439 the radicals at Basel declared Eugenius deposed. And not only did they declare him deposed; they elected Amadeus VIII of Savoy as Felix V. Felix is an utterly forgettable character with one exception. He gets a footnote in the history books—he's the last antipope. There would never be another one, and nobody really paid much attention to him at that time either. It was to everyone's great relief that the Great Schism didn't pop open once more. In other words, Felix and Eugenius did not split Europe the way we saw had happened in the case of Urban VI and Clement in 1378. Thus far, the course of the Great Schism: it broke out; two men claiming to be pope, then a third man claiming to be pope; then it was composed, only one pope; and then briefly that pope had a rival or that line of popes had a rival. But the schism didn't break open again.

What kind of papacy emerged from the Great Schism? What was the church going to look like? What was its ecclesiology to be? What would its governing structure be after the Great Schism? In certain respects, this is going to be a theme that we'll see worked out over the next four or five lectures that we'll be having in this course. But for the moment, we want to just try to see these developments, these events, in their 14th and early 15th century contexts. I think you'll agree with me if I say that the papal monarchy of the high Middle Ages, with that tremendously structured hierarchical thought that was so characteristic of it, didn't leave much room for shared governance of the church. In antiquity the ecumenical council was the great agency. It was the great agent of church government, and it was widely understood that its decisions, the decisions of the great ecumenical councils—Nicaea and Constantinople and so on—were to be received by everyone. That's the technical term, "the decisions of the councils were to be received by everyone."

We also saw that popes tried to assert that councils only sat with their approval and on their summoning, but there were many who knew that the facts were otherwise. Emperor Constantine had assembled the council of Nicaea, for example. There's also the fact that beginning with Pope Gregory VII, smack in the middle of the Investiture Controversy, Rome promoted the idea that papal decisions governed the church and that papal decisions were to be received by everyone. So we have two conflicting, two competing ecclesiologies: a collegial model, and a monarchical model. As the ecumenical councils of antiquity had been very much imperial ventures—one after another, emperors called those councils, sometimes in close cooperation with the church, sometimes in real opposition, but the emperors had called them—the Lateran councils—1123, 1139, 1179, 1215, 1245, 1274—the Lateran councils of the high Middle Ages were very much papal ventures.

Already in the 12th and 13th centuries, there were writers who understood the implication of the notion of the papal *plenitudo potestatis*, the fullness of power. Those terms, those ways of thinking, emerge already in late antiquity. But what did the pope's fullness of power mean? If he has a fullness of power, what's the theory behind it on the one hand, and how does he exercise it on the other? The great canonist Gratian—remember, we talked about Gratian's *Decretum*, the great law book issued in 1140 in the 12th century—Gratian had said the pope cannot be judged by anyone unless he is found to have deviated from the faith. What would be the point of that qualification? Well, let's pursue it just a bit. The great canonist Huguccio of Pisa—he died about 1210—once said that if a pope were to fall into heresy he would cease to be pope and therefore could be judged like anyone else. So if the pope became a heretic, he immediately ceased to be pope.

This may have something to do with our friends Virgilius and Honorius in the 6th and 7th centuries who in earlier times had lapsed from the faith and the church always knew that that had happened. But what we're seeing here is people are trying to find, not some wiggle room—that's unfair; that's cynical—they're trying to find a legal formula that says if the pope can't be judged by anybody, is that true always in every imaginable circumstance? Would there be any circumstances in which anybody anywhere, any competent authority could actually sit in judgment of a pope? So Gratian says heresy and Huguccio says, "If the pope's a heretic he stops being pope." In other words, you still can't judge the pope.

But the increasing study of Roman law—remember we talked about Roman law producing on the one hand "what pleases the prince has the power of law" has the force of law; that could be a prince or pope—but there were also principles in Roman law—it came from the Roman law of corporations, for instance—that says, "What touches all ought to be approved by all" *Quod omnes tangit approbetur ab omnibus)*. For some, this led in a very radical direction—that the church ought to be governed by all its members acting for the common good. That's nice as a theory. How would that work in practice? There was no polling in the Middle Ages; there was no Harris poll or Gallup poll. How would you know what everybody thought? Through what means would they manifest themselves? For others, the "body", the corpus, could act in cases where, for example, serious reform was needed, but not necessarily on a regular basis. In other words, the body of the church could come together to deal with a big problem such as, for example the Great Schism. But who would decide when it was a big problem? Who would decide who qualifies to come together to participate?

The schism, in other words, raised problems to which a "conciliar" ecclesiology—a church run by councils as opposed to by a monarch—seemed to be a satisfactory answer. Theologians at the University of Paris argued that the church consisted of the "totality of the faithful," the *universitas fidelium*, and only a general council represented the *universitas fidelium*, the "totality of the faithful." Some went further; they said that theologians and canonists should participate with bishops in the decision-making process. There were longstanding Gallican currents. The French—Gaul, France—had always been very jealous of their own rights, their own powers, their own privileges, their own responsibilities. They've never really quite liked the idea of being bullied by the popes. Lawyers at Bologna said that if a pope could be judged for heresy, then certainly schism was a like offense. A pope could be judged for schism. That's how you could depose some of these guys claiming to be pope.

The fact that Pisa had tried to solve the schism, and that Constance did so, conferred a considerable legitimacy and prestige on Conciliarism as an operative theory. But the precise implications of *Haec Sancta*—a council is superior to a pope—and of Basel's even stricter *Dudum sacrum*—this dubious council at Basel, which also declared councils much superior to popes—the practical implications of those decisions were a little hard to grasp. How was that going to work in practice? Basel's condemnation of Eugenius IV and its election of Felix V—as an antipope, moreover—actually sapped a lot of the momentum of the conciliar movement. It brought it into discredit. The combination of Avignon and the Great Schism, however, these two great crises from 1305 until 1418, or indeed into the 1430s and '40s, these two great crises usher the papacy in the church into the era that we call the Renaissance. So in our next lecture, we want to turn to what it was like to be a pope and what the papacy was like, as the heirs of Avignon and the schism, and in the midst of this remarkable efflorescence we call the Renaissance.

Lecture Twelve
The Renaissance Papacy—Politics

Scope:

Rome and the papacy made important contributions to the dynamic set of movements that we call the Renaissance. Statecraft constitutes one kind of contribution, and we will examine the place of the popes in the public culture, war, diplomacy, and government of the 15th-century world in this first of two lectures on the Renaissance. Culture constitutes the second, and more familiar, element of the Renaissance. We turn to that subject in the next lecture.

Papal activity during the Renaissance did little to bring credit to the institution. Still, one can discern some traditional areas of activity. The fall of Constantinople to the Turks in 1453 spurred a renewed interest in crusades. The definitive return of an unrivaled papacy to Rome led to attempts to put the Papal States in order. Many customary sources of revenue having dried up, the popes needed the revenues from the Papal States. But, as in the Middle Ages, the independence of the Papal States was believed to guarantee papal freedom of action. Renaissance popes were, therefore, engaged repeatedly in wars with Italian powers. The Renaissance popes also ruthlessly promoted their own families, handing out lands, offices, and incomes with a free hand. Within the Church, popes and cardinals engaged in a long-running and unsavory battle for power. Almost every Renaissance pope was more prince than priest.

Outline

I. The old, but not contemporary, term *Renaissance* may be used in either of two ways.

   A. It may be applied somewhat imprecisely to some chunk of the period, roughly, 1300 to 1600, with the chunk usually lopped off according to the dictates of particular disciplines (painting, sculpture, literature, philosophy, and so on). But the focus here is on cultural phenomena.

   B. The term can also be used, just as imprecisely, to refer to general historical developments in that same long period or some segment of it.

II. In this lecture, we will look at the papacy as an institutional, political, and diplomatic actor in what we might otherwise call the later Middle Ages.

III. Let us begin by attempting to characterize the popes of the Renaissance.

    A. When Eugenius IV was elected in 1431, 6 of 12 cardinals were Italian, but when Alexander VI was elected in 1492, 23 of 24 were Italian.

    B. Not only was papal Rome becoming more Italian, but quasi-dynasties were emerging in the Roman Church.

    C. The Renaissance period was not a time when the popes reached a very high standard of moral rectitude.

    D. The papacy became a secularized institution during the Renaissance.

IV. Let us set the national and international stage for the Renaissance papacy because, as we have learned, this background is essential to understanding other aspects of papal history.

    A. In the early 15th century, Milan's leaders were the Visconti family, followed by the Sforza family.

    B. In 1452, Venice attacked Milan, but the fall of Constantinople to the Turks in 1453 was sufficiently shocking that the major parties in Italy made peace at Lodi in 1454.

    C. Italy's peace was broken when the French invaded in 1494.

    D. In 1527, an army of German mercenaries, nominally in the service of Habsburg ruler Charles V of Spain, terrorized Italy and sacked Rome.

        1. Pope Clement VII (r. 1523-1534) finally joined an alliance of Milan, Florence, Venice, and France against Charles V, which resulted in peace in 1529.

        2. As a consequence of that peace, Clement crowned Charles emperor in Bologna in 1530, the last time a pope would crown a Holy Roman Emperor.

V. No less important than the general historical situation was always the particular situation of the Papal States in central Italy.

    A. The popes tried hard to maintain and even expand the Papal States, partly to provide independence in Italy and partly to provide revenues.

    B. Popes often named either relatives or people from their home districts as rulers of various segments of the Papal States.

    C. During the foreign occupations after 1494, several popes tried cleverly to expand the Papal States but without lasting success.

    D. Down to the 19th century, the Papal States remained a top priority for the popes but represented an insignificant factor in Italian politics.

VI. The position of the pope within the Church was altered in subtle ways during the Renaissance.

    A. The epoch of the Great Schism and conciliarism had somewhat contradictory results.

        1. Basel partially discredited conciliarism, but in France (1438) and Germany (1448), rulers opportunistically imposed concordats that cut off revenues to Rome, some kinds of papal appointments, and some appeals to the papacy.

        2. The popes meanwhile tried to quash conciliarism definitively, and Pius II issued the bull *Execrabilis* forbidding appeals to councils.

        3. Julius II assembled Lateran V (1512–1517) to counter the French-inspired Council of Pisa (1512), which sought to restore *Haec Sancta* and *Frequens*. He effectively put *Unam Sanctam*, the powerful statement that Boniface VIII issued at the end of his failed pontificate, back in force, but it was clearly an empty letter in terms of practical effect.

    B. The very calling of Lateran V points to other key issues.

        1. There had been powerful calls for reform and a council for decades, even among ardent supporters of the papacy.

2. Fearful of the precedents set by Constance and, especially, Basel, the popes were reluctant to call councils at all.

VII. The basic institutions of the Roman Church changed relatively little.

   A. Practically every pope agreed to an electoral capitulation and quite frequently dispensed money. Technically, this made simonists of popes and cardinals.

   B. Grasping for new revenues, offices began to be sold.

   C. The popes gradually assumed greater responsibility for governing Rome itself, which furthered the secularization of the Church.

VIII. The Renaissance papacy can be viewed in European perspective by looking at failed attempts to mount a new crusade.

   A. Popes tried unsuccessfully several times to rally support in the Balkans for wars against the Turks.

   B. The fall of Constantinople in 1453 did not have the kind of effect that some expected.

   C. Pius II called a congress at Mantua in 1459 to launch a crusade, but virtually no one attended, and Venice had already concluded a lucrative commercial treaty with the Turks.

   D. The continuing fragmentation of anything that might reasonably be called Christendom was ongoing, unstoppable, and dangerous for the long-term interests of the papacy.

Recommended Reading:

Prodi, *The Papal Prince*.

Thomson, *Popes and Princes, 1417–1517*.

Questions to Consider:

1. If you viewed them purely as secular rulers, how would you evaluate the Renaissance popes?

2. The popes were generally unsuccessful with their diplomatic ventures. Why?

Lecture Twelve—Transcript
The Renaissance Papacy—Politics

Hello once again, and welcome to the twelfth lecture in our series on the history of the popes and of the papacy. This time we're going to turn our attention to the popes in the age of the Renaissance. That word, the term *Renaissance* is old; it's not exactly contemporary with the Renaissance itself. It's first used in Italian in the middle of the 16th century by Giorgio Vasari, *rinascita*, but eventually it became the name in its French form, *renaissance*, for the period as a whole. We can use this term in two different ways. We could apply it, somewhat imprecisely, to some chunk of the period between roughly 1300 and 1600, with the chunk lopped off according to the particular interest we had at the moment. For instance, if we're interested in painting or in sculpture or in literature or in philosophy, we would give this Renaissance a slightly different chronology. But the point is that in any understandings of the term "Renaissance" such as that, the focus is on a cultural phenomenon or on a variety of cultural phenomena.

The term can also be used just as imprecisely to refer to kind of general historical developments in that same long period—or in some segment of it—where the connection isn't necessarily or obviously to cultural phenomena, but we're again talking about the period from about 1300 to 1500 or 1600 or thereabouts. In this lecture we're going to look at the papacy as an institutional, political, and diplomatic actor in what we might otherwise call the late Middle Ages. In the next lecture we're going to look at the popes as participants in the great cultural movement to which we attach the word "Renaissance" a little bit more familiarly. But we are, in this lecture, going to take our lead from cultural history because it was with Eugenius IV, who was the pope at the time of the Council of Basel that the papacy came into contact for the first time with the movement of humanism. We're going to end with Clement VII, not because the Renaissance in general—or papal participation in or interest in the Renaissance—ended with Clement VII, but by the time we get to Clement, the papacy is almost fully engaged with the phenomenon we know as the Protestant Reformation. So basically we're going to go over about a century's time in terms of our Renaissance.

Let's begin by doing what we have done in a number of earlier lectures: to characterize the popes of this period. How might we try to grasp the popes of the Renaissance era? When Eugenius IV was elected in 1431, six of the 12 cardinals were Italian; only 12 cardinals, six of them were Italian. When Alexander VI was elected in 1492, 23 of 24 were Italian. Obviously the Italians were beginning to dominate the College of Cardinals in a way that they had not done for some time. Not only was papal Rome becoming more Italian, but quasi-dynasties were emerging inside the Roman Church. Let me just give you a few examples. For instance: Paul II, Pietro Barbo, was a nephew of Eugenius IV; Alexander VI, Rodrigo Borgia, Spanish pope, was a nephew of Callistus III; Pius III, Francesco Todeschini, was a nephew of Pius II; Julius II, Giuliano delle Rovere, was a nephew of Sixtus IV; and, finally, the Medici family produced two popes in this period, Leo X and Clement VII.

One interesting phenomenon that I'll just drop in as a kind of footnote is these great Roman families rarely produced a lot of popes. In fact, it's extremely rare for more than one or two to come from a family. It was thought that once you had your pope, that individual would have done everything he could possibly do for your family and then other families would be able to hold the papal office. So it was very rare for the families such as the Borghese and the Barberini and the others to have pope after pope after pope. That just didn't happen.

There is another way we can look at the kind of dynastic politics of Renaissance papal Rome. Eugenius IV named six nephews cardinals. He married his nieces and nephews into some of the great families of Rome and of Italy. He made his favored nephew, Giuliano—who later became Pope Julius II—get this—Archbishop of Avignon and Bologna; Bishop of Lausanne, Coutances, Viviers, Monde, Ostia, and Velletri; and also abbot of Nonantola and Grottaferrata. This is probably the biggest case of pluralism in the entire history of the church. This one man had all these positions. Alexander VI was, in some ways maybe, the most dubious of the Renaissance popes. We'll have more to say about him as we go along. He made his son Cesare bishop of several sees, and he named Cesare, along with Alessandro Farnese, who was the son of one of his many mistresses—not his son, but the son of Giulia Farnese—he named Cesare and Alessandro cardinals at the age of 19. He wasn't 19; they were. Influential families such as the Colonna—for example, they had Martin V, and they couldn't have a pope elected in this period—but they could often block candidates they didn't like.

When family connections weren't enough, money was spent quite freely. For example, Cardinal Pietro Riario secured the election of his uncle Sixtus IV, and Alexander VI spent a fortune on his own behalf having himself elected. Money talks. The Renaissance was not a period, on the whole, where it's possible to say that the popes came up to a very high moral standard; in fact, perhaps on the contrary. Alexander VI lived openly with a series of mistresses in the Vatican, and it was said that prostitutes were readily available in the Vatican in his time. Julius II had three daughters. Popes were often away hunting at country residences and doing things such as that, leaving masses and religious celebrations to subordinates and others in the city.

The Corpus Christi procession—this was on Corpus Christi Sunday every year, the "feast of the body of Christ"—there was a great procession through the area of Rome called the Borgo. The Borgo is the area in Rome that basically runs from Saint Peter's down to the Tiber, and there was a procession that wove its way through that neighborhood. Well, perhaps not under Leo X but certainly in the Renaissance period anyway, the Corpus Christi procession had minstrels in it. Under Leo X, whom I started to mention a moment ago, the Sistine chapel choir was performing comedies, which is not with that choir was founded to do. Sixtus IV, to look at a slightly different kind of case, managed to get himself involved in the murderous, brutal Pazzi Conspiracy in Florence in 1478. What we can say is this. During this Renaissance period, the papacy became, in fundamental respects, a very much secularized institution. The popes didn't behave better or worse than the secular rulers all around Europe and all around Italy with whom they were contemporary. One might have supposed, however, that the popes should have behaved somewhat differently.

Now, let's set the national and international stage for the Renaissance papacy for, as I think we have been learning, papal history is always tied to, in fundamental respects, whatever else is going on in Rome, in Italy and in the wider world. The first thing we would notice is this. In the early 15th century, Milan's leaders—first of all the Visconti family, and then subsequently the Sforza—were seeking to dominate Italy. They were really trying to establish hegemony in Italy. Their efforts at domination distressed Florence and Venice. In a certain way, northern Italy is a congeries of small towns, each fiercely independent, each jealous of its rights *vis à vis* its neighbors. Having said that, Milan and Florence and Venice are in a sense the three big ones here, and they are always trying to dominate the towns in their immediate region and then trying to gain advantages *vis à vis* one another. When the Visconti and the Sforza of Milan attempted to impose their authority more widely in Italy, Florence and Venice basically allied against them.

Now, the church was also a little worried about Milan imposing its authority very widely in Italy because the dukes of Milan had a long tradition of controlling the church with an iron hand, and the popes did not want to have an iron hand controlling them. In 1452 the Venetians attacked the Milanese, without immense significance at that very moment, but in 1453 the city of Constantinople fell to the Turks. This was sufficiently shocking in Italy; the Italian powers decided they probably ought to compose their difficulties. They had no idea whether the Turks were coming after them next, and at Lodi in 1454, Milan, Venice and Florence concluded peace. Very soon, Naples and the papacy also signed on to the Peace of Lodi.

Now, there are a couple of interesting things going on here. There was always a certain amount of petty local skirmishing; we're talking about Italy, after all. But the Peace of Lodi inaugurated 40 years of sustained large-scale peace in Italy, 1454–94. It was brought to an end when the French invade Italy. We'll have more to say about that in just a second. If you were to go through a list of great writers, a list of great philosophers, a list of great painters, a list of great architects, this is the high Renaissance, this moment of peace in Italy inaugurated by the Peace of Lodi. Well, as I said just a second ago, Italy's piece was broken in 1494 when the French invaded Italy. Well, you know the French have had interest in southern Italy for a long time. Generally speaking however, we've seen that it was the Germans who had interest in northern Italy.

King Charles VIII of France laid claim to Naples in succession to the Angevins, who had been the Angevin French princes, and had been involved in Naples and its region since the 13th century. So Charles VIII laid claim to Naples, then he laid claim to Milan through marriage alliances. The French armies come to Italy in 1494. Italy's peace in a sense was ruptured, and once again foreign actors were upon the Italian stage. The French continued, we might say, from an Italian point of view, meddling in Italian affairs down to 1525, when the Hapsburg ruler, Charles V of Spain, and his army defeated King Frances I of France's army just outside the city of Pavia. In 1527, however, an army of German mercenaries—nominally in Charles's service, but there were Spaniards in this army, there were Germans in this army, there were all kinds of people in this army—put Rome to a hideous and appalling sack. It was worse than when the Visigoths took Rome in 410, and something that people in Rome did not soon forget.

Pope Leo X, who was the pope at the time of the German attack—of the Hapsburg attack of 1527—tried to find a German prince to counter the Hapsburgs. He turned, interestingly enough, to Elector Frederick of Saxony. Frederick turned him down, and we're going to meet Frederick of Saxony in a later lecture as the man who protected Martin Luther. But anyway, Leo X hadn't quite figured out that Frederick was not going to be a good bet to help him out in Italy. Clement VII finally joined an alliance of Milan, Florence and Venice—and France, for that matter—against Charles V, and this resulted in peace being concluded, sort of a general peace in Europe but also a particular peace in Italy in 1529. In consequence of this peace, Clement crowned Charles emperor in Bologna in 1530. That was the last time a pope crowned a Holy Roman Emperor, although the Holy Roman Empire would continue struggling along until 1806, but this was the last time a pope crowned a Holy Roman Emperor.

The papacy continued to be at the beck and call of wide international circumstances over which basically the popes didn't have much control. No less important than the general historical situation was always, as we've had occasion to see, the particular situation of the popes in the Papal States in central Italy. What was that situation during the Renaissance? The popes, of course, always tried very hard to maintain and to expand the Papal States.

They did that for a number of reasons. One of the reasons, of course, was that as much as they could expand the size and scope of the Papal States, by that measure they created a buffer zone for themselves to keep whoever was in southern Italy and whoever was in northern Italy a little bit away from them. But it's also true that the Papal States provided the majority of papal revenues. At least they did when the popes were in a position effectively to administer and to exploit the Papal States. When other powers were doing so or when the Papal States were in open rebellion of course, then the papacy's ability to extract revenue from the Papal States was very much diminished. So protection, independence and revenue—those were the three big deals with respect to the Papal States. It's also true in this particular period that the popes were sometimes losing some other resources that they had customarily had at their disposal. We'll have a little bit more to say about that as we go along here, but the Papal States were always prominent in papal thinking. Suffice it to say that's the key point here.

The popes during the Renaissance period very often named relatives or else people from their own home districts as rulers of various segments of the Papal States—various duchies and counties and principalities and so on inside the Papal States. The policy was in some ways an intelligent one. It was in some ways a policy that had a certain rationale, primarily this. If the popes could put their own relatives—or people from the towns they came from or the regions they came from—in control of significant parts of the Papal States, they might be able to keep powerful Roman families from dominating the Papal States and then using their domination of the Papal States, and the revenue they could extract from the Papal States, to play in the games of Roman politics. The fact is that over a period of years, many powerful Roman families had come into vast tracts of papal land.

Now, in the course of the 15th and into the early years of the 16th century, a number of these families had been turning a great deal of arable land—in other words, land where green or other crops were planted—they had been turning that land into pasture. This was more profitable for them, but it raised some rather serious and interesting problems from the popes' points of view. First of all, from the popes' points of view, Roman noble rivals controlling land out there in hinterland Rome was a bad idea, period. The pope never liked that. But in the immediate circumstances that we're talking about now, there was this problem—small farmers were being driven off the land. When arable land was being turned into pasture, small farmers were being driven off the land. This impoverished them, it brought them into Rome, where they hade no jobs, they had no work, they required to be fed, they became volatile politically. Plus, I mean, the popes felt, I think quite legitimately, quite sincerely, that this was just wrong.

But a closely related phenomenon was this. If the land around Rome was no longer planted in cereal grains, where did Rome obtain its food? Well, bread is the staff of life. I mean, fundamentally, cereal grains feed any city. That's true in the 21st century; it was certainly true in 15th. But other things enter the food supply as well, so the popes were very concerned that Rome's food supply was in danger, that the poorer, more vulnerable elements of the rural population was in danger, and the Roman nobility was aggrandizing its power. Sixtus IV attempted to implement land reforms, but the nobles—led by the Colonna family—opposed him at every turn, and basically the popes over the next several decades struggled again and again and again to try to implement some kind of reforms of the situation in the Italian countryside, often without success. They often faced opposition from these powerful aristocratic interests in Rome.

During the course of the foreign occupations after 1494, a series of popes tried very cleverly to expand the Papal States with French backing, or in opposition to the French—they could play both sides of the street here—but generally speaking without much success. They weren't really able to profit from the French presence in Italy to expand their own interests in the peninsula, but they tried rather hard to do so. Again, there is nothing new about that in the 15th century. Popes trying to expand their influence in the Papal States in central Italy is a constant theme of papal history. Indeed, it was going to remain a constant theme in papal history right down to the point in the 19th century where the popes finally lost the Papal States to the newly emerging Italian Republic. But when we come to the 19th century in a later lecture, and we see how tenaciously the popes held on to the idea of temporal rule, we may want to remember how long and how hard they had fought to establish and maintain that temporal rule in the first place. So the Renaissance popes didn't invent temporal rule, didn't invent the Papal States, didn't invent the political and economic conditions of the Papal States. They inherited it and they bequeathed it.

The position of the pope inside the church was altered in some subtle ways during the Renaissance. The epic of the Great Schism and Conciliarism, as we saw, had rather contradictory results. The Council of Basel for example, particularly after 1439 or thereabouts—when it kind of went into its radical phase, when it elected an antipope and so on—had discredited Conciliarism in some ways, had brought the whole theory of the council into a measure of disrepute. But the rulers of France in 1438 and in Germany in 1448 rather opportunistically took advantage of the fraught political circumstances to impose concordats on the popes that cut off some kinds of papal appointments—always remember these battles between secular rulers and the popes: who can name the bishops, who can name the abbots, who can make the great appointments—so they were able to impose some controls on papal appointments, and they were able to curb some appeals to the pope. The churchmen in their particular realms would be able to appeal controversies to the pope; they managed to curtail appeals. They also cut off some revenues, so this is the point I was making a moment ago, that managing the Papal States was increasingly important in this period because these concordats imposed on the pope in 1438 and 1448 in Germany also had the result of cutting papal revenues a little bit.

The popes themselves also took a rather aggressive posture with respect to Conciliarism. What they really wanted to do was quash it. They wanted to quash it in two distinct respects. They wanted to quash conciliar theory and re-establish a more monarchical, a more hierarchical kind of theory as the central operating ecclesiology of the church, and they wanted to quash the particular effects of the councils. Pius II, for example issued the bull *Execrabilis*, forbidding appeals to councils—in other words, forbidding anyone to appeal over the head of a pope to a council. One of the things that the decree *Haec Sancta* of Constance, making a council superior to a pope, one of the forces of the decree *Haec Sancta* as that people could appeal over the pope to a council. Pius then issued *Execrabilis* and said, "No appealing over the pope to a council."

Julius II assembled the Fifth Lateran Council. It kind of met off and on from 1512–1517. What he was trying to do was counter a council that had been assembled in Pisa, interestingly enough, where the council that first had the Great Schism going toward resolution had been held in the 15th century. Anyway, the French assembled the Council at Pisa in 1512. That Council attempted to reinstitute the great decrees of Constance: *Haec Sancta*, making council superior to popes; and *Frequens*, requiring frequent councils. This was the sort of thing that Julius II, in calling his Counsel the Fifth Lateran, was trying to put an end to. Julius actually put *Unam Sanctam*—this powerful statement of Boniface VIII issued at the end of his failed pontificate—he actually put that decree back into effect, but it was dead on arrival. It simply couldn't have the kind of effect in the early years of the 16th century that it might have had in the early 13th, and heaven knows in the early 14th century Boniface didn't get much mileage out of it either.

The calling, however, of the Fifth Lateran Council—which was not, we would have to say, a terribly important or a terribly successful Council in the grand scheme of things—points to one or two other issues that were, themselves, of some interest and consequence. There had been powerful calls for reform and for a council for decades. There was a widespread sense that there were many issues in the church that needed to be addressed, that many issues needed to be reformed. We've had occasion in earlier lectures to reflect on this word "reform" and how different figures in the history of the church, over a long period of time, have used that word. But suffice it to say, there were calls for reform in this period. People really had a sense that something needed to be done. Even among ardent supporters of the papacy, even among some of the most papal of thinkers, there was an awareness that there were reforms that simply needed to be introduced.

Now imagine yourself looking at this situation through the eyes of a pope in the late 15th and the early 16th century. The last thing you were going to do was to call a council. They had the memory, after all, of Constance—which yes, it had put an end to the Great Schism, but it issued *Haec Sancta* and *Frequens*. If you were a pope, you didn't like that much. Then there was the Council of Basel, which was the council that sort of went totally out of control. How could a pope expect that he might be able to control a council? So one of the things that the popes just were really worried about was that possibility—all the unforeseen possibilities—if a council were to be called. The Fifth Lateran ended in 1517. Some other interesting things happened in October of 1517. A young university professor in Germany named Martin Luther tacked some propositions to the door of the castle church in Wittenberg and so on. We're going to see in a later lecture that one of the bitter inheritances of this Conciliarism was that papal Rome was paralyzed in the face of the need to address some profound religious issues in Europe.

Julius II seems to have had an ambitious plan for the reform of the curia, for example and for spiritual reform quite generally, but nothing came of it. As far as we can tell, really nothing very much came of it. Yet if we go back to, say, 1450, which was declared a Holy Year in Rome, a Jubilee Year, pilgrims and money came streaming into the city. The popes could continue to draw on deep reservoirs of respect and affection. That just never changed. That's one of the great and interesting, fascinating elements of this papal story. No matter how bad things were, they may not like the pope very much, but the papacy seemed to maintain an enormous kind of strength and solidity.

The basic institutions of the Roman Church actually changed rather little in this Renaissance period. Practically every pope had to agree to an electoral capitulation. We described electoral capitulations a while ago when we were talking about the Avignonese popes. Virtually every one of these had to agree to an electoral capitulation. Quite often, not always, but quite often those electoral capitulations involved spending money. One of the things that was interesting here is that spending money in that way technically made most of the Renaissance popes simonists, and one of the things that the Investiture Controversy had been about was putting an end to simony. This was a slightly awkward situation in the 16th century.

Popes needed money. One can't think of rulers who don't. Grasping for new revenues became a real scramble in Rome, and one thing that they began to do was to sell offices. Pope Sixtus IV created 244 new offices that could be sold. By the time of Leo the X, there were 2,150 offices in the papal government that could be sold, worth annually three million ducats. Scholars called this the "Venality of Office," the selling of offices. In point of fact, every government in Europe at the time did it. A lot of these posts were sinecures; they simply gave people inflated and pompous titles, and they didn't necessarily do anything. In some instances, however, important jobs were actually sold in this way, but it was a way that governments all over Europe at that time raised money. The popes gradually assumed greater responsibility for governing the City of Rome itself. This further secularized the church and its government. The popes had as many or more secular officers, for example, working under them as ecclesiastical ones.

We can conclude, I think, our view of the popes in their Roman, Italian and European setting by taking a quick look at their failure to mount a crusade, for this once again will tell us something about the great currents of the age and what popes could do and what they couldn't do. We saw, remember, that part of the problems that poor old Frederick II of Hohenstaufen had had in the 13th century was that he kept promising to go on a crusade and refusing to go and promising to go and refusing to go. That had been his problem. In the 14th century the Avignon popes wanted to persuade the French and English to stop fighting each other, so they would mount a crusade against the Muslims in the East. Well, not surprisingly, the conquest of Constantinople by the Turks in 1453 sent a certain kind of shockwave through Europe, but not exactly the one the popes wanted or expected. Basically people didn't respond very much. The popes thought, "Surely now people will see we simply have to march east and meet this grave threat." But people simply had other priorities.

It's true that an army was raised, for instance, and the Turks had been pressing across the Balkans, and were temporarily expelled from the city of Belgrade in 1456. It's true, for example, that Cardinal Ludovico Trevisa led a fleet into the Aegean Sea and had a few momentary victories, but no long-term results. Pope Pius II called a Congress at Mantua in northern Italy for people to come together to proclaim a crusade, but virtually no one came. Venice, moreover, had already concluded a very lucrative commercial treaty with the Turks. The Venetians were a little nervous about all this talk about a crusade against the Turks—bad for business.

A good indicator of prevailing conditions is provided by the Turkish succession battle. When Sultan Mehmet II died in 1481—this is the very sultan whose forces had conquered Constantinople in 1453—there was a succession crisis—that's not particularly unusual—and eventually a man by the name of Bayazid II won out over the person who would have been presumed to be Mehmet's natural successor. Djem was his name. Djem fled; he went to Rhodes. He was captured there. He was sent to Rome, and Innocent VIII imprisoned him. Bayazid then had the bright idea that he would pay Innocent an annual subsidy—popes always need cash—he would pay Innocent an annual subsidy as long as he kept Djem in prison. That was what his desire to formulate a crusade had resulted in. The continuing fragmentation of anything that could be plausibly called

Christendom was ongoing, unstoppable and dangerous for the long-term interests of the papacy.

Let's give the last word here to the famous Cambridge University historian Eamon Duffy. "After the arc of achievement on which Leo IX had set them, the popes were once again trapped within the politics of Italy, obliged to concede control of local churches to kings and princes, under fire from the best informed and most devout churchmen of the age, and once again perceived as the chief obstacle to desperately needed reform. The papacy, it seemed, had come full circle." But there is also another side to the popes in the Renaissance, and to that we'll turn next time.

Timeline

c. 6 B.C.–30 A.D............Life and ministry of Jesus Christ.

c. 4 B.C. ....Birth of Peter (Simon).

c. 28 A.D. ....Peter meets Jesus.

42–67 A.D.....................Dates traditionally given for Peter's term as the first pope, though their accuracy is questionable.

64–67 A.D.....................Peter's crucifixion takes place sometime during this period.

c. 150...........................Sources speak of "monarchical bishops," suggesting that the bishops had come to be significant figures in the cities of the Roman world.

180–284 ....Crisis of the 3rd century: civil wars and succession crises, barbarian incursions along frontiers, rampant inflation, systematic persecution of Christians.

284–600 ....The world of late antiquity; Christian culture becomes dominant.

306–337 ....Reign of Constantine.

313 ....Constantine issues the Edict of Milan, making Christianity legal.

343 ....Council of Serdica decrees that appeals of unjust judgments against bishops could go to Rome.

381 ....Council of Constantinople I.

410 ....Pope Innocent I ministers to Rome after the sack of the city by the Goths.

451 ....Council of Chalcedon.

452 ....Pope Leo I persuades Attila the Hun not to sack Rome.

455 ....Pope Leo I persuades Gaiseric the Vandal not to sack Rome.

prelate's office and his position as a landed magnate and vassal of the crown.

1130 .... Struggle for power between papal candidates backed by the powerful Pierleoni and Frangipani families.

1140 .... Issuance of the *Concordantia Discordantium Canonum* (usually called Gratian's *Decretum*) as a rationalized compendium of Church law down to its time.

1145–1147 .... Second Crusade.

1159–1180 .... Papal schism centering on tensions between popes and German kings.

1176 .... Lombard League forces defeat of Frederick Barbarossa at Legnano.

1177 .... Peace of Venice; the German king and Roman emperor Frederick Barbarossa makes peace with Pope Alexander III.

1179 .... Alexander III and the Lateran Council decree that popes will be elected by the *sanior pars* ("wiser part"), meaning a two-thirds majority.

1188–1192 .... Third Crusade.

1192 .... Cencius Savelli, as *camerarius*, draws up the *Liber Censuum*, a listing of virtually all revenues due to the papacy.

1204 .... Fourth Crusade, during which Constantinople is taken.

1212 .... Pope Innocent III elevates Frederick II to the throne of Germany.

1215 .... Pope Innocent III's Fourth Lateran Council forms the basis for the *Clericis laicos*, forbidding taxation of the clergy.

1217	Fifth Crusade, including the conquest of Damietta.
1228–1239	Sixth Crusade.
1249–1252	Seventh Crusade.
1270	Eighth Crusade.
1297	Pope Boniface VIII permits taxation of the clergy "in an emergency."
1300–1600	Period of the Renaissance; religious reformation.
1305–1378	Avignon papacy.
1337–1453	Hundred Years War.
1378–1417	Great Schism.
1414–1418	Council of Constance, which ended the Great Schism.
1438	French rulers impose a concordat that cuts off revenues to Rome, some kinds of papal appointments, and some appeals to the papacy.
1448	German rulers impose a concordat that cuts off revenues to Rome, some kinds of papal appointments, and some appeals to the papacy.
1453	Fall of Constantinople.
1454–1494	Peace of Lodi.
1506	Pope Julius II issues the *Cum tam divino*, which voids any papal selection tainted by simony.
1509	Erasmus writes his widely read *In Praise of Folly*, an indictment of the contemporary Church.
1512	French-inspired Council of Pisa, seeking to restore *Haec Sancta* and *Frequens*.

1512–1518 .... Lateran V council, seeking to reestablish *Unam Sanctam*, in essence quashing the Council of Pisa.

1517 .... Erasmus writes *Julius Exclusus*, another indictment of the Church.

1517 .... Martin Luther posts his Ninety-five Theses on the church door in Wittenberg.

1520 .... Pope Leo X issues the bull *Exsurge Domini*, condemning Martin Luther's teaching on 41 specific points.

1524 .... St. Cajetan and Giovanni Pietro Caraffa (later Pope Paul IV) form the Theatine order of priests, explicitly focused on reforming the Church.

1525 .... Charles V of Spain defeats Francis I of France near Pavia, then puts Rome to an eight-day sack.

1530 .... Pope Clement VII crowns Charles V emperor of Rome, the last time a pope will crown a Holy Roman Emperor.

1534 .... The Act of Supremacy makes Henry VIII head of the Church in England, although he does not embrace Protestant theology.

1534 .... Ignatius Loyola forms the Society of Jesus (the Jesuits).

1536 .... Commission created under Pope Paul III to determine what aspects of the Church need reform.

1542 .... Roman Inquisition reinstated under Caraffa.

1545–1563 .... Council of Trent affirms traditional Catholic teachings and institutes many reforms.

1548 .... Confraternity of the Most Holy Trinity founded by Philip Neri (the "Apostle of Rome," 1515–1595) to care for pilgrims and the ill.

1555	Peace of Augsburg, the first example of religious toleration in Europe.
1570	Pope Pius V excommunicates the Protestant Queen Elizabeth I of England.
1582	Pope Gregory XIII introduces the Gregorian calendar.
1600–1700	Baroque era.
1618–1648	Thirty Years War between the Catholic Habsburgs and Protestant powers of Germany.
1633	Pope Urban VIII condemns Galileo's writings and commits him to imprisonment.
1700	War of the Spanish Succession.
1700–1800	Era of the Enlightenment.
1789–1799	French Revolution.
1815	Congress of Vienna.
1860	Pope Pius IX loses the Papal States.
1864	Pope Pius IX writes his *Syllabus of Errors* to counter the "progress, liberalism, and modern civilization" seen as corrupting tradition.
1869	Vatican I opened in the presence of more than 700 bishops, the largest council in the Church's history.
1870	Vatican I adopts *Dei Filius*, a decree on faith that essentially affirms the teachings expressed in Pope Pius IX's *Syllabus* of 1864, and *Pastor Aeternus*, defining papal infallibility and making the pope universal ordinary.
1870	Pope Pius IX loses Rome.
1900–present	Modern era of the Church.

1908	French theologian Alfred Loisy excommunicated.
1914–1918	World War I.
1920	Pope Benedict XV canonizes Joan of Arc as a concession to France in the wake of hostility following the pope's efforts to keep Italy out of World War I.
1929	Lateran Treaty turns the Papal States into Vatican City and puts the pope's political position in the modern world on a new footing.
1933	Pope Pius XI negotiates controversial concordat with Nazi Germany.
1939–1945	World War II.
1942	The Vatican opens relations with Japan.
1960	Pope John XXIII creates a Secretariat for Christian Unity.
1961	Pope John XXIII sends envoys to the World Council of Churches meeting in Delhi.
1962–1965	Second Vatican Council (Vatican II).
1963	Pope Paul VI appoints a study commission to examine the use of artificial contraception, banned by the Church.
1964	Pope Paul VI signals papal interest in Asian Catholics by attending a Eucharistic congress in Bombay.
1965	Pope Paul VI addresses the United Nations, pleading for an end to war.
1965	Pope Paul VI and Orthodox Patriarch Athenagoras I issue a joint resolution regretting the mutual excommunications of 1054.
1988	Pope John Paul II institutes the apostolic constitution *Pastor Bonus*.

1994 ....Pope John Paul II hailed as *Time* magazine's "Man of the Year."

1996 ....Pope John Paul II makes changes to the procedures for electing a pope.

Glossary

Allocution: A solemn form of address or speech used by the pope on certain occasions.

Antipope: A false claimant of the Holy See in opposition to a pontiff canonically elected.

Arianism: See **Arius** in Biographical Notes.

Augsburg, Peace of: A settlement made in 1555 between Lutherans and Catholics in Germany, which included the principle *cuius regio, eius religio* ("whose the rule, his the religion"). Princes could dictate the religion of their lands, and people were free to stay and practice that religion or migrate elsewhere. The settlement ignored Calvinists yet was the first example of religious toleration in Europe.

Babylonian Captivity: Derisive name for the period when the papacy resided in Avignon (1305–1378).

Baroque: Period in the history of Western culture and art roughly coinciding with the 17th century. The work that distinguishes the Baroque period is stylistically complex and strives to evoke emotional states. Qualities associated with the Baroque are sensuous richness, drama, vitality, tension, and emotional exuberance

Bishops: "Overseers" in Greek, the chief religious and administrative officers of the Christian Church.

Breviary: A priest's daily prayer book.

Camera/Camerarius: The pope's chamberlain, responsible for writing, recordkeeping, and overseeing the financial machinery of the Church.

Cardinals: Key officers of the Catholic Church. Emerged in late antiquity and achieved institutional prominence in the 12th century. Served as papal electors.

Carolingian: Dynasty of Frankish rulers whose most famous member was Charlemagne (Carolus Magnus). The Carolingians came to power in 751 and ruled until 911 in Germany and 987 in France.

Cistercians: Monks of Citeaux, in Burgundy, or their allies; a community of reformed Benedictine monks who sought primitive purity. Their influence spread rapidly in the 12th century.

Clericis laicos: Order issued by Pope Boniface VIII forbidding taxation of the clergy.

Cluny: Great monastery founded in Burgundy in 910 to be free of all lay control. Tremendously influential well into the 12th century, not least because of its famous abbots.

Conciliarism: Doctrine spawned during the Great Schism, which maintained that Church councils, not the popes, are supreme in the Church.

Conclave: Assembly of the cardinals for the purpose of electing a new pope.

Concordantia Discordantium Canonum: A rationalized compendium of Church law developed in 1140. Thereafter, several new collections of decretals were issued.

Concordat of Worms: Compromise arranged in 1122 between Pope Calixtus II and Roman Emperor Henry IV marking the end of the first phase of the Investiture Controversy. The Concordat of Worms made a clear distinction between the spiritual side of a prelate's office and his position as a landed magnate and vassal of the crown.

Confraternity of the Most Holy Trinity: Order founded by the "Apostle of Rome," Philip Neri, that devoted itself to caring for pilgrims and the ill.

Consistory: Session in which the cardinals and the popes formally meet to discuss and make decisions about the affairs of the Church.

Constitutiones: Documents issued by the pope without his being asked to do so.

Council of Constance (1414–1418): Broad program of Church reform that ended the Great Schism. Two critical decrees declared that the authority of councils was superior to that of popes and called for a new council in 5 years, another in 7 years, then one every 10 years.

Council of Trent (1545–1563): Most important Catholic Church council of the Reformation era. Affirmed traditional Catholic teachings and instituted many reforms.

Counter Reformation: From the 1560s, an effort by the Catholic Church to win back areas lost to Protestants. Most effective in Poland and southern Germany.

Crusades: Long series of "armed pilgrimages" between 1095 and 1291 designed to liberate the Holy Land from the "infidels" (Muslims). The French were most prominent in the Crusades. Papal leadership was sometimes effective, but the overall results were limited.

Curia Romana: General reference to the papal court, the Church's government, or specifically, to the pope and the cardinals sitting in consistory.

Decretals: A form of document and practice derived directly from Roman imperial procedure.

Defensores: Church officials who possessed minor judicial authority.

Diocese: The territory under the authority of any bishop; the word comes from Roman imperial administration.

Dominicans: Mendicant order founded by Dominic de Guzman (1170–1221) in southern France. The ideal of the monks was to combat heresy by acquiring great learning and living exemplary lives. The order produced many great scholars.

Donatism: Christian movement, named for Bishop Donatus, that arose in Africa after Constantine granted legal status to Christianity. The movement objected to forgiving Christians who knuckled under during times of persecution and opposed welcoming them back to the fold.

Ecclesiology: The theory of Church government.

Edict of Milan: Decree in 313 whereby Constantine granted legal toleration to Christianity.

Eirenicism: Theology aiming at religious unity.

Encyclical: A papal letter addressed to bishops or to the Church hierarchy of a specific country.

Enlightenment: An intellectual movement in the late 17th and 18th centuries characterized by an abiding faith in the power of human reason.

Excommunication: Ecclesiastical punishment in which a person is denied the sacraments of the Church and forbidden most kinds of ordinary human interaction.

Febronianism: A politico-ecclesiastical system outlined by Johann Nikolaus von Hontheim (1701–1790), auxiliary bishop of Trier (under the pseudonym Justinus Febronius), that attempted a reconciliation of Protestants with the Church by proposing diminished papal power.

Franciscans: Mendicant order founded by Francis of Assisi (1181/1182–1226) based on poverty and service to outcasts. Tremendously popular but riven by factional strife over the question of individual versus corporate property.

Gallicanism: A French movement with the intent of diminishing papal authority and increasing the power of the state over the Church. It was viewed as heretical by the Roman Catholic Church.

Great Schism (1378–1417): Period during which two or even three rivals claimed to be the legitimate pope. Generally considered the greatest crisis in papal history, the schism grew out of the papacy's period of residence in Avignon (see **Babylonian Captivity**).

Holy See: The authority of the pope to govern the Church.

Huguenots: Name for French Protestants of the Calvinist variety; derives from a medieval romance about King Hugo.

Humanism: Movement encompassing love for the literary culture of antiquity, concern for human beings, and interest in secular rather than theological issues. Often associated with the Renaissance.

Hundred Years War: Conflict between France and England (1337–1453) rooted in the longstanding controversy over English royal holdings in France. The English won most battles, but the French won the war.

Indulgences: In Catholic theology, the remission of some portion of the temporal punishment for sin. Subject to massive abuses in the late Middle Ages.

Inquisition: Ecclesiastical judicial process for the identification and reconciliation of heretics. Followed basic principles of Roman law.

Interdict: Ecclesiastical censure whereby most sacramental services are forbidden in a defined area to pressure the rulers of that region.

Interregnum: The period between the end of a sovereign's (or a pope's) reign and the accession of his successor.

Investiture Controversy: Institutional and ideological battle between popes and German emperors in the 11th and 12th centuries; finally won by the popes at great cost to the Germans.

Jansenism: Christian teaching of Cornelius Jansen, which held that people are saved by God's grace, not by their own willpower, because all spiritual initiatives are God's. Jansenism divided the Roman Catholic Church in France in the mid-17th century.

Jesuits: Common name for the religious order called the Society of Jesus, founded in 1534 by Ignatius Loyola. The order is dedicated to poverty, chastity, and obedience to the pope. Its members are famous as teachers, scholars, and missionaries.

Josephism: Religious reform movement developed by Joseph II of Austria (1741–1790). Like Febronianism, Josephism focused on minimizing papal authority.

Lateran Councils: Councils called by the popes to facilitate the governance of the Church. The most important was the Fourth Lateran Council in 1215.

Lateran Treaty of 1929: Agreement between the papacy and Mussolini's government that turned the Papal States into Vatican City and put the pope's political position in the modern world on a new footing.

Lay investiture: The investing of a clergyman with both the symbols and the reality of his office by a layman.

Legate: One whom the pope sends to sovereigns or governments or only to the members of the episcopate and faithful of a country, as his representative, to handle Church matters or on a mission of honor.

Liberation theology: Doctrine, often Marxist tinged, teaching that Christians must work for social and economic justice for all people.

Lombards: Germanic people who entered Italy in 568 and gradually built a strong kingdom with a rich culture, especially in law, only to fall to the more powerful Franks in 773–774.

Modernism: Artistic and cultural movement that generally includes progressive art and architecture, music, and literature, emerging in the decades before 1914, as artists rebelled against late-19th-century academic and historicist traditions.

Monoenergism: Christian doctrine holding that Jesus Christ had two natures but a single will. Proposed as a compromise between the Monophysitist view and that of the Council of Chalcedon.

Monophysitism: Christian heresy prominent in the eastern Mediterranean world holding that Jesus Christ had only one true (divine) nature. Condemned by the Council of Chalcedon in 451. Still influential among West Asian Christians.

Nuncio: A permanent representative of the pope, vested with both political and ecclesiastical powers, first appearing in the 16th century. The nuncio's office is limited to a specific district (his *nunciature*), wherein he must reside; his mission is general, embracing all interests of the Holy See.

Papal States: Lands in central Italy ruled by the papacy beginning in the 8th century.

Peace of Lodi: A 40-year period (1454–1494) of relative peace and prosperity in Italy; an important background to the cultural side of the Renaissance.

Penitentiara: The Church's court for dispensations.

Peter's pence: The annual voluntary laymen's contribution to the support of the pope.

Petrine theory: Idea advanced by Roman bishops that, just as Peter was leader of the apostles, so, too, is the successor to Peter the leader of the Church. Based on Matthew 16:16–19.

Pontificate: The term of office of a pope.

Pope: The bishop of Rome who, on the basis of the Petrine theory, the historical resonances of Rome, and various historical circumstances, achieved a leading position in the Catholic Church.

Protestant: Latin word meaning "they protest" that appeared in a document of 1529. Became a catchall designation for persons who left the Catholic Church and the descendants of such people.

Religious (noun): A person who belongs to a religious order.

Renaissance: Generally means "rebirth," specifically of the literary culture of Greco-Roman antiquity. The term was traditionally applied to Italy during the period 1300 to 1550 but is increasingly applied to all periods of significant cultural efflorescence.

Rota Romana: The second highest tribunal of the Roman Catholic Church.

Schemata: Documents spelling out issues for discussion in a council.

Schism of 1130: The struggle between popes supported by the powerful Pierleoni and Frangipani families.

Simony: Selling the gifts of the Holy Spirit, especially religious offices.

Spiritualia: The spiritual, sacramental, or holy side of a churchman's office.

Syllabus of Errors: Document written by Pope Pius IX to counter the "progress, liberalism, and modern civilization" that he saw as corrupting tradition.

Temporalia: The temporal dimensions of the authority that churchmen have by dint of investiture. These responsibilities might be legal, financial, or military.

Theatines: Order of priests formed by St. Cajetan and Giovanni Pietro Caraffa (later Pope Paul IV), aimed explicitly at reforming the Church.

Thirty Years War: Series of European conflicts from 1618 to 1648, primarily based on the profound religious antagonism engendered among Germans by the events of the Protestant Reformation.

Tropaion: A special tomb or a cenotaph, a monument to a deceased person whose remains are interred elsewhere.

Ultramontanism: Policy of supporting papal authority.

Uniate churches: Eastern Christian communities that were in full communion with Rome but retained all their rites, customs, and languages. They are found throughout Eastern Europe and in the Middle East.

Vatican II: The Second Vatican Council was an ecclesial, theological, and ecumenical congress convened from 1962 through 1965. The council produced 16 documents and marked a fundamental shift toward the modern Church.

Vatican City: An independent state within Rome, the product of the Lateran Treaty of 1929, that is ruled by the pope and serves as world headquarters of the Roman Catholic Church.

Vernacular: Languages or other cultural manifestations that are not in Latin.

Vestararius: A financial officer of the Church.

Zelanti: Extremely conservative 18th-century cardinals.

Biographical Notes

The biographical sketches in this appendix cover nonpapal personages who figure prominently in the history of the papacy. Individual popes spotlighted in various course lectures are listed below. For further information, refer to http://www.newadvent.org/cathen/12272b.htm, a website that provides links to details about most of the popes.

Peter, Lecture One
St. Leo I (the Great), Lecture Two
Gregory I (the Great), Lecture Three
Hadrian I, Lecture Four
Sylvester II, Lecture Six
Gregory VII, Lecture Seven
Pius II, Lecture Thirteen
Julius II, Lecture Thirteen
Paul III, Lecture Fourteen
Paul IV, Lecture Fifteen
Paul V, Lecture Fifteen

Urban VIII, Lecture Sixteen

Benedict XIV, Lecture Sixteen
Pius IX, Lecture Seventeen
Leo XIII, Lecture Eighteen
Pius X, Lecture Eighteen
Benedict XV, Lecture Eighteen
Pius XI, Lecture Eighteen
Pius XII, Lecture Nineteen
John XXIII, Lecture Twenty
Paul VI, Lecture Twenty-One
John Paul I, Lecture Twenty-Three
John Paul II, Lecture Twenty-Three
Benedict XVI, Lecture Twenty-Four

Alberic II (d. 954): A son of Marozia and Alberic I; on his deathbed, he insisted that his 18-year-old son, Octavian, be elected pope.

Albornoz, Gil (1310–1367): Cardinal noted for his administrative genius and often reckoned the "Second Founder" of the Papal States.

Anacletus II (d. 1138) Antipope supported by the Pierleoni family, who had been the papacy's bankers since the 11th century. Discord over whether he or Innocent II should hold the papal office forced Innocent to flee Rome temporarily.

Aquinas, Thomas (1225–1274): Italian Dominican, trained at Paris and Cologne, taught in Paris and Rome, produced *Summa theologiae* and *Summa contra gentiles*. Greatest scholastic philosopher and theologian.

Arius (c. 250–336): Priest of Alexandria who, in an attempt to preserve absolute monotheism, taught that Jesus Christ was slightly subordinate to God the Father. Condemned by the Council of Nicaea in 325 but influential among Germanic peoples who were converted to Arianism.

Athenagoras I (1886–1972): Patriarch of Constantinople (1948–1972). In December 1965, he and Pope Paul VI issued a joint resolution regretting the mutual excommunications of 1054.

Augustine (354–430): Prolific Christian theologian and greatest of the Latin Church fathers. One of the most influential writers in Christian history.

Benedict XII (r. 1394–1409): The second of four antipopes (paralleling the legitimate Boniface XI [r. 1389–1404], Innocent VII [r. 1404–1406], and Gregory XII [r. 1406–1415]) during the Great Schism.

Benedict XIV (r. 1425–1430): The last of four antipopes (paralleling the legitimate Martin V [r. 1417–1431]) during the Great Schism.

Bonaparte, Napoleon (1769–1821): French emperor (1796–1815) whose dictatorship ended the French Revolution, while consolidating the reforms it had brought about.

Cajetan, St. (1480–1547): With Giovanni Pietro Caraffa (later Pope Paul IV), formed the Theatine order of priests, explicitly aimed at reforming the Church.

Calvin, John (1509–1564): French scholar and theologian, author of *Institutes of the Christian Religion*, founder of the "reformed" tradition of Christianity, and leader of the reform of the Church in French Switzerland.

Caraffa, Giovanni Pietro (Gianpietro) (1476–1559): With St. Cajetan, formed the Theatine order of priests, explicitly aimed at reforming the Church. Later elected pope, taking the name Paul IV.

Cavour, Camillo (1810–1861): Sardinian statesman and chief architect of Italy's unification.

Charlemagne (747–814): Greatest member of the Carolingian dynasty. King from 768 to 800; emperor from 800 to 814. Secured the frontiers of the Frankish kingdom, promoted cultural and institutional reform, and formulated the ideology of Christendom.

Charles V (1500–1558): The last Holy Roman Emperor crowned by a pope (Clement VII).

Clement VI (r. 1378–1394): The first of four antipopes (paralleling the legitimate Urban VI [r. 1378–1389] and Boniface XI [r. 1389–1404]) during the Great Schism.

Clement VII (r. 1409–1417): The third of four antipopes (paralleling the legitimate Gregory XII [r. 1406–1415]) during the Great Schism.

Conrad III of Hohenstaufen (1093–1152): Succeeded Lothar of Supplinburg as king in Germany (1138–1152) but never secured the imperial crown. Excommunicated by German bishops.

Constantine I (228?–337): Roman emperor (306–337) who continued the reforms of Diocletian, restructured the Roman army, granted toleration to Christianity, and became Christian himself.

Constantine IV (652–685): Roman emperor (668–685) who held the Sixth Ecumenical Council, which repudiated Monothelitism.

Constantius II (317–361): Roman emperor (337–361) who pushed the Arianist philosophy.

de Cramaud, Simon (1360–1422): Patriarch of Alexandria and administrator of the diocese of Avignon. With Peter Philarghi, the archbishop of Milan, oversaw the meeting of a council of the majority of Avignonese and Roman cardinals in Pisa in 1409.

Donatus (d. 355?): Bishop of Carthage in north Africa; founder of the Donatist sect.

Elizabeth I (1533–1603): Protestant Queen of England (1558–1603); excommunicated by Pope Pius V in 1570.

Febronius, Justinus (1701–1790): Pseudonym for Johann Nikolaus von Hontheim, auxiliary bishop of Trier, who published a proposed politico-ecclesiastical system featuring diminished papal power in an attempt to reconcile Protestants with the Catholic Church.

Francis of Assisi (1181/1182–1226): Founder of the Franciscan monastic order; devoted himself completely to a life of poverty.

Frederick (I) Barbarossa (1123–1190): The German king (1152–1190) and Roman emperor (1155–1190) whose efforts to control northern Italy called into being the Lombard League. The league's forces dealt Frederick a humiliating defeat at Legnano.

Frederick II of Hohenstaufen (1194–1250): Ward of the pope; elevated by Innocent III to the throne of Germany in 1212. His rule was marked by poor relations with Rome.

Galilei, Galileo (1564–1642): Scientist and astronomer; demonstrated mathematically that the Earth moves; was censured by the Church.

Garibaldi, Giuseppe (1807–1882): Italian nationalist revolutionary and leader in the struggle for Italian unification and independence.

Henry III (1017–1056): The German king (1039–1056) and Holy Roman emperor (1046–1056) who, in 1046, rode triumphantly into Italy; at Sutri, he deposed three rival contenders for the papacy and imposed a choice of his own.

Henry IV (1050–1106): The German king (1056–1105) and Holy Roman emperor (1084–1105) with whom Pope Gregory VII battled regarding whether clergymen could be invested by a layman.

Henry VIII (1491–1547): King of England (1509–1547) whose marriages and divorces led to a break with the Roman Catholic Church and creation of the Anglican Church.

Hostiensis (d. 1271): Thirteenth-century canonist known for saying that priestly dignity is exactly 7,644½ times greater than the royal, based, no doubt, on Ptolemy's claim that the Sun is 7,644½ times brighter than the Moon.

Jansen, Cornelius (1510–1576): In his intensive study of St. Augustine, Bishop Jansen came to a series of theological positions contrary to the customary teachings of the Catholic Church and close, in many ways, to the ideal of John Calvin. In 1640, his *Augustinus* was posthumously published but soon condemned, by the Sorbonne in 1649 and by Pope Innocent X in 1653.

Joseph II of Austria (1741–1790): German emperor (1765–1790) who developed religious reforms centered on reduction of the pope's authority.

Justin I (c. 450–527): Devout Catholic Roman emperor (518–527) who worked with Pope Hormisdas (r. 514–523) on the "Formula of Hormisdas," meant to achieve unity among different factions of the Church.

Justinian II (669–711): Roman emperor (685–695, 705–711) who called the Quinisext Council, which issued many decrees that were unacceptable in Rome.

Leo III (c. 680–741): Roman emperor (717–741) who campaigned against icons, spurring his zealous followers—Iconoclasts—to destroy them. In response to the papacy's condemnation of Iconoclasm, Leo stripped the papacy of critical revenues from southern Italy and the western Balkans.

Loisy, Alfred (1857–1940): French theologian, biblical scholar, and leader of the Modernist movement, which sought to apply the developments of modern science, philosophy, and criticism to Roman Catholic theology.

Lorenzo de' Medici (1449–1492): Financier and administrator; a virtual dictator in Florence but a great promoter of cultural life and booster of his city.

Lothar of Supplinburg (1075–1137): German king (1125–1137), favorably inclined toward the papacy, who helped Pope Innocent II wrest control of Rome from antipope Anacletus II.

Louis XIV (1638–1715): King of France (1643–1715), known as the Sun King. Louis expanded the effectiveness of the central government, increased the boundaries of France to the north and east, and placed one of his grandsons on the throne of Spain, but these successes cost the nation dearly. The economy suffered during the long years of war, taxes increased, and the countryside was left vulnerable to punishing famines.

Loyola, Ignatius (1491–1556): Spanish nobleman who founded the Society of Jesus (the Jesuits).

Luther, Martin (1483–1536): German-born Augustinian priest who became alienated from the Catholic Church over the issues of free will, good works, and indulgences. Initiated Church reform in Germany.

Machiavelli, Niccolò (1469–1527): Florentine politician and writer best known for *The Prince*, an intensely practical guide to the exercise of raw political power over a Renaissance principality. (The model for Machiavelli's *Prince* was Alexander VI's son Cesare Borgia.) Patronized by the Medici pope Leo X.

Malachy (1094–1148): Irish bishop who traveled to Rome and allegedly had visions pertaining to 112 popes, including predictions of who would be elected. He supposedly transcribed his visions— now known as the "Prophecies of St. Malachy"—and gave them to Pope Innocent II.

Marozia (c. 892–c. 937): Daughter of Theophylact and mistress of Pope Sergius III, by whom she had a son who was later elected pope as John XI. Marozia also married in succession three powerful men who, in concert with her, named and removed popes at will.

Mazzini, Giuseppe (1805–1872): Italian revolutionary, political theorist, and advocate of Italian unification. The highpoint of Mazzini's career came during the revolutions of 1848–1849, when he returned to Italy and was elected one of the leaders of the new Roman Republic.

Michelangelo Buonoratti (1475–1564): Florentine artist who mastered the techniques, styles, and influences of his time to produce breathtakingly original works of art, such as the statue of David and the ceiling of the Sistine Chapel.

Neri, Philip (1515–1595): Known as the "Apostle of Rome," a Florentine who embraced asceticism and founded the Confraternity of the Most Holy Trinity.

Otto I (912–973): German king (936–962) and Holy Roman Emperor (962–973) who confirmed the Carolingian territorial privileges for Rome.

Philarghi, Peter (1328–1423): Archbishop of Milan. With Simon de Cramaud, patriarch of Alexandria, he oversaw the meeting of a council of the majority of Avignonese and Roman cardinals in Pisa in 1409. He was elected pope, taking the name Alexander V.

Philip IV (1268–1314): King of France (1285–1314) known for his conflict with Pope Boniface VIII, which grew out of Philip's attempt to levy taxes against the clergy.

Pippin III (714–768): First Carolingian to become king (751–768). He allied with the popes, defeated the Lombards in Italy, and fostered Church and cultural reform.

Roger II of Sicily (1095–1154): Invaded and seized Apulia and Calabria, lands nominally held as papal fiefs. Pope Honorius II mounted a military expedition against Roger, but it was a dismal failure.

Savonarola, Girolamo (1452-1498): Fiery Florentine Dominical preacher who called for Church reform and was excommunicated by Pope Alexander VI.

Sigismund of Bohemia (1361–1437): King of Germany and Holy Roman Emperor responsible for the great reform councils of Constance (1414–1418) and Basel (1431).

Suleiman the Magnificent (1495–1566): Turkish sultan (1520–1566) who signed an anti-Habsburg pact with Francis I of France in 1536.

Theophylact (d. 920): A 9th-century duke and "Master of the Soldiers," as well as *vestararius*, or financial officer of the Church. Father of Marozia, who was mistress of one pope and mother of another.

Wibert of Ravenna (c. 1029–1100): Installed by Henry IV as an antipope (Clement III) after Pope Gregory VII excommunicated Henry in 1080.

Zeno (474–491): Roman emperor who bullied Pope Felix III (483–492) over Monophysitism.

Bibliography

Papal history is a vast subject with an immense bibliography, only a minor portion of which is available in English. Accordingly, the following bibliography is organized in sections that should prove helpful to those who wish to secure more information for themselves. Many of the works listed here contain rich bibliographies in European languages. Please note that some of the references are arranged chronologically by historical period rather than alphabetically. Books that themselves contain rich bibliographical information are marked with an asterisk (*).

Reference Tools:

Cross, F. L., and E. A. Livingstone, eds. *Oxford Dictionary of the Christian Church*. 3rd ed. Oxford, UK: Oxford University Press, 1997. By far, the best brief encyclopedia of all matters Christian.

Kelly, J. N. D. *The Oxford Dictionary of Popes*. Oxford, UK: Oxford University Press, 1986. By far, the best single-volume biographical dictionary.

Levillain, Philippe, ed. *The Papacy: An Encyclopedia*. New York: Routledge, 2002. An outstanding reference work with both biographical and topical entries.

The New Catholic Encyclopedia. New York: Thomson, Gale, 2002–. Fifteen volumes to date (replacing the *New Catholic Encyclopedia* of 1967). Excellent, reliable, and balanced.

General Histories (Large-Scale):

Creighton, Mandell. *A History of the Papacy from the Great Schism to the Sack of Rome*. 6 vols. London: Longmans Green, 1901. Sensible, reliable account by an Anglican bishop of London and formidable scholar.

———. *A History of the Papacy during the Period of the Reformation*. 5 vols. London: Longmans Green, 1892. Again, a sensible, reliable account by an Anglican bishop of London and formidable scholar.

Grisar, Hartmann, S.J. *A History of Rome and the Popes in the Middle Ages*. Translated by Luigi Cappadelta. London: Kegan Paul, Trench, and Trübner, 1911–1912. Dense but learned, based on the sources, and interesting on Rome.

Mann, Horace K. *The Lives of the Popes in the Early Middle Ages.* 18 vols. London: Kegan Paul, Trench, and Trübner, 1925–1932. Organized biographically and reliable in details if not always up to date in interpretation.

Pastor, Ludwig. *The History of the Popes from the Close of the Middle Ages.* 40 vols. London: J. Hodges, 1891–1953. Massive but judicious and readable; satisfying to browse in.

Ranke, Leopold von. *The Ecclesiastical and Political History of the Popes of Rome during the Sixteenth and Seventeenth Centuries.* 3 vols. Translated by Sarah Austin. London: J. Murray, 1840. A masterpiece by one of the founders of modern historical scholarship, who although Lutheran, believed he could write with objectivity.

General Histories (Smaller Scale):

Baumgartner, Frederick J. *Behind Locked Doors: A History of the Papal Elections.* New York: Palgrave Macmillan, 2003. Readable and fascinating.

Belitto, Christopher M. *The General Councils: A History of the Twenty-One General Councils from Nicaea to Vatican II.* New York: Paulist Press, 2002. Solid book on an important topic for papal history.

Cheetham, Nicholas. *Keepers of the Keys: A History of the Papacy from St. Peter to John Paul II.* New York: Scribners, 1982. Accessible, manageable, and balanced.

Collins, Michael. *The Fisherman's Net: The Influence of the Popes on History.* Blackrock, Ireland: Columba, 2003. More popular than scholarly, the book is true to its title.

*Duffy, Eamon. *Saints and Sinners: A History of the Popes.* 2nd ed. New Haven: Yale University Press, 2002. Outstanding!

Jalland, Trevor Gervase. *The Church and the Papacy: A Historical Study.* London: Society for Promoting Christian Knowledge, 1944. Balanced treatment of history and theology from a moderate Protestant point of view.

Kittler, Glenn D. *The Papal Princes: A History of the Sacred College of Cardinals.* New York: Funk and Wagnalls, 1960. Perhaps the best of a small selection on this vast topic; now dated.

*La Due, William J. *The Chair of St. Peter: A History of the Papacy.* Maryknoll, NY: Orbis Books, 1999. Emphasizes the changing bases of papal authority.

Lo Bello, Nino. *The Incredible Book of Vatican Facts and Papal Curiosities: A Treasury of Trivia.* Ligouri, MO: Ligouri, 1998. Great fun!

*Maxwell-Stuart, P. G. *Chronicle of the Popes: The Reign-by-Reign Record of the Papacy from St. Peter to the Present.* London: Thames and Hudson, 1997. Lavishly illustrated with many quotations from primary sources.

Schatz, Klaus. *Papal Primacy from Its Origins to the Present.* Collegeville, MN: Liturgical Press, 1996. Comprehensive, fair, and readable.

Seppelt, Franz Xaver. *A Short History of the Popes.* St. Louis: Herder, 1932. An abridgement of his superb multivolume history in German.

Walsh, Michael J. *An Illustrated History of the Popes: St. Peter to John Paul II.* New York: St. Martin's, 1960. Readable and accessible.

————. *Conclave: A Sometimes Secret and Occasionally Bloody History of Papal Elections.* London: Sheed and Ward, 2003. Informative and a good read.

Wills, Garry. *Papal Sin: Structures of Deceit.* New York: Doubleday, 2000. Relentlessly negative but thought-provoking.

Primary Sources (Selective):

Carlen, Claudia. *Papal Encyclicals.* 5 vols. Wilmington, NC: McGrath, 1981. A rich source for the period from 1740 through Paul VI. For information on John Paul II, consult the Internet Resources listed at the end of this section.

Davis, Raymond. *Liber Pontificalis*: Translated as: *The Book of Pontiffs.* Rev. ed. Liverpool: Liverpool University Press, 2000; *The Lives of the Eighth-Century Popes.* Liverpool: Liverpool University Press, 1992; *The Lives of the Ninth-Century Popes.* Liverpool: Liverpool University Press, 1995. Well-translated and helpfully annotated version of the crucial source for early papal history.

Flannery, Austin, O.P. *Vatican Council II: The Conciliar and Post-Conciliar Documents.* Northport, NY: Costello, 1975. The standard English translation of the Latin texts with only limited commentary and annotation.

Gregory the Great. *The Letters of Gregory the Great*. 3 vols. Translated by John R. C. Martyn. Toronto: Pontifical Institute of Mediaeval Studies, 2004. Papal letters are always valuable sources, and no pope is more interesting than Gregory I.

Shotwell, James T., and Louise Ropes Loomis. *The See of Peter*. New York: Columbia University Press, 1927; reprinted, 1991. Outstanding collection of documents from the first four centuries.

Tanner, Norman P., S.J., ed. *The Decrees of the Ecumenical Councils*. 2 vols. Washington, DC: Georgetown University Press, 1990. Convenient edition of a major source for papal and Church history.

Tierney, Brian. *The Crisis of Church and State, 1050–1300*. 1964. Reprinted, Toronto: University of Toronto Press, 1988. Excellent on the historical and ideological dimensions of the Investiture Controversy and its aftermath.

Studies of Particular Periods or Topics (Chronologically Arranged):

Weltin, Edward George. *The Ancient Popes*. Westminster, MD: Newman Press, 1964. Good on the neglected early period.

Guarducci, Margherita. *The Tomb of St. Peter: New Discoveries in the Sacred Grottoes of the Vatican*. New York: Hawthorn, 1960. Aggressively positive in its interpretation of the finds.

*O'Connor, Daniel William. *Peter in Rome: The Literary, Liturgical, and Archaeological Evidence*. New York: Columbia University Press, 1969. Reliable, readable, and balanced.

Brown, Raymond E., Karl P. Donfried, and John Reumann, eds. *Peter in the New Testament*. Minneapolis: Augsburg Publishing House, 1973. A collaborative ecumenical treatment of a controversial topic.

Richards, Jeffrey. *The Popes and the Papacy in the Early Middle Ages*. London: Routledge and Kegan Paul, 1979. Detailed account of the papacy's traverse from antiquity to the Middle Ages.

Llewellyn, Peter. *Rome in the Dark Ages*. 2nd ed. New York: Barnes and Noble, 1996. A solid narrative history of Rome and Italy from the 6th century to the 10th.

Ullmann, Walter. *A Short History of the Papacy in the Middle Ages*. London: Methuen, 1972. Excellent, manageable account by a major scholar.

Ullmann, Walter. *The Growth of Papal Government in the Middle Ages*. 3rd ed. London: Methuen, 1970. Standard but controversial account of papal institutions and ideology.

*Schimmelpfennig, Bernhard. *The Papacy*. New York: Columbia University Press, 1992. Poorly translated but a good history down to 1534.

*Noble, Thomas F. X. *The Republic of St. Peter: The Birth of the Papal State, 680–825*. Philadelphia: University of Pennsylvania Press, 1984. The origins of papal temporal rule and the early papal government.

Partner, Peter. *The Lands of St. Peter*. Berkeley: University of California Press, 1972. Comprehensive treatment of the Papal States to the end of the Middle Ages.

*Blumenthal, Uta Renate. *The Investiture Controversy: Church and Monarchy from the Ninth to the Twelfth Centuries*. Philadelphia: University of Pennsylvania Press, 1988. Fine treatment of an important and difficult subject.

Tellenbach, Gerd. *Church, State, and Christian Society at the Time of the Investiture Controversy*. New York: Harper, 1970. Brilliant and penetrating.

*Morris, Colin. *The Papal Monarchy: The Western Church from 1050 to 1300*. Oxford, UK: Oxford University Press, 1989. Emphasizes the papacy within a remarkable period.

Robinson, Ian S. *The Papacy, 1073–1198: Continuity and Innovation*. Cambridge, UK: Cambridge University Press, 1990. Clear, comprehensive, and detailed.

Tierney, Brian. *The Origins of Papal Infallibility, 1150–1350: A Study in the Concepts of Infallibility, Sovereignty, and Tradition in the Middle Ages*. Leiden, Netherlands: Brill, 1972. Fundamental.

Gill, Joseph. *Byzantium and the Papacy, 1198–1400*. New Brunswick, NJ: Rutgers University Press, 1979. Informative on an important topic.

Mollat, Guillaume. *The Popes at Avignon, 1305–1378*. London: T. Nelson, 1963. One of the two standard studies on the topic (see below).

Renouard, Yves. *The Avignon Papacy, 1305–1403*. Hamden, CT: Archon Books, 1970. The second major study; treats the period after the restoration of the Roman line.

Smith, John Holland. *The Great Schism*. London: Hamish Hamilton, 1970. Still the only single-volume treatment.

Tierney, Brian. *Foundations of the Conciliar Theory*. Cambridge, UK: Cambridge University Press, 1955. Seminal study now only slightly dated.

*Oakley, Francis. *The Conciliarist Tradition: Constitutionalism in the Catholic Church, 1300–1870*. Oxford, UK: Oxford University Press, 2003. Learned and impressive history of a crucial topic.

Stinger, Charles. *The Renaissance in Rome*. Bloomington, IN: Indiana University Press, 1985. Essential and readable.

*Prodi, Paolo. *The Papal Prince: One Body and Two Souls—The Papal Monarchy in Early Modern Europe*. Cambridge, UK: Cambridge University Press, 1987. Fascinating study of the princely papacy.

Thomson, John A. F. *Popes and Princes, 1417-1517: Politics and Polity in the Late Medieval Church*. Boston: Allen & Unwin, 1980. This book complements Prodi's (above) in giving a solid account of the nature of late medieval politics in general, with papal politics always in focus.

Signorotto, Gianvittorio, and Maria Antonietta Visceglia, eds. *Court and Politics in Papal Rome, 1492–1700*. Cambridge, UK: Cambridge University Press, 2002. Wide-ranging essays by major scholars.

*Wright, A. D. *The Early Modern Papacy: From the Council of Trent to the French Revolution*. Harlow, UK: Longman, 2000. Excellent brief survey.

Jedin, Hubert. *A History of the Council of Trent*. 2 vols. London: Nelson, 1957–1961. The standard history of this major council.

O'Connell, Marvin. *The Counter-Reformation: 1559–1610*. New York: Harper, 1974. Superseded in details but still the best survey.

Evennett, Henry O. *The Spirit of the Counter Reformation*. Notre Dame, IN: University of Notre Dame Press, 1970. Dated now in some details but a brilliant book.

Gross, Hanns. *Rome in the Age of Enlightenment: The Post-Tridentine Syndrome and the Ancien Regime*. Cambridge, UK: Cambridge University Press, 1990. Treats both the Roman scene in the Enlightenment period and the papal response to a changing intellectual culture.

*Coppa, Frank J. *The Modern Papacy since 1798*. Harlow, UK: Longman, 1998. An excellent introduction.

Hales, Edward Elton Young. *Revolution and Papacy, 1769–1846*. Garden City, NY: Hanover House, 1960. Fine account of a difficult period for the popes.

*Chadwick, Owen. *The Popes and European Revolution*. Oxford, UK: Oxford University Press, 1981. Brilliant and readable by a major scholar.

*Chadwick, Owen. *A History of the Popes, 1830–1914*. Oxford, UK: Oxford University Press, 1998. The best overall book on the 19th century.

Holmes, J. Derek. *The Triumph of the Holy See: A Short History of the Papacy in the Nineteenth Century*. London: Burns and Oates, 1978. Readable but half as long as Chadwick and less acute in judgment.

Butler, Edward Cuthbert. *The Vatican Council*. 2 vols. London: Longmans Green, 1930. Insider's account based on the letters of a participant.

Mondin, Battista. *The Popes of the Modern Age: From Pius IX to John Paul II*. Vatican City: Urbaniana University Press, 2004. Brief, lively, and informed by an Italian perspective.

Holmes, J. Derek. *The Papacy in the Modern World, 1914–1978*. New York: Crossroad, 1981. Readable and informative on the same scale as Mondin.

Falconi, Carlo. *The Popes in the Twentieth Century from Pius X to John XXIII*. Boston: Little Brown, 1968. Solid book by a major Italian scholar.

Vidler, Alexander Roper. *The Modernist Movement in the Roman Church*. Cambridge, UK: Cambridge University Press, 1934. Still the best overall book on an important subject.

Jemolo, Arturo Carlo. *Church and State in Italy, 1850–1950*. Oxford, UK: Blackwell, 1960. Unbiased account of an important and much-contested subject.

Hebblethwaite, Peter. *1978: The Year of Three Popes*. New York: Collins, 1979. Fascinating account of the two elections of 1978.

Tentler, Leslie Woodcock. *Catholics and Contraception: An American Story*. Ithaca: Cornell University Press, 2004. An outstanding discussion of the background to and aftermath of *Humanae Vitae*.

Noonan, John T. *Contraception: A History of Its Treatment by the Catholic Theologians and Canonists.* Cambridge, MA: Harvard University Press, 1986. Fundamental treatment of the most controversial subject in modern Catholicism.

Reese, Thomas J. *Inside the Vatican: The Politics and Organization of the Catholic Church.* Cambridge, MA: Harvard University Press, 1996. Sensitive account of *how* things work.

Ratzinger, Joseph Cardinal. *The Salt of the Earth: The Church at the End of the Millennium. An Interview with Peter Seewald.* San Francisco: Ignatius Press, 1997. Keen insights into the mind of the man who was elected Pope Benedict XVI.

Allen, John L., Jr. *All the Pope's Men: The Inside Story of How the Vatican Really Thinks.* New York: Doubleday, 2003. Perhaps the best starting point for "Vaticanology."

Allen, John L., Jr. *The Rise of Benedict XVI.* New York: Doubleday, 2005. An "instant book" but excellent nevertheless.

Selected Biographies (Chronologically Arranged):

Jalland, Trevor Gervase. *The Life and Times of St. Leo the Great.* London: Society for Promoting Christian Knowledge, 1941. The only reasonably full study of this key pope.

*Markus, Robert. *Gregory the Great and His World.* Cambridge, UK: Cambridge University Press, 1997. Of the many books on Gregory, this one is the best.

*Cowdrey, H. E. J. *Pope Gregory VII, 1073–1085.* Oxford, UK: Clarendon Press, 1998. The fruit of a life's work by a major historian.

*Sayers, Jane. *Innocent III: Leader of Europe, 1198–1216.* London: Longman, 1994. Readable, intelligent, and comprehensive in a modest scope.

Boase, T. S. R. *Boniface VIII.* London: Constable, 1933. Still worthwhile.

Boureau, Alain. *The Myth of Pope Joan.* Chicago: University of Chicago Press, 2001. Brilliant, riveting, and important; the one book to read on the subject.

Wood, Diana. *Clement VI: The Pontificate and Ideas of an Avignon Pope*. Cambridge, UK: Cambridge University Press, 1989. Difficult but an entrée into the Avignon period.

Mitchell, Rosamond Joscelyne. *The Laurels of the Tiara: Pope Pius II, 1458–1564*. London: Harvill Press, 1962. More popular than scholarly, this book is nonetheless valuable.

Shaw, Christine. *Julius II: The Warrior Pope*. Oxford, UK: Blackwell, 1993. A good book and a great read.

Bainton, Roland. *Here I Stand: A Life of Martin Luther*. New York: Abingdon-Cokesbury Press, 1950. Dated, perhaps, but still the most readable biography of the Great Reformer.

Hales, Edward Elton Young. *Pio Nono*. New York: P.J. Kenedy, 1954. Still the best book in English.

Soderini, Eduardo. *The Pontificate of Leo XIII*. London: Burns and Oates, 1934. Old but not superseded on a crucial pope.

Giordani, Igino. *Pius X: A Country Priest*. Milwaukee: Bruce, 1954. Perhaps the best of a bad lot of ultra-pious books.

Rope, Henry Edward George. *Benedict XV: The Pope of Peace*. London: J. Gifford, 1941. Uncritical but solid on details.

Fontenelle, René. *His Holiness Pius XI*. Cleveland: Sherwood, 1939. Still serves in the absence of a scholarly book.

Halecki, Oskar. *Eugenio Pacelli: Pope of Peace*. New York: Creative Age Press, 1951. Written well before Pius died, this book provides a conventionally positive view.

Falconi, Carlo. *The Silence of Pius XII*. London: Faber, 1970. Critical but not harsh.

Cornwell, John. *Hitler's Pope: The Secret History of Pius XII*. New York: Penguin Books, 2000. The more one despises Pius, the more one will like this book.

*Sánchez, José M. *Pius XII and the Holocaust: Understanding the Controversy*. Washington, DC: Catholic University of America Press, 2002. Fair on a subject for which there has been only passion recently.

Hebblethwaite, Peter. *John XXIII*. London: Geoffrey Chapman, 1984. Well-crafted book by a major interpreter of the recent papacy.

Johnson, Paul. *Pope John XXIII*. Boston: Little, Brown, 1974. Solid book by a popular writer.

Hebblethwaite, Peter. *Paul VI: The First Modern Pope.* New York: Paulist Press, 1993. Excellent and likely to remain the standard book for a long time.

Szulc, Tad. *Pope John Paul II: The Biography.* New York: Scribner, 1995. In fact, an interim report, very good on the early life and background.

Weigel, George. *Witness to Hope: The Biography of John Paul II.* New York: Cliff Street Books, 1999. Another interim report, with the active collaboration of its subject, and uncritical in a scholarly sense.

Internet Resources:

Catholic-Pages.com. www.catholic-pages.com. This is a Catholic website with a wide array of information and a rather pious orientation.

The Holy See. www.vatican.va/index.htm. This is the official website for the Vatican. With a little navigation, it will yield vast stores of information.

New Advent. www.newadvent.org. This is also a Catholic website with a great deal of useful information, including an online version of the "old" *New Catholic Encyclopedia.*